The Psychology of S
in Sport and Physic.

International Perspectives on Key Issues in Sport and Exercise Psychology is a series of edited books, with a global focus, that reflect the state of the art in areas of current and emerging interest in the study of sport and exercise psychology. Each volume in the series contributes to the better understanding of a key issue facing researchers and practitioners in sport psychology.

This volume in the series focuses upon the sociocultural issues that challenge and often undermine participation, performance, and well-being in sport. Contributors address a number of important issues, such as exclusion, miscommunication, and ineffective practice in sport. The book extends the recent interest in culture within sport psychology by using a critical approach to highlight less mainstream sports, such as martial arts and extreme sports, and will help sports participants and social scientists to gain an understanding of these marginalized sporting identities. By highlighting "subcultural" contexts, with their individual practices and values, it is hoped that the volume will promote the goal of achieving a more just, inclusive, and ethical sport psychology.

The Psychology of Sub-Culture in Sport and Physical Activity will be ideal reading for sport and exercise academics and practitioners, advanced students of applied sport psychology, and those interested in related fields such as sport science, critical studies, sociology, cultural studies, and social anthropology.

Robert J. Schinke is Professor and Canada Research Chair in Multicultural Sport and Physical Activity at Laurentian University, Canada.

Kerry R. McGannon is Assistant Professor at Laurentian University, Canada.

**International Perspectives on Key Issues in
Sport and Exercise Psychology**
Series Editors: Athanasios Papaioannou and
Dieter Hackfort

International Perspectives on Key Issues in Sport and Exercise Psychology is a series of edited books published in partnership with the International Society of Sport Psychology. Each title reflects cutting-edge research in the psychological study of high-level sport, and is written by key researchers and leading figures in the field of sports psychology.

Books in this series:

Athletes' Careers Across Cultures
Edited by Natalia B. Stambulova and Tatiana V. Ryba

**Routledge Companion to Sport and Exercise Psychology:
Global Perspectives and Fundamental Concepts**
Edited by Athanasios G. Papaioannou and Dieter Hackfort

**The Psychology of Sub-Culture in Sport and Physical Activity:
Critical Perspectives**
Edited by Robert J. Schinke and Kerry R. McGannon

The Psychology of Sub-Culture in Sport and Physical Activity

Critical perspectives

Edited by Robert J. Schinke and Kerry R. McGannon

Routledge
Taylor & Francis Group

LONDON AND NEW YORK

First published 2015
by Routledge
27 Church Road, Hove, East Sussex BN3 2FA

and by Routledge
711 Third Avenue, New York, NY 10017

Routledge is an imprint of the Taylor & Francis Group, an informa business

British Library Cataloguing in Publication Data
A catalogue record for this book is available from the British Library

Library of Congress Cataloging in Publication Data
The psychology of sub-culture in sport and physical activity :
critical perspectives / edited by Robert J. Schinke, Kerry R. McGannon.
    pages cm. — (International perspectives on key issues in
    sport and exercise psychology)
    Includes bibliographical references and index.
    1. Sports—Psychological aspects.   2. Exercise—Psychological aspects.
    3. Sports—Social aspects.   4. Subculture.   I. Schinke, Robert J.
    II. McGannon, Kerry R.
    GV706.4.P716 2014
    796.01'9—dc23   2014007682

ISBN: 978-1-84872-157-9 (hbk)
ISBN: 978-1-84872-158-6 (pbk)
ISBN: 978-1-315-77849-5 (ebk)

Typeset in Times New Roman
by RefineCatch Limited, Bungay, Suffolk

Printed and bound in the United States of America by Publishers Graphics, LLC on sustainably sourced paper.

Contents

Contributors

The editors

Robert J. Schinke, EdD, has been awarded the Canada Research Chair in Multicultural Sport and Physical Activity. This title is bestowed on Canadian scholars with a strong international reputation in their field. In 10 years as a faculty member, Robert has become a full professor, and has been awarded the Canadian Sport Science Research Award for Community Research. As a scholar, Robert has over 80 publications to his name, and has been published in a wide range of international sport science journals, including *Psychology of Sport and Exercise*, the *Journal of Applied Sport Psychology*, *The Sport Psychologist*, the *International Journal of Sport and Exercise Psychology*, the *Journal of Clinical Sport Psychology*, the *Journal of Sport and Social Issues*, and *Quest*. Robert is presently Editor of *Athletic Insight*, an Associate Editor with the *Journal of Sport and Social Issues*, and an Editorial Board Member with the *Journal of Clinical Sport Psychology* and *Qualitative Research in Sport, Exercise and Health*. Robert has also guest co-edited the *International Journal of Sport and Exercise Psychology*, the *Journal of Sport and Social Issues*, the *Journal of Clinical Sport Psychology* and *Qualitative Research in Sport, Exercise and Health*. He has also edited or co-edited the following textbooks: *Cultural Sport Psychology* (2009), *The Cultural Turn in Sport Psychology* (2010), *Contemporary Sport Psychology* (2009), *Sport Psychology: Training, Competition and Coping* (2011), *Sport for Development, Peace and Social Justice* (2012), *Sport Psychology Insights* (2012), *Athletic Insights* (2012), and *Case Studies in Sport for Peace and Social Justice* (2012). In addition, Robert is presently the section editor pertaining to cultural diversity for the forthcoming *Encyclopaedia of Sport and Exercise Psychology*, a President Elect Candidate with the Association for Applied Sport Psychology, and elected to the managing council of the International Society of Sport Psychology. Finally, Robert is a former major games athlete and a consultant to Olympic and professional sport organizations.

Kerry R. McGannon, PhD, has an extensive background in cultural sport psychology and the sociocultural analysis of sport and exercise participation. Kerry has 11 years of experience as a researcher and educator. She began her career as a research associate with the Alberta Centre for Active Living (University of Alberta, Edmonton, Canada), worked as an assistant professor at the University of Iowa, USA, for seven years, and is now in her fourth year as an assistant professor at Laurentian University, Canada. She is a leading figure in work that bridges sport and exercise psychology and cultural studies to understand physical activity promotion and participation. Her work uses interpretive qualitative methodologies (e.g., discourse analysis, narrative) to explore the social construction of gender in sport and exercise and to study the media as a cultural site that constructs self and identity within the context of health promotion. Her peer-reviewed scholarship includes empirical and theoretically driven contributions to 61 national and international academic conferences, and over 50 publications in prominent international sport science journals (e.g., *Psychology of Sport and Exercise*, *Quest*, *Journal of Sport Sciences*, *International Journal of Sport and Exercise Psychology*, *Sociology of Sport Journal*) and scholarly books pertaining to sport and exercise psychology and/or cultural sport psychology (e.g., *Cultural Sport Psychology*, *The Cultural Turn in Sport Psychology*). She is also co-editing a special issue of *Qualitative Research in Sport, Exercise and Health* on community research in physical activity, with Robert J. Schinke and Brett Smith. In addition to serving on the editorial boards of *Psychology of Sport and Exercise*, *Qualitative Research in Sport, Exercise and Health*, and *Athletic Insight*, she is also on the advisory board of *Qualitative Research in Sport, Exercise and Health*, and is the section editor of Qualitative Methodologies, Critical and Cultural Approaches for *Athletic Insight*. She also serves as Chair of the Cultural Diversity Committee of the Association for Applied Sport Psychology.

Contributors

Shannon Baird, PhD, United States Army, United States

Ted M. Butryn, PhD, San José State University, United States

David Carless, PhD, Leeds Metropolitan University, United Kingdom

Hamish Crocket, PhD, University of Waikato, New Zealand

Kitrina Douglas, PhD, University of Bristol, United Kingdom

Leslee A. Fisher, PhD, University of Tennessee, Knoxville, United States

Alicia J. Johnson, MA, University of Tennessee, Knoxville, United States

Cindra S. Kamphoff, PhD, Minnesota State University, United States

Gretchen A. Kerr, PhD, University of Toronto, Canada

Anthony P. Kontos, PhD, University of Pittsburg, United States

Vikki Krane, PhD, Bowling Green State University, United States

Matthew A. Masucci, PhD, San José State University, United States

Anthony Papathomas, PhD, Loughborough University, United Kingdom

Marie-Josee Perrier, PhD, Loughborough University, United Kingdom

Erin Reynolds, PsyD, University of Pittsburg, United States

Brett Smith, PhD, Loughborough University, United Kingdom

Ashley E. Stirling, PhD, University of Toronto, Canada

Kelsey Timm, BA, Minnesota State University, United States

Jennifer J. Waldron, PhD, University of Northern Iowa, United States

Series editors' foreword

In our foreword to the first volume in this series, we emphasized that the typical character of an individual book in the series is an edited book bringing together contributions from different perspectives, and not just the most up-to-date knowledge on current key issues. Our hope is that this series will initiate discussion and stimulate research and further consideration in teaching and applied practice, and on sensitivity and awareness issues to open up further understanding of such issues. The present (second) volume, *The Psychology of Sub-Culture in Sport and Physical Activity*, edited by Robert Schinke and Kerry McGannon, turns this hope into a reality by way of a critical approach. The focus of this volume is sociocultural issues that challenge and often undermine participation, performance, and well-being in sport.

As the second volume in the series, it is another book on cultural issues following the first volume, *Athletes' Careers Across Cultures*. The inclusion of this second volume allows for cultural issues in sport and exercise psychology to be futher emphasized and explored. We, the editors of the series (and the publisher as well), obviously share the feeling that this perspective has been either neglected or remained marginalized for far too long, and is important and relevant to providing further insight and improving our understanding and orientation in the field of sport and exercise research and practice. The neglect is somewhat astonishing given that as early as 1900 Wilhelm Wundt (1832–1920), the founder of experimental psychology in Germany, had presented a series of 10 volumes on "Völkerpsychologie," which would be translated today as "cultural psychology." The International Society of Sport Psychology (ISSP) brought to the awareness of its members and the international sport psychology community that a consideration of cultural perspectives was needed by inviting a keynote on cross-cultural psychology and organizing a symposium at the 2001 World Congress in Skiathos, Greece. Both of the editors of this series (Dieter Hackfort as the organizer of the symposium, and Athanasios Papaioannou as the organizer of the congress) have been involved in this initiative, and we are very happy about the awareness that has been raised. Maybe this book also can be regarded as an outcome of this initiative. We hope to be able to publish further consequences of such initiatives by the ISSP, and we are already planning volumes to cover further key issues in international sport and exercise psychology.

Importantly, this book helps draw our attention to such issues in sport as abuse, hazing, and concussion, which represent and demonstrate subcultural phenomena and developments to be analyzed and discussed by the announced critical approach, or which have been described and explained by perspectives and models that need to be discussed critically. Along these lines, the editors have devoted the final part of the book to the topic of self-reflection and reflexivity in sport psychology practice and research.

Being among the critical sport psychology movement, the editors of this volume invited researchers to illuminate several examples of traumatic sport experiences that often remain obscure both in sport settings and in mainstream science, partly because practitioners and scientists rarely reflect on issues of sociocultural difference, power, ethics, and politics in sport. In the first chapter of the book, the editors make it very clear that their mission is not to create a new or alternative (with regard to mainstream or other, i.e., ecological, clinical) branch of sport psychology, but to contribute to the theoretical and applied-oriented differentiation of sport psychology.

The editors have done a fine job, putting together, in the first part of the book, chapters that make it very clear which issues characterize those subcultures in sport that urgently need sport psychology consideration. Generally speaking, such a subculture is identified by lesser-known and/or marginalized sport and physical activity contexts of action, and by the involvement of minorities or under-privileged/non-privileged groups. Participants or actors in such action contexts are characterized not only by being deviant or resistant to dominant cultural settings and groups, but also by opposing the exclusive acceptance of the mainstream. A key characteristic of actions or individuals in such a subculture might be to oppose power that is perceived to be a compulsion and/or to be misleading, manipulative, or encroaching. In the second part of the book, the chapters argue critically against certain models, understandings, and definitions of sport culture and approaches in sport research. The third and final part of the book provides examples of self-reflection and reflexivity in and for sport psychology practice and research, which together suggest a more appropriate political and ethical orientation.

To be critical is not only the goal of the contributions to this book but also a fundamental attitude in science and research. Furthermore, it should be targeted not only toward others or certain issues but also and especially toward oneself, and also being aware of the particular concept, approach, and consequences. In this regard the contributions to this book may be regarded as an example of questioning common or established perspectives, adding further and sometimes alternative perspectives, but also reflecting on one's own point of view and, most significant for the readers of this volume, opening it up for discussion.

Science and research are not in the business of finding *the* truth; rather, they are part of a system that is looking or striving for answers in the awareness that there is no single truth and that we build up something by our endeavors that cannot be evaluated in its truth exclusively by ourselves. The endeavor to achieve a better or more appropriate understanding of a certain phenomenon by means of theoretical and methodological approaches is always embedded in a cultural context, and there is always a less accepted, marginalized part of this culture that is the subculture. Interpretations, explanations, predictions, and further actions are all and always contextualized. This is an essential consideration in sport and all other psychology research and practice. We would like to thank the editors of the volume and the authors of the individual chapters for making this very clear and exciting for the sport psychology community and beyond.

Dieter Hackfort   Athanasios Papaioannou
Munich, December 2013   Trikala, Thessaly, December 2013

1 Situating the subculture of sport, physical activity and critical approaches

Kerry R. McGannon and Robert J. Schinke

Sport psychology researchers have challenged the lack of inclusion of culture and/or cultural identities within sport psychology for many years (e.g., Butryn, 2002; Duda & Allison, 1990; Fisher, Butryn, & Roper, 2003; Gill, 2001; Krane, 2001; Martens, Mobley, & Zizzi, 2000). Recently there has been a further push toward a more culturally inclusive sport psychology, with a "community" of scholars (see Sparkes, 2013) advocating for culture's rightful place within the discipline. Known as *cultural sport psychology* (CSP), scholars within this genre challenge mainstream sport psychology's assumptions to facilitate contextualized understandings of marginalized topics and cultural identities (Ryba, Schinke, & Tenenbaum, 2010; Ryba, Stambulova, Si, & Schinke, 2013; Schinke & Hanrahan, 2009; Stambulova & Ryba, 2013). While CSP is a relatively new trajectory within sport psychology, such work is creating dialogue among sport and physical activity participants and social scientists to open up new and additional understandings concerning solutions to sociocultural challenges that limit physical activity participation and performance.

Although in its infancy, the rationale for CSP is firmly established. Three special journal issues in sport psychology have been devoted to CSP. *Athletic Insight* showcased articles on culturally relevant practice (Schinke, Michel, Danielson, & Gauthier, 2005), the *International Journal of Sport and Exercise Psychology* highlighted articles that used "decolonizing methodologies" to address issues of power and sociocultural difference in research (Ryba & Schinke, 2009), and the *Journal of Clinical Sport Psychology* opened up areas of discussion concerning cultural awareness and competence in clinical, counseling, and applied sport psychology (Schinke & Moore, 2011). Recently, the *International Journal of Sport and Exercise Psychology* published the International Society of Sport Psychology's position stand on culturally competent research and practice (Ryba et al., 2013). In late spring 2014, we will co-edit a special issue on intersecting cultural identities in CSP for the journal *Psychology of Sport and Exercise*. Two edited volumes have also brought together CSP scholarship to examine how sport psychology is (re)presented via a sociocultural lens to challenge the domain's assumptions and practices (Ryba et al., 2010; Schinke & Hanrahan, 2009). The recently published *Athletes' Careers Across Cultures* brought together a collection of essays using a sociocultural lens to explore sport careers literature in relation to how social and cultural discourses shaped their development across national boundaries (Stambulova & Ryba, 2013).

Important for continued growth within the CSP movement is that either less considered or not previously considered topics are included and explored using a critical lens (Ryba et al., 2010). While more will be said about what a critical lens may encompass, for now it can be noted that the contributions within this book add to CSP by highlighting lesser-known and/or marginalized sport and physical activity contexts and the participants within them, using a *critical approach*. We hope that this collection will open up further dialogue about and exploration of uncharted sport and physical activity subcultures. Moreover, we hope that the chapters are accessible and authoritative – though not viewed as definitive – on a range of critical "takes" intended to continue to open up new ways of thinking and doing in sport psychology.

Critical humility: contextualizing a critical approach and the subculture of CSP

To further contextualize the contributions to the book, an overview of our thinking concerning the parameters of a *critical approach* is first necessary. In keeping with the interpretive and cultural turn that informs the critical CSP movement (Ryba et al., 2010), we acknowledge that the notion of a *critical approach* is neither straightforward nor value-free, and that it does not have a singular meaning. Critical approaches are difficult to define because they have historical and political roots within the social sciences, there are multiple critical theories, the critical tradition is in flux, and laying out a set of fixed characteristics for what constitutes "being critical" is the antithesis of such approaches (Kincheloe & McLaren, 2000). Scholars have also problematized the various strands of the critical theory, research, and practice movement from its inception to the present day (Canella & Steinberg, 2011; Kincheloe, McLaren, & Steinberg, 2011).

Within the sport studies literature there is a rich dialogue informing critical scholarship that has its roots in cultural studies (e.g., Andrews & Loy, 1993; Birrell & McDonald, 2000; Cole, 1993). Despite the differences in specific orientations and subject matter, such research has a built-in activist and social justice component, drawing attention to marginalized identities and inequalities through a focus on contemporary sport culture(s) as sites of the (re)construction of embodied selves and lives (Birrell & McDonald, 2000). In an effort to draw attention to social difference, distribution of power, and social justice as interrelated concerns, sport psychology scholars have also advocated for a critical cultural studies approach (Butryn, 2002; Fisher et al., 2003, Krane, 2001; McGannon & Johnson, 2009; Roper, 2001; Ryba & Wright, 2005). This work has its roots in broader social science "takes" on the meaning(s) of being critical (e.g., Agger, 1998; Kincheloe & McLaren, 2000) and the sport studies literature grounded in cultural studies (e.g., Birrell & McDonald, 2000; Sage, 1998).

The notion of *subculture* has been less explicitly discussed within the CSP literature, but it warrants mention here, as sport studies scholars have problematized the term to examine the implications for research and practice using critical cultural studies scholarship (e.g., Crosset & Beal, 1997; Donnelly, 1985). Drawing upon early critiques in sociology that viewed subculture as a way for groups to distinguish themselves in various ways from dominant cultural norms and practices (e.g., Fine & Kleinman, 1979), sport studies scholars suggested that subcultures are more than just forms of deviance and/or resistance to dominant culture. Though sport subcultures can (and very often do) include people who collectively resist the values and practices of a dominant or mainstream culture, Donnelly (1985) urged sport studies scholars to be more critical by conceptualizing and interpreting subcultures within the context of historical, social, cultural, and political forces. Crosset and Beal (1997) further articulated that an element of marginalization is assumed when one refers to a *subculture* – regardless of whether or not a subculture is viewed as a form or resistance against dominant cultural norms. Forms of subcultural resistance can be positive (e.g., the sub-culture's meanings and practices result in social justice for those marginalized within the subculture) or negative (e.g., the subculture's practices result in further isolation and marginalization resulting in less access to opportunities within society), and are interpreted as such depending on the sociocultural and political context (Crosset & Beal, 1997).

While the CSP movement is interested in subcultures within which marginalized sporting identities and practices are formed and framed, we also position CSP as a subculture in light of the goals and topics it espouses in contrast to mainstream sport psychology. As a subculture, CSP has undergone growth and is currently in a state of flux as it continues to develop. As with other subcultures positioned as deviant, the CSP movement remains on the fringes of sport psychology in relation to the ways of thinking that prevail within the field (e.g., post-positivist, performance based, White, male). However, we reiterate that culture can no longer be ignored in sport psychology, and thus we position this book and its chapters within an overarching, fundamental belief: *we cannot step outside culture, thus to ignore it would be to ignore a key matter that shapes all of us.*

Given the multiple meanings of critical approaches, we are overwhelmed and humbled to outline the precise parameters of a critical approach. In light of this disclaimer, what follows is our attempt to provide one idiosyncratic view (see Kincheloe & McLaren, 2000) of the critical approach that frames this book. This view is not offered as definitive or prescriptive of what critical approaches *should be*; rather, in the spirit of adding to the growing discourse within the CSP movement, we offer our take on what it *could* mean to be critical. We remain open, and we hope that the reader will as well, to the possibility of additional critical "takes" on each chapter, above, beyond, and even in spite of the critical approach we suggest and what each author puts forward. Our "take" on the critical will draw upon one specific development within CSP – cultural praxis (Ryba & Wright, 2005) – that we see as being at the heart of the critical CSP movement (Schinke, McGannon, Parham, & Lane, 2012). Following an overview of cultural praxis, we summarize the chapters within this book that exemplify various elements of the cultural praxis parameters outlined, and conclude with our final thoughts.

Cultural praxis: opening up critical dialogues

Cultural praxis grew, in part, out of earlier sport psychology writings that drew upon cultural studies to highlight issues of power and privilege in research and practice that excluded certain individuals (e.g., gay, lesbian, non-White, low socio-economic status) while privileging others (e.g., heterosexual, male, middle class, the researcher or consultant) (e.g., Butryn, 2002; Fisher et al., 2003; Krane, 2001). The privileging of some people over others was largely the result of a taken-for-granted way of "doing" sport psychology steeped in a post-positivist, White, European, male, performance-based discourse (Ryba & Wright, 2005; Schinke & Hanrahan, 2009). By problematizing what was taken for granted as "truth" through a cultural studies lens, sport psychology researchers and practitioners were encouraged to step outside of the disciplinary box – and this crossing and blurring of disciplinary boundaries is the starting point of being critical that frames this book. As a result of this critical reflection in sport psychology, space was opened up to include multiple cultural identities and plurality of difference (e.g., race, ethnicity, class, gender, sexuality, ability, physicality, nationality) within the context of the ideological, moral, and ethical implications of Westernized knowledge.

Cultural praxis follows in the above critical cultural studies tradition, operating as a "heuristic" (Ryba & Wright, 2010, p. 14) to draw attention to and/or "smash" the status quo in sport psychology through a blending of theory, lived culture, and social action with a reflexive sensibility (McGannon & Johnson, 2009; Ryba & Wright, 2010; Schinke et al., 2012). Through cultural praxis, researchers and practitioners strive to consider their own, as well as others', cultural identities, to be critical by highlighting issues of sociocultural difference, power, ethics, and politics, and to facilitate a more contextualized understanding of marginalized voices (Ryba & Schinke, 2009; Ryba et al., 2013; Schinke et al., 2012).

Self-identity as a sociocultural construction

Ryba and Wright (2010) further suggest not only that cultural praxis embraces intersecting cultural identities and difference, but also that such differences make up psychological "realities" that have real consequences in the everyday lives of people (e.g., athletes, coaches, practitioners, researchers). As such, issues concerning self-identity come to the fore, with psyche and self-identity conceptualized as *simultaneously* social and cultural and the product of multiple discourses and narratives, rather than being reduced to decontextualized mechanisms within the mind, as with mainstream sport psychology (McGannon & Mauws, 2000; Smith, 2010). Subjectivity – of athletes, practitioners, and researchers – is thus fluid, multiple, and ever changing because who we "are" is the product of multiple discourses (e.g., race, sexuality, gender, physicality, nationality) (McGannon

& Spence, 2010) and our membership of local, social, and cultural groups (Ryba & Wright, 2010; Schinke, McGannon, Battochio, & Wells, 2013). Beyond the narratives and discourses that people draw upon to frame and fashion their self-identities are sport practices and institutions that can limit how we think, feel, and behave (McGannon & Spence, 2010).

Critical pedagogy and reflexivity

The above conception of subjectivity and self-identity opens up new and additional understandings of athletes' and practitioners' experiences, with the potential for developing new and innovative interventions in applied sport psychology (Busanich, McGannon, & Schinke, 2012; Douglas & Carless, 2008; Papathomas & Lavallee, 2012; Smith, 2013). Important to realizing this goal is the engagement of researchers and practitioners in "critical pedagogy" (Kincheloe et al., 2011, p. 163), which emphasizes co-participatory research and practice to create inclusive and equitable outcomes through the clarification and levelling of power relations in sport and physical activity settings (Schinke, Smith, & McGannon, in press).

An important pathway toward critical pedagogy and practice is reflexivity. Within applied sport psychology, Anderson, Knowles, and Gilbourne (2004) defined reflective practice as "an approach to training and practice that can help practitioners explore their decisions and experiences in order to increase their understanding of (self) and manage themselves and their practice" (p. 189). We recently linked reflective practice with reflexivity within the CSP literature (Schinke et al., 2012). Reflexivity is a nuanced form of reflective practice based upon an emerging innovation in qualitative methodology whereby researchers situate their own personal identities and biases to explore surprises and un-doings in the research process (i.e., unexpected turns in the research process) (McGannon & Johnson, 2009). Reflexivity has a further goal of drawing attention to power issues in the research and consulting process by raising such questions as "how do my identity and social position lead me to ask particular questions and interpret phenomena in particular ways?" and "how do my own self-related views and identities, values, and social position privilege some choices in the research or consulting process over others?" Such questions shape the research and practice process and outcomes in political, social, and cultural ways.

We propose that asking the above questions may result in both researcher and practitioner producing narratives and practices that challenge or (re)produce power structures, which may empower or disempower consultants and/or athletes. Such questions have further implications for how (or even if) marginalized cultures and identities are researched and portrayed (McGannon & Johnson, 2009) or included in the applied realm (Schinke et al., 2012). Through reflexivity, researchers and practitioners can move beyond merely delivering services and interventions in the same way to everyone, and can strive to be more culturally sensitive and inclusive (Ryba et al., 2013). Additionally, through an awareness of how their own taken-for-granted beliefs and social identities impact sport and physical activity participants in relation to the categories to which they belong, power issues can begin to be acknowledged and attended to in research and consulting contexts.

Cultural praxis as theory and research

Given the aforementioned conception of self-identity and critically reflexive pedagogy, the theories and associated methodologies within cultural praxis need to align with these conceptions (Ryba & Wright, 2010; Schinke et al., 2012). In this regard, praxis as a form of theory-driven research aligns closely with post-modernist and social constructionist conceptions of participants' identities and the social and cultural worlds they inhabit (McGannon & Johnson, 2009; Schinke et al., 2012). By way of a caveat concerning our use of the terms *post-modernist* and *social constructionist*, we acknowledge that what is presented here is an oversimplification, and what some might even argue is a misrepresentation, of distinct, complex, and contested terms steeped in different historical and philosophical traditions (see Kincheloe & McLaren, 2000). Despite this caveat, we use the terms *post-modernist* and *social constructionist* in a pragmatic way to further outline the commonalities of the various critical theoretical perspectives (e.g., critical cultural studies, critical feminist, post-structuralism) that may be used in CSP to illuminate understandings of cultural identities and power issues. We position critical theories used in cultural praxis under the umbrella of post-modernism and social constructionism because they converge on three points. First, critical theories falling under these umbrellas are committed to social justice through the illumination of socially constructed cultural identities, economics, politics, and power issues. Second, following on from this point, critical theories with a post-modernist or social constructionist sensibility question the notion that the application of any one particular method, theory, discourse, or worldview is the only way to learn about people, subculture, and culture (McGannon & Johnson, 2009). Critical theories thus maintain an openness to variation of self, others, and culture, seeking to represent "realities" as multiple, competing, in flux, and fluid, and never as the "one" correct or final representation or interpretation. Finally, related to this second point, truth and knowledge claims are regarded as serving particular interests that are located in local, cultural, and political struggles. Thus, although researchers can claim to know something about people, that knowledge is partial, local, historical, political, and fragmented (Kincheloe et al., 2011).

Given that critical theories within cultural praxis assume that experiences are (re)produced by complex contexts (e.g., political, economic, gendered, racial, sexuality), multiple qualitative approaches that capture this richness of experience and context tend to be advocated and highlighted. Examples of qualitative research within sport psychology using a variety of methodological approaches that fit this description are growing, and include narrative research (Smith, 2013), critical discourse analysis (McGannon & Schinke, 2013), visual methods

(Blodgett et al., 2013), authoethnography (Douglas, 2009), and community approaches (Schinke et al., in press). These and other forms of critical methodology will no doubt continue to grow as their transformative power is demonstrated (Ryba & Wright, 2010).

The structure and contributions in the book

The chapters in this book are committed to "being critical," with such commitment being achieved through all chapters problematizing taken-for-granted "truths" to encourage researchers and/or practitioners to continue to step outside of the disciplinary and subcultural box. Not all chapters adhere to every element of what we have outlined as our critical approach. Instead, each of the chapters approaches sport and physical activity subcultures and the participants within them using different critical perspectives, with the goal of expanding the critical CSP discourse. Further, all chapters take a critical approach as each is committed to creating safe and/or socially inclusive spaces for sport and physical activity participants in order to promote psychological well-being and an ethically and socially just sport psychology. The book is divided into three parts that cut across multiple aspects of our critical approach (i.e., concern for marginalized identities, social justice and political and ethical concerns, the use of critical theories and/or methodologies and reflexivity). We recognize that despite the organization of these separate parts, many chapters cross-cut more than one part or could cluster within a part not used or considered. Ultimately, we invite the reader to reflect upon the possible and multiple intersections within and across chapters, particularly from a critical perspective.

Part I: sociocultural dimensions of inclusion/exclusion in sport

Chapters within this part highlight the dark side of sport in terms of what (and implicitly who) is being silenced in sport psychology (e.g., emotional abuse, sex variation, hazing, vulnerability and playfulness, women's access to endurance ultramarathon running) due to intersecting sociocultural dimensions (e.g., history, social influences, cultural narratives and discourses, policies and politics) that (re)produce exclusionary practices. Each chapter offers possibilities for challenging various sociocultural dimensions in order to raise awareness and create positive participation experiences and/or opportunities in sport and physical activity settings.

In Chapter 2, "Applying a critical ecological approach to the issue of athlete abuse in sport," Gretchen Kerr and Ashley Stirling explore the less often addressed issue of the emotional abuse of young athletes using a critical ecological approach to highlight individual and contextual influences (e.g., parents, coaches, the sport system and policies) that make an athlete vulnerable to such abuse. The concept of "willful blindness" is examined, and the landscape of coaching policy and practice in Canada is reviewed as a risk environment. Recommendations for the professionalization of coaching are proposed as a strategy for preventing incidents of athlete abuse in sport. In Chapter 3, "A post-structuralist approach to hazing in sport," Jennifer Waldron uses post-structuralism to show how hazing is discursively and socially constructed, and how the use of particular language creates and maintains power relationships that encourage certain hazing practices. The chapter concludes with three case studies to illustrate how researchers and practitioners could use post-structuralism in their work. In Chapter 4, "Gender nonconformity, sex variation, and sport," Vikki Krane uses a critical transfeminist perspective to explore the interplay among sex, gender, and fair play in sport. After outlining critical concepts for understanding the issues surrounding gender nonconformity and sex variation in sport, Krane explores the attitude toward transgender, transsexual, and intersex athletes through recent sport policy decisions. A critical view of these policies in elite sport reveals that they often reinforce gender and sex stereotypes, and are exclusionary despite attempts at being inclusionary. The chapter ends by reframing issues surrounding transgender, transsexual, and intersex athletes through an ethics of inclusion. In Chapter 5, "'The dark side' and beyond: narrative inquiry in professional golf," Kitrina Douglas and David Carless use a critical narrative approach to illuminate the relationships between life as *lived* and life as *storied*, to reveal how sport culture influences these relationships. Using two examples of stories often silenced in elite sport culture (those about playfulness and those about vulnerability in professional golf), the authors consider how these stories "work" for the storyteller, and, more broadly within sport culture, which has political dimensions and wider implications. In Chapter 6, "Ultraempowering women: a feminist analysis of the ultramarathoning culture," Cindra Kamphoff and Kelsey Timm use a feminist standpoint approach to trace the history of women's exclusion from long-distance running until the late 1970s and early 1980s, highlighting women's exclusion from ultramarathons in the present day. Despite this exclusion, a rare glimpse of ultramarathoning women reveals the experience to be both liberating and complicated. The chapter concludes with a discussion of how ultramarathoning breaks down barriers to women's participation in sport, as they push their bodies, enjoy the adventure and challenges, and become part of a supportive community.

Part II: critiques of the medical model, sport culture and sport research

In common with those in the first part of the book, chapters within this part highlight cultural identities and/or sport-related issues that are silenced. Here, however, the medical model and current medical understandings are explicitly discussed as (re)producing certain ideals, beliefs about people, and/or topics that compromise understanding and athlete well-being. Taken-for-granted aspects of sport culture and dominant lines of inquiry in sport research are also highlighted and problematized within each chapter as contributing to the marginalization of certain identities and ideas. Each chapter offers its own critical take on possibilities for challenging conventional and taken-for-granted ways of thinking about such topics as disability sport, male athletes' eating disorders, and sport concussion. All chapters conclude that asking new and different questions from a critical perspective is necessary to spark novel research and practice to enhance understanding.

In Chapter 7, "Disability, sport, and impaired bodies: a critical approach," Brett Smith and Marie-Josee Perrier identify the lack of a critical approach to the study of disability sport, and address this gap by problematizing the medical model that dominates sport psychological work on disability. Critical disability studies literature is also drawn upon to provide an example of a critical study of disability through the examination of "exercise as medicine." The social relational model for developing a critical study of the psychology of disability, sport, and physical activity is highlighted. Future directions for continued critical work on the psychology of disability and sport conclude the chapter. In Chapter 8, "A few good men: male athlete eating disorders, medical supremacy and the silencing of a sporting minority," Anthony Papathomas discusses the principal reasons why male athletes' eating disorders are marginalized by problematizing the supremacy of medical science in eating disorders research. Competitive sport itself is also discussed as a dangerous paradox that promotes unhealthy eating behaviors in males while simultaneously stigmatizing such behaviors. The chapter concludes with recommendations for how sport psychology scholars could conduct more culturally sensitive research in order to gain insights that could inform and de-stigmatize male athlete eating disorders. In Chapter 9, "Sport-related concussion: critical issues moving forward," by Anthony Kontos and Erin Reynolds, the growth in concussion attention by way of specialized clinics, special journal issues, quick-fix solutions, and media coverage is problematized by highlighting five key challenges faced by sport concussion researchers and clinicians. These include the need for evidence-based approaches to assessment and management; a lack of awareness of psychological issues that may accompany concussion; health disparities in concussion management; and a movement toward a more targeted approach to assessing and managing concussion. These issues are used to make future recommendations for research in order to dispel various myths and move the understanding of sport concussion forward.

Part III: self-reflection and reflexivity in sport psychology practice and research

The chapters within this part of the book focus on the critical pedagogy and reflexivity aspects of cultural praxis in both applied (e.g., teaching/classroom, consultancy) and research settings. Chapters within this part adhere to the underlying assumption that the cultural identities of researcher, practitioner, and participant are socially constructed (i.e., identities are part and parcel of cultural discourses and institutional practices, which can facilitate or inhibit certain forms of thought and behavior). Each chapter also adheres to the underlying assumption that it is important to attend to "the self" reflexively in various ways in order to illuminate the political and ethical implications of sport psychology practice and/or research.

In Chapter 10, "BE, KNOW, DO model of consulting: an exploration of how experiences with soldiers affected me and how my notions of self affected soldiers' experiences," Shannon Baird uses self-reflexivity to examine her applied work with soldiers in the United States Army in an effort to illustrate how one's own self-stories, personal and cultural narratives, and taken-for-granted notions can impact effectiveness and have ethical implications. In Chapter 11, "'Standing in the question': teaching a critical perspective to developing sport psychology consultants," Leslee Fisher and Alicia Johnson engage in critical reflexive pedagogy. Leslee first addresses her own position as a teacher/professor trying to facilitate graduate student engagement in/with sociocultural difference and the development of a critical perspective about sport and sport psychology practice. Alicia self-reflexively writes about her own experiences as a student who presented these concepts to classmates. In Chapter 12, "Caged quandaries: mixed martial arts and the politics of research," Matthew Masucci and Ted Butryn provide a nuanced critical interrogation of the process of investigating the sport of mixed martial arts (MMA). Through cultural praxis and self-reflexive autoethnography, these authors explore personal and ethical tensions that arise when faced with a research topic imbued with social and political issues. In Chapter 13, "Confessions of the disc: a Foucauldian analysis of ethics within Ultimate Frisbee," Hamish Crocket develops a critical psychological perspective on ethics within the sub-culture of Ultimate Frisbee through a Foucauldian analysis of subjectivities, focusing on the self-confession as a theoretical tool to understand oneself as an ethical athletic subject. The chapter concludes with possibilities for a critical psychology of ethics within sporting subcultures.

Conclusion

The chapters in this book add to the growing subcultural critical discourse of CSP. We are indebted to the authors, who have contributed their critical "takes" on each of their topics. We are also indebted to the numerous scholars who have paved the way for this book, and to those who continue to pave the way for a more culturally inclusive, sport psychology. As CSP continues to grow and gain prominence, we hope that the subcultural practices and values will continue working toward achieving a more socially just, inclusive, and ethical sport psychology, and that this results in the continued recognition and embracing of diversity and difference – in cultural identities, research, and practice.

References

Agger, B. (1998). *Critical social theories: An introduction*. Boulder, CO: Westview.
Anderson, A., Knowles, Z., & Gilbourne, D. (2004). Reflective practice for sport psychologists: Concepts, models, practical implications, and thoughts on dissemination. *The Sport Psychologist, 18*, 188–203.
Andrews, D., & Loy, J. (1993). British cultural studies and sport: Past encounters and future possibilities. *Quest, 45*, 255–275.

Birrell, S., & McDonald, M. G. (2000). *Reading sport: Critical essays on power and representation*. Boston: Northeastern University Press.

Blodgett, A. T., Coholic, D. A., Schinke, R. J., McGannon, K. R., Peltier, D., & Pheasant, C. (2013). Moving beyond words: Exploring the use of an arts based method in Aboriginal community sport research. *Qualitative Research in Sport, Exercise and Health, 5*, 312–331.

Busanich, R., McGannon, K. R., & Schinke, R. J. (2012). Expanding understandings of the body, food and exercise relationship in distance runners: A narrative approach. *Psychology of Sport & Exercise, 13*, 582–590.

Butryn, T. M. (2002). Critically examining white racial identity and privilege in sport psychology consulting. *The Sport Psychologist, 16*, 316–336.

Canella, G., & Steinberg, S. (2011). *Critical qualitative research: A reader*. New York: Peter Lang.

Cole, C. L. (1993). Resisting the canon: Feminist cultural studies, sport and technologies of the body. *Journal of Sport and Social Issues, 17*, 77–97.

Crosset, T., & Beal, B. (1997). The use of "subculture" and "subworld" in ethnographic works on sport: A discussion of definitional distinctions. *Sociology of Sport Journal, 14*, 73–85.

Donnelly, P. (1985). Sport subcultures. *Exercise and Sport Sciences Review, 13*, 539–578.

Douglas, K. (2009). Storying my self: Negotiating a relational identity in professional sport. *Qualitative Research in Sport and Exercise, 1*, 176–190.

Douglas, K., & Carless, D. (2008). Using stories in coach education. *International Journal of Sports Science and Coaching, 3*, 33–49.

Duda, J. L., & Allison, M. T. (1990). Cross-cultural analysis in exercise and sport psychology: A void in the field. *Journal of Sport and Exercise Psychology, 12*, 114–131.

Fine, G. A., & Kleinman, S. (1979). Rethinking subculture: An interactionist analysis. *American Journal of Sociology, 85*, 1–19.

Fisher, L. A., Butryn, T. A., & Roper, E. A. (2003). Diversifying (and politicizing) sport psychology through cultural studies: A promising perspective. *The Sport Psychologist, 17*, 391–405.

Gill, D. (2001). Feminist sport psychology: A guide to our journey. *The Sport Psychologist, 15*, 363–372.

Kincheloe, J. L., & McLaren, P. (2000). Rethinking critical theory and qualitative research. In Norman K. Denzin & Yvonna S. Lincoln (Eds.), *Handbook of qualitative research* (2nd ed., pp. 279–313). Thousand Oaks, CA: Sage.

Kincheloe, J. L., McLaren, P., & Steinberg, S. R. (2011). Critical pedagogy and qualitative research: Moving to the bricolage. In Norman K. Denzin & Yvonna S. Lincoln (Eds.), *Handbook of qualitative research* (4th ed., pp. 163–177). Thousand Oaks, CA: Sage.

Krane, V. (2001). One lesbian feminist epistemology: Integrating feminist standpoint, queer theory and cultural studies. *The Sport Psychologist, 15*, 401–411.

Martens, M. P., Mobley, M., & Zizzi, S. J. (2000). Multicultural training in applied sport psychology. *The Sport Psychologist, 14*, 81–97.

McGannon, K. R., & Johnson, C. R. (2009). Strategies for reflective cultural sport psychology research. In R. J. Schinke & S. J. Hanrahan (Eds.), *Cultural sport psychology* (pp. 57–75). Champaign, IL: Human Kinetics.

McGannon, K. R., & Mauws, M. K. (2000). Discursive psychology: An alternative approach for studying adherence to exercise and physical activity. *Quest, 52,* 148–165.

McGannon, K. R., & Schinke, R. J. (2013). "My first choice is to work out at work; then I don't feel bad about my kids": A discursive psychological analysis of motherhood and physical activity participation. *Psychology of Sport and Exercise, 14,* 179–188.

McGannon, K. R., & Spence, J. C. (2010). Speaking of the self and physical activity participation: What discursive psychology can tell us about an old problem. *Qualitative Research in Sport and Exercise, 2,* 17–38.

Papathomas, A., & Lavallee, D. (2012). Eating disorders in sport: A call for methodological diversity. *Revista de Psicología del Deporte, 21,* 387–392.

Roper, E. A. (2001). The personal becomes political: Exploring the potential of feminist sport psychology. *The Sport Psychologist, 15,* 445–449.

Ryba, T. V., & Schinke, R. J. (2009). Methodology as a ritualized eurocentrism: Introduction to the special issue. *International Journal of Sport and Exercise Psychology, 7,* 263–274.

Ryba, T. V., & Wright, H. K. (2005). From mental game to cultural praxis: A cultural studies model's implications for the future of sport psychology. *Quest, 57,* 192–212.

Ryba, T. V., & Wright, H. K. (2010). Sport psychology and the cultural turn: Notes toward cultural praxis. In T. V. Ryba, R. J. Schinke, & G. Tenenbaum (Eds.), *The cultural turn in sport and exercise psychology* (pp. 3–27). Morgantown, WV: Fitness Information Technology.

Ryba, T. V., Schinke, R. J., & Tenenbaum, G. (Eds.). (2010). *The cultural turn in sport and exercise psychology.* Morgantown, WV: Fitness Information Technology.

Ryba, T. V., Stambulova, N., Si, G., & Schinke, R. J. (2013). ISSP position stand: Culturally competent research and practice in sport and exercise psychology. *International Journal of Sport and Exercise Psychology, 11,* 123–142.

Sage, G. H. (1998). *Power and ideology in American sport: A critical perspective.* Champaign, IL: Human Kinetics.

Schinke, R. J., & Hanrahan, S. J. (Eds.). (2009). *Cultural sport psychology.* Champaign, IL: Human Kinetics.

Schinke, R. J., & Moore, Z. (2011). Culturally informed sport psychology: An introduction to the special issue. *Journal of Clinical Sport Psychology, 5,* 283–294.

Schinke, R. J., Smith, B., & McGannon, K. R. (in press). Future pathways for community researchers in sport and physical activity research: Criteria for consideration. *Qualitative Research in Sport, Exercise and Health.*

Schinke, R. J., McGannon, K. R., Battochio, R. C., & Wells, G. (2013). Acculturation in elite sport: A thematic analysis of immigrant athletes and coaches. *Journal of Sports Sciences, 15,* 1676–1686.

Schinke, R. J., McGannon, K. R., Parham, W. D., & Lane, A. (2012). Toward cultural praxis: Strategies for self-reflexive sport psychology practice. *Quest, 64,* 34–46.

Schinke, R. J., Michel, G., Danielson, R., & Gauthier, A. (2005). Introduction to cultural sport psychology. Retrieved from http://www.athleteinsight.com/Vol7Iss3/introduction.htm.

Smith, B. (2010). Narrative inquiry: Ongoing conversations and questions for sport and exercise psychology research. *International Review of Sport and Exercise Psychology, 3,* 87–107.

Smith, B. (2013). Disability, sport, and men's narratives of health: A qualitative study. *Health Psychology, 32*, 110–119.

Sparkes, A. C. (2013). Qualitative research in sport, exercise and health in the era of neoliberalism, audit and new public management: Understanding the conditions for the (im)possibilities for a new paradigm dialogue. *Qualitative Research in Sport, Exercise and Health, 5*, 440–459.

Stambulova, N. B., & Ryba, T. V. (Eds.). (2013). *Athletes' careers across cultures*. London and New York, NY: Routledge/Taylor & Francis Group.

Part I

Sociocultural dimensions of inclusion/exclusion in sport

2 Applying a critical ecological approach to the issue of athlete abuse in sport

Gretchen A. Kerr and Ashley E. Stirling

Introduction of context

Sport is a social institution, with over 2 million children and adolescents participating in organized sport in Canada annually (Clarke, 2008). In 2005, 51% of youth between 5 and 14 years of age engaged in sports regularly outside of school (Clarke, 2008). A plethora of research indicates that sport has the potential to contribute to the health and development of young people. More specifically, previous researchers have indicated that sport has the potential to enhance self-esteem, self-efficacy, leadership development, and positive body image (Adams-Blair, 2002; Pate, Trost, Levin, & Dowda, 2010; Pedersen & Seidman, 2004; Slutzky & Simpkins, 2009). Young people who participate in school sports have been found to have a greater commitment to and identification with school (Adams-Blair, 2002; Eccles & Barber, 1999). Sport participation is also associated with lower rates of cigarette and substance use, and other delinquent behaviours (Cohen, Taylor, Zonta, Vestal, & Schuster, 2007; Hartmann, 2012; Melnick, Miller, Sabo, Farrell, & Barnes, 2001). Furthermore, those who participate in sport are less inclined to suffer from such mental health challenges as depression and anxiety (Harrison & Narayan, 2003; Steiner, McQuivey, Pavelski, Pitts, & Kraemer, 2000). For females specifically, sport participation is associated with enhanced body image, delayed sexual behaviour, and unwanted pregnancies (Lehman & Koerner, 2004; Pate et al., 2010; Sabo, Miller, Farrell, Melnick, & Barnes, 1999; Taliaferro, Rienzo, & Donovan, 2010).

While acknowledging the potential benefits offered by sport, it is also important to recognize the potential for sport to have negative influences on the health and development of young people. A substantial body of literature highlights the harm experienced by many young people in sport, in such forms as excessive physical training, serious and long-term injuries (David, 2005), emotional abuse (Stirling & Kerr, 2008), and sexual abuse (Brackenridge, 2001) within the coach–athlete relationship. The focus of this chapter will be on young athletes' experiences of emotional abuse within the coach–athlete relationship. Given the influence that childhood experiences have on long-term health and development, including continued participation in sport and physical activity (Fraser-Thomas, Cote, & Deakin, 2005), particular attention will be paid to athletes under the age of 18 years. Using a critical ecological approach, individual and contextual influences that make the sport environment conducive to emotional abuse within the coach–athlete relationship are reviewed, and recommendations are made for enhancing athlete welfare. As proposed by Bronfenbrenner (1999), a critical ecological approach is one in which the influence of various environments on an individual's development are considered; these environments range from the proximal level of the family to the macro level of the culture in which one lives. Further, these environments interact with one another across time.

What do we know about emotional abuse in sport?

Previous research has revealed that in some sporting contexts, athletes are vulnerable to emotional abuse (Gervis & Dunn, 2004; Stirling & Kerr, 2007). Common examples of emotionally abusive behaviours include the experience of threats, humiliation, demeaning comments, degradation, harsh criticisms, and belittlement (Stirling, 2009). These harmful experiences can lead to a number of reported negative psychological effects, including depressed mood, anger, anxiety, low self-efficacy, and low self-esteem (Stirling & Kerr, 2013).

Emotionally abusive coaching practices are commonly interpreted as normal sporting behaviours and are appraised as necessary for attaining optimal athletic performance. Accordingly, these harmful coaching behaviours are often taken for granted as a required part of athlete development (Boocock, 2002; Gervis & Dunn, 2004; Stirling & Kerr, 2007, 2014). Researchers have reported that emotional abuse of athletes tends to occur in public sporting contexts, in the presence of adults who are in a position of responsibility and authority, including coaches, sport administrators and practitioners, and parents of the young athletes (Stirling, Bridges, Cruz, & Mountjoy, 2011; Stirling & Kerr, 2010). The finding that adults in positions of responsibility for the welfare of young people observe emotionally abusive behaviours and do not intervene lends support to the proposition that emotional abuse in sport is normalized.

With specific reference to parents, researchers have indicated that parents watch their child's training and have observed the coach engage in emotionally abusive practices with their child, including such behaviours as yelling, intimidation, and humiliation, but have not intervened (Kerr & Stirling, 2012). Furthermore, in this same study, these parents were found to be well educated, highly involved in their children's sport experiences, and well intentioned with respect to their parental responsibilities. One wonders, therefore, why such responsible parents have been complicit in their child's emotionally abusive experiences.

It is also perplexing that other coaches and sport practitioners are complicit in these abusive experiences. In previous focus group research on ethical concerns faced by coaches in the sport environment, coaches were described as witnessing the use of training methods and techniques that can harm the athletes and may be classified as physically or mentally abusive (Haney, Long, & Howell-Jones, 1998). It was reported in a recent survey of over 3700 coaches that 78% of the coaches had been exposed to situations involving athlete emotional abuse

(Stirling, Kerr, & Cruz, 2012). Similarly, in survey-based research of sport psychology consultants' exposure to various forms of athlete harm in sport, it was reported that 87% had previously witnessed an athlete cry as a result of his/her coach's or parent's behaviour, and over 70% had witnessed harmful coaching behaviours that could be classified as emotionally abusive (Stirling & Kerr, 2010). Other personnel in sport, such as medical professionals, may also encounter occurrences of athlete abuse in sport (Stirling et al., 2011).

Why then are emotionally abusive behaviours taken for granted as part of the elite sport culture? Furthermore, why do adults in positions of responsibility and authority for the welfare of youth in sport overlook or choose not to intervene when they become aware of or observe emotionally abusive practices?

Critical approach: ecological systems theory

Bronfenbrenner (1979, 1999), through his ecological systems theory, addressed individual action and development within a system of contextualized relation-ships. More specifically, Bronfenbrenner (1999) identified five environmental systems with which an individual interacts: microsystem, mesosystem, exosys-tem, macrosystem, and chronosystem. At the most proximal level, what Bronfenbrenner termed the microsystem, an individual's development is influ-enced by those with whom they have direct contact, such as family members, school teachers, or coaches. In the case of emotional abuse, for example, the microsystem would refer to the child's parents' and coaches' attitudes and conduct regarding the treatment of children. The mesosystem involves interactions between the microsystems such that experiences in the home can influence or be influenced by experiences in school or in sport. The parent who does not tolerate emotionally abusive conduct from the coach is one example. The exosystem refers to the larger social system of communities in which the child functions and by which she or he is impacted. The extent to which coaches are educated and monitored with respect to appropriate conduct with youth athletes is an example. The macrosystem refers to the culture in which one lives, including its socio-economic conditions, cultural values, and ethnicity. In sport, the macrosystem may also include the particular society's views on the purpose of sport for young people and the resultant emphases placed on holistic development and perform-ance outcomes. And finally, the chronosystem refers to the patterning of environ-mental events and changes across time; the increase in opportunities for females to participate in sport observed over the past few decades in developed countries would be an example. Consistent with Bronfenbrenner's theory, an ecological approach suggests that individuals are embedded in and affected by a social context that influences their experiences and behaviours. This is proposed as an appropriate approach for examining the occurrence of athlete abuse as it has been used previously as a guiding framework for understanding child maltreatment etiology (Belsky, 1993), community violence (Cicchetti & Lynch, 1993), and positive youth development through sport (Côté, Strachan, & Fraser-Thomas, 2008). As well, referring specifically to the need for an ecological approach to understanding athlete abuse, other researchers have proposed the need for a more holistic, ecological interpretation of abuse (Calder, 2000), and the need to consider the social and cultural systems that surround the athlete's abusive experiences (Brackenridge, 2003).

Intersection of athlete emotional abuse with a critical ecological approach

From the application of Bronfenbrenner's (1979, 1999) ecological systems theory, it follows that athlete abuse may exist and persist in the sport environment due to a myriad of influences, from the level of the individual to the broader culture of sport. Looking first at the level of the individual, the concept of "wilful blindness" may help us understand why adults who are in positions of care over the welfare of young people fail to intervene on the child's behalf when emotional abuse is observed. Wilful blindness originated as a legal term, and refers to the act of turning a blind eye to crime, injustice, and immoral or unethical behaviour. As Heffernan (2011, p. 2) wrote: "you are responsible if you could have known, and should have known, and instead strove not to see." Within a legal framework, if you could and should have known, then you are responsible; in other words, in certain contexts not knowing is not an excuse. Although the term was first used in the legal world, it has since been used to account for the fact that a large number of people knew of such tragedies as the sexual abuses within the Catholic Church, the crimes committed in Nazi Germany, the Enron scandal, and the unethical practices of subprime mortgage lenders in the United States, and yet failed to intervene. It may be argued that adults in positions of power and authority in sport, such as coaches, sport administrators, and parents, are also guilty of wilful blindness when they fail to recognize emotionally abusive practices as such, and to intervene when these practices are used with children.

From a systems theory perspective, there are several proposed explanations for the occurrence of wilful blindness. At the individual level, we cannot notice and cognitively process everything in our perceptual field, and, as a result, we filter or edit information. We also have a preference for information that makes us feel good about ourselves and confirms an image or characteristics of ourselves that are positive. As such, we "turn a blind eye" to feel safe, to avoid conflict and change, and to protect our images of ourselves (Heffernan, 2011). It may be the case that parents turn a blind eye to emotionally abusive coaching practices in order to maintain an image of themselves as "good" parents who provide opportunities for their children to pursue athletic dreams. As Bazerman and Tenbrunsel (2011) explained in their book *Blind Spots*:

> Across most major scandals of the last decade, many people—members of boards of directors, auditing firms, rating agencies, and so on—had access to the appropriate data and should have noticed and acted on the unethical behavior of others. Yet they did not do so, at least in part because of the psychological tendency not to notice bad data that we would prefer not to see.
>
> (p. 81)

Just as Bronfenbrenner (1999) emphasized the interrelationship between the various ecological processes, it is suggested that there are social, environmental, and cultural influences that encourage wilful blindness. The influences of positions of authority and organizational hierarchies make it difficult to "see" things that are in plain sight. In the sport culture, the power and the authority of the coach has been well documented (Bringer, Brackenridge, & Johnston, 2001; Burke, 2001; Tomlinson & Yorganci, 1997) and proposed as a reason athletes give for their failure to report incidences of abuse in the coach–athlete relationship (Brackenridge, 2001; Stirling & Kerr, 2009). Parents have also described the authority of the coach and a fear of repercussions associated with intervening (Kerr & Stirling, 2012). Moving to the broader sub-culture of sport, the vast literature on cultures can assist us in enhancing our understanding of why and how emotionally abusive coaching practices occur and are permitted to persist in sport. In every culture, there are foundational values that are deeply embedded, often not well articulated, and yet guide behaviour in important ways. These values inform members of a particular culture about what is right and wrong, acceptable and not acceptable, rewarded and penalized (Townley, 2008). The values that typically characterize elite sport are performance-oriented, such as winning, often at the exclusion or neglect of other, more athlete-focused values, such as holistic development (Miller & Kerr, 2002). Such performance-oriented values are reflected in what is known as the "sport ethic", which encourages athletes to make personal sacrifices for the sake of the game and winning, to take risks, to obey authority, and to challenge limits (Hughes & Coakley, 2001). Consideration of the sport ethic and performance-centred values, which are at the heart of the sport culture, may help us to understand why yelling at a child or humiliating him or her as a way of pushing the child to perform better is interpreted by athletes as necessary and simply what it takes to become a good athlete (Gervis & Dunn, 2004; Hughes & Coakley, 2001; Stirling & Kerr, 2007). It may, in part, also account for the inaction of other coaches, parents, sport administrators, and medical/psychological consultants.

Not only are cultures characterized by values, but also these values are typically shared by its members. As Schein (1991) wrote, culture is:

> a pattern of shared basic assumptions, invented, discovered, or developed by a given group, as it learns to cope with its problems of external adaptation and internal integration, that has worked well enough to be considered valid and therefore, is to be taught to new members of the group as the correct way to perceive, think, and feel in relation to those problems.
>
> (p. 247)

While broad-based prevalence data regarding emotionally abusive experiences are lacking, previous findings indicate that athletes report these experiences as being common – in fact, the most commonly experienced form of athlete maltreatment (Stirling & Kerr, 2008, 2009). Researchers have reported that parents and athletes who are new to the elite sport environment learn about acceptable behaviours in this environment through the observation of other parents' and athletes' tolerance of these potentially harmful incidents (Brackenridge, 1998; Kerr & Stirling, 2012; Stirling & Kerr, 2014). Further, when reflecting on their own past use of harmful coaching practices, coaches attributed their own acceptance of such practices to personal histories of maltreatment as athletes from parents and past coaches, exposure to other coaches' harmful coaching techniques, lack of knowledge of alternative developmental strategies, and the athletes' acceptance of these coaching techniques in sport (Stirling, 2011).

The values of a given culture tend to be implicit, and, as such, individuals tend to behave in ways that are consistent with these values, but which may be below the level of consciousness (Townley, 2008). Within the culture of elite sport, this is exemplified by the findings that coaches are often well intentioned in their actions and do not recognize their emotionally abusive practices as harmful (Stirling, 2011), that athletes do not identify abusive behaviours as such until they leave the sport environment (Stirling & Kerr, 2007), and that parents experience guilt and remorse about not intervening or protecting their child once the child retires from sport (Kerr & Stirling, 2012). In sum, one potential consequence of the value-driven, shared, and implicit nature of cultures is that inappropriate behaviours can go unchecked. No other example in sport is so poignant as the recent case involving Jerry Sandusky and others at Pennsylvania State University. In 2011, the assistant football coach, Jerry Sandusky, was arrested and charged with over 50 counts of sexual abuse of young boys that extended over a period of 15 years. In 2012, Sandusky was found guilty on most of these counts, and was given a life sentence. Furthermore, and very importantly, independent investigators of the scandal concluded that the head coach, the athletic director, a campus administrator, and the university president knew of Sandusky's abuses of young people and actively endeavoured to conceal them; all of these individuals were subsequently fired from the university. At a press conference announcing the investigation findings, the lead investigator, Louis Freeh, stated: "The most powerful men at Penn State failed to take any steps for 14 years to protect the children Sandusky victimized." He said they "never demonstrated, through actions or words, any concern for the safety and well-being of Sandusky's victims" until after he was arrested in 2011 (www.nytimes.com/2012/07/13/opinion/).

One possible interpretation of this tragedy is that the cultural values of collegiate sport in a top 10 US university, namely the priorities of performance superiority, revenue generation, and alumni relations, encouraged those in positions of power and authority, who had the ability to intervene and did not, to engage in wilful blindness. This high-profile case is also an illustration of the positions of power held by males, and more specifically white males, in the domain of American football. We propose that the influence of the sport ethic extends to the normalization of abuse and the seemingly wilful blindness of adults who are in positions of authority and responsible for the care of young people.

Recommendations

To date, within the sport-related literature, numerous recommendations have been made in attempts to reduce and/or prevent the occurrence of emotionally abusive practices in elite sport. Several of these recommendations pertain to coach education (Australian Sport Commission, 1998; Gervis & Dunn, 2004; Kerr & Stirling, 2008; Kidman, 2005; Stirling & Kerr, 2009; www.nspcc.org.uk), specifically to enhance the awareness of coaches about abuse and abusive coaching behaviours. These educational initiatives also aim to expose coaches to alternative coaching behaviours that are more ethically sound and promote the health and development of the athlete. Programmes such as the National Coaching Certification Program (www.coach.ca) and Respect in Sport (www.respectinsport.org) in Canada, Play by the Rules (www.playbytherules.net.au) in Australia, and Safe4Athletes (www.safe4athletes.org) in the United States are examples of attempts to educate coaches about distinctions between unethical or illegal behaviours and more ethical, athlete-centred coaching behaviours. At the core of these educational interventions are the goals of enhancing the awareness of coaches about their positions of power and teaching coaches to use this power constructively. Other recommendations proposed previously to address emotionally abusive coaching practices include enhanced monitoring, surveillance, and reporting mechanisms (David, 2005; Gervis & Dunn, 2004; Kerr & Stirling, 2008). More specifically, to enhance the detection and reporting of abusive coaching practices, such recommendations as having athlete advocates and trained athlete welfare or harassment officers available to young athletes have been proposed (Brackenridge, 2001; Kerr & Stirling, 2008).

Together, these recommendations focus on the individual level, specifically to change the behaviour of the coach in order to reduce or eliminate the harm experienced by young people. While these recommendations point to critical components of an ecological approach to harm reduction, such a focus neglects the social and contextual influences in which the coach, in this case, functions. With the recent shift in our understanding of health promotion and harm, from an individual or behavioural focus to a broader, ecological emphasis, the responsibility for harm and the focus for change has moved to social situations and structures in which individuals find themselves (Marmot, 1998; Rhodes, 2002). This broader lens on social and environmental influences includes the study of "risk environments", which may help us better understand the contextual influences on the occurrences of harm to young people in sport. A focus on risk environments has previously been used to address the prevalence of such harmful behaviours as intravenous drug use, and the transmission of sexually transmitted infections (Des Jarlais, 2000; Rhodes, 2002). Shifting the focus of attention and agent of change from individuals to the environment changes how we think about responsibility for the occurrence of harm. As Rhodes (2002) wrote: "A focus on the risk environment encourages us to think about the social situations and places in which harm is produced and reduced" (p. 88). Such a shift in focus maximizes harm reduction at a community level. Although not previously applied in the context of sport, a focus on risk environments removes the focus of prevention and intervention from the coach and emphasizes interventions at the broader exosystem and macrosystem levels. Furthermore, by better understanding the social, environmental, and cultural determinants of harm, we also encourage thinking about ways to create enabling environments for harm reduction (Rhodes, 2002), and, in this case, harm prevention.

With this approach in mind, our question about preventing the occurrence of emotional abuse in sport shifts from "how can we keep coaches from using emotionally abusive practices?" to "how can we structure sport for children in ways that encourage coaches to use developmentally positive and healthy pedagogical practices?"

A possible structural method to help protect children may be to professionalize the practice of coaching. Professionalization refers to a social process that distinguishes between qualified and unqualified individuals, and establishes norms for entry, conduct, and professional development. Lyle (1998) wrote the following:

> Professional practice is characterized by skilled behaviour, not normally available to members of the public, which is developed over an extensive period of time of education and training and is conducted within identified codes of ethics and conduct. Professions are concerned to protect their boundaries and mark their territories through control of access accreditation of training, professional bodies and the licensing of practice.
>
> (p. 134)

Professionalizing an occupation is important for improving the profession and protecting the public interest. As such, professionalizing coaching is proposed as a method of effecting change at various levels within the ecological approach, from the individual to the broader values that characterize the elite sport context.

Improving an occupation through professionalization tends to be characterized by several criteria. First, there is a requirement for substantial education and training, and an identification of foundational knowledge, skills, or competencies. As the use – or misuse – of power by the coach is cited as the root cause of athlete abuse in the coach–athlete relationship, the complicity of parents and other bystanders, and the apparent silencing of athletes, such educational experiences would provide opportunities to develop more constructive ways of using positions of power. Humanistic or athlete-centred approaches to developing youth athletes may be promoted through such educational opportunities. Further, entry to professions is typically controlled through a licensing or registration process; this would ensure that coaches have the requisite education and skills. Quality assurance within a profession is pursued through the establishment of standards of conduct and boundaries of practice, a process to oversee these standards, and requirements for ongoing professional development. Additionally, specific grounds for misconduct are identified and a system of accountability is established. Typically, a professional, regulatory body oversees entry to the profession, maintenance of standards of ethical conduct of members, independence, and professional development (Hodkinson, 1995; Lyle, 2002; Middlehurst, 1995). By extending interventions from the coach to a regulatory body, there is a greater likelihood of affecting the values that characterize the youth sport context. More specifically, the presence of a regulatory body may help to counter the sport or performance ethic that currently characterizes the youth sport context, and may instead engender an ethic of care for young people in sport, one in which the primary focus is the enhancement of athletes' overall health and development.

In addition to improving the profession, professionalization serves to protect the public interest. It may be argued that the need to protect the public is greatest in the case of such vulnerable people as the children and youth who participate in sport.

Coaching in Canada and internationally is a long way from being professionalized. Presently, no specified qualifications or educational requirements are needed to become a coach in Canada; although some sport organizations require some National Coaching Certification Program (NCCP) certification, for others, this is optional. The organization Coaches of Canada has a published Code of Conduct that identifies standards of behaviour for coaches, and yet membership in this organization is optional; instead, it serves as an advocacy group and has no regulatory authority. Further, neither Coaches of Canada nor the Coaching Association of Canada has accountability measures in place to sanction coaches who do not comply with the expected standards of conduct. Unless a coach's misconduct falls into the criminal category, and thus becomes the responsibility of the justice system, there is no regulatory body in sport to receive and address concerns. Finally, there are no requirements for the professional development of coaches. All things considered, we argue that the landscape of the coaching occupation is such that we are left without assurances that the coaches of young people are well prepared, are adhering to the expected standards of conduct, or are up to date with respect to their knowledge and skills.

One could also argue that coaches are placed in an impossible position – being expected to perform well in very competitive environments without receiving adequate training and education. It is perplexing that our society accepts the lack of preparation, oversight, and regulation of coaches, who have influence over millions of young people in Canadian sport annually, when there are strict regulations in place for other professions that deal with young people, such as teachers and early childhood educators. The Ontario College of Teachers, for example, licenses, governs, and regulates the Ontario teaching profession in the public interest. Teachers who work in publicly funded schools in Ontario must be certified to teach in the province, and must be members of the College (www.oct.ca). Further, the College is accountable to the public for how it carries out its responsibilities. The social situation of sport is thus very different from the social situation of schools. Lyle (2002), who has written extensively about coaching, argued that "insufficient attention" has been paid to the issue of professionalizing coaching (p. 199).

So, while previous literature on the prevention of emotional abuse has appropriately and understandably targeted coach education and monitoring, it has done so at an individual level. While this approach is an important piece of the puzzle, it has a limited impact and neglects the more socio-environmental influences on coaching. We propose that one of the most significant ways in which to protect public interest – in this case, the public interest of young people – is to take a broader ecological approach to harm reduction, one that addresses changes at the individual level, as well as the social and environmental levels. This, we suggest, can best be done by professionalizing and thus regulating coaching. Only when coaches are held to consistent standards with respect to knowledge, skills, and conduct, and are accountable for their behaviours, will we have some assurances that young people are protected from poor practices and maltreatment.

Conclusion

For millions of youth around the world, organized sport offers the potential to grow in positive ways – physically, psychologically, and socially. Regrettably, however, harm has been known to occur to young people in this environment. Emotional abuse in particular has been reportedly experienced by young athletes, and has been associated with several detrimental outcomes for athlete well-being (Stirling & Kerr, 2013). Further, athletes' experiences of emotionally abusive coaching practices are typically observed by other adults, including the athletes' parents, other coaches, sport administrators, and other practitioners in sport, unfortunately without intervention.

The proposed normalization of such athlete abuse may be attributed to the "wilful blindness" of persons in sport – a tendency to turn a blind eye to what is known to be inappropriate, illegal, or unethical. The culture of competitive sport, with its emphasis on such performance outcomes as winning, is thought to contribute to this wilful blindness and the subsequent perception of emotional abuse as an acceptable practice. Previous researchers focused on the prevention of emotional abuse in sport have emphasized the need to increase the awareness of coaches about maltreatment and the substantial power they hold over athletes, and to educate coaches about ways in which to use this power constructively (Brackenridge, 2001; Burke, 2001; David, 2005; Tomlinson & Yorganci, 1997). These interventions, while important and necessary, fail to acknowledge the social environments in which coaches work. It is proposed in this chapter that the current landscape of coaching in Canada and other countries represents a risk environment. Taken together, the fact that coaches need not be trained or educated in a specified manner, that they are not obliged to adhere to standards of conduct or to engage in professional development, and that there is not a specific body responsible for hearing and addressing concerns about coach conduct leaves young people at risk of experiencing harm. Accordingly, in order to prevent the harm associated with athlete abuse, we propose the professionalization of coaching. Such a development would enhance the preparation of coaches at the level of the individual, better equipping them to be agents of social change. Further, professionalization may encourage the infusion of values associated with healthy child development and the creation of an ethic of care throughout the youth sport context, thus affecting other agents of change, such as parents and sport administrators.

By way of a comparison, at the turn of the nineteenth century, teaching was not viewed as a profession. Ryerson (1847), who was instrumental in developing the profession of teaching, wrote: "There cannot be good schools without good teachers; nor can there be, as a general rule, good teachers . . . unless persons are trained for the profession" (p. 55). Perhaps the same can be said about coaching: without good coaches who are trained for the profession, we will not have good sports – sports that protect young people from harm and promote their holistic health.

References

Adams-Blair, H. (2002). The importance of physical education and sport in the lives of young females. *International Sports Journal, 6*(1), 45–50.

Australian Sport Commission (1998). *Harassment-free sport: Guidelines for coaches.* Australian Sport Commission, Australia.

Bazerman, M., & Tenbrunsel, A. (2011). *Blind spots: Why we fail to do what's right and what to do about it.* Princeton, NJ: Princeton University Press.

Belsky, J. (1993). Etiology of child maltreatment: A developmental-ecological analysis. *Psychological Bulletin, 114*, 413–434.

Boocock, S. (2002). NSPCC report reveals concern over child abuse in swimming. Retrieved from www.nspcc.org.

Brackenridge, C. (1998). Healthy sport for healthy girls? The role of parents in preventing sexual abuse. *Sport, Education and Society, 3*, 59–78.

Brackenridge, C. H. (2001). *Spoilsports: Understanding and preventing sexual exploitation in sport.* London: Routledge.

Brackenridge, C. H. (2003). Dangerous sports? Risk, responsibility and sex offending in sport. *Journal of Sexual Aggression, 9*, 3–12.

Bringer, J., Brackenridge, C., & Johnston, L. (2001). The name of the game: A review of sexual exploitation of females in sport. *Current Women's Health Reports, 1*, 225–231.

Bronfenbrenner, U. (1979). *The ecology of human development: Experiments by nature and design.* Cambridge, MA: Harvard University Press.

Bronfenbrenner, U. (1999). Environments in developmental perspective: Theoretical and operational models. In S. L. Friedman & T. D. Wachs (Eds.), *Measuring environment across the lifespan* (pp. 3–28). Washington, DC: American Psychological Association.

Burke, M. (2001). Obeying until it hurts: Coach–athlete relationships. *Journal of the Philosophy of Sport, XXVIII*, 227–240.

Calder, M. (2000). *The complete guide to sexual abuse assessment.* Lyme Regis, UK: Russell House Publishing.

Cicchetti, D., & Lynch, M. (1993). Toward an ecological/transactional model of community violence and child maltreatment: Consequences for child development. *Psychiatry: Interpersonal and Biological Processes, 56*, 96–119.

Clarke, W. (2008). *Kids Sports. Canadian Social Trends.* Statistics Canada. Catalogue No. 11-008.

Cohen, D., Taylor, S., Zonta, M., Vestal, K., & Schuster, M. (2007). Availability of high school extracurricular sports programs and high-risk behaviors. *Journal of School Health, 77*, 80–86.

Côté, J., Strachan, L., & Fraser-Thomas, J. (2008). Participation, personal development and performance through youth sport. In N. L. Holt (Ed.), *Positive youth development through sport* (pp. 34–47). New York, NY: Routledge.

David, P. (2005). *Human rights in youth sport: A critical review of children's rights in competitive sports.* New York, NY: Routledge.

Des Jarlais, D. (2000). Structural interventions to reduce HIV transmission among injecting drug users. *AIDS, 14* (Supplement 1), S41–S46.

Eccles, J. S., & Barber, B. L. (1999). Student council, volunteering, basketball, or marching band: What kind of extracurricular involvement matters? *Journal of Adolescent Research, 14*, 10–43.

Fraser-Thomas, J., Côté, J., & Deakin, J. (2005). Youth sport programs: An avenue to foster positive youth development. *Physical Education and Sport Pedagogy, 10*, 19–40.

Gervis, M., & Dunn, N. (2004). The emotional abuse of elite child athletes by their coaches. *Child Abuse Review, 13*, 215–223.

Haney, C. J., Long, B. C., & Howell-Jones, G. (1998). Coaching as a profession: Ethical Concerns. *Journal of Applied Sport Psychology, 10*, 240–250.

Harrison, P., & Narayan, G. (2003). Differences in behaviours, psychological factors and environmental factors associated with participation in school sports and other activities in adolescence. *Journal of School Health, 73*(3), 113–120.

Hartmann, D. (2012). Beyond the sporting boundary: The racial significance of sport through midnight basketball. *Ethnic and Racial Studies, 35*, 1007–1022.

Heffernan, M. (2011). *Willful blindness.* Toronto: Doubleday Canada.

Hodkinson, P. (1995). Professionalism and competence. In P. Hodkinson & M. Issitt (Eds.), *The challenge of competence: Professionalism through vocational education and training* (pp. 58–69). London: Casell.

Hughes, R., & Coakley, J. (2001). Positive deviance among athletes: The implications of overconformity to the sport ethics. In A. Yiannakis & M. Melnick (Eds.), *Contemporary issues in sociology of sport* (pp. 361–374). Champaign, IL: Human Kinetics.

Kerr, G. A., & Stirling, A. E. (2008). Child protection in sport: Implications of an athlete-centred philosophy. *Quest, 60*, 307–323.

Kerr, G. A., & Stirling, A. E. (2012). Parents' reflections on their child's experiences of emotionally abusive coaching practices. *Journal of Applied Sport Psychology, 24*, 191–206.

Kidman, L. (2005). *Athlete-centred coaching: Developing inspired and inspiring people.* Riccarton, New Zealand: Innovative Print Communications.

Lehman, S. J., & Koerner, S. S. (2004). Adolescent women's sports involvement and sexual behavior/ health: A process-level investigation. *Journal of Youth and Adolescence, 33*, 443–455.

Lyle, J. (1998). The coaching process. NCFB2001. Leeds: National Coaching Foundation.

Lyle, J. (2002). *Sports coaching concepts. A framework for coaches' behavior.* New York, NY: Routledge.

Marmot, M. (1998). Improvement of social environment to improve health. *Lancet, 351*, 57–60.

Melnick, M. J., Miller, K. E., Sabo, D., Farrell, M. P., & Barnes, G. M. (2001). Tobacco use among high school athletes and nonathletes: Results of the 1997 Youth Risk Behavior Survey. *Adolescence, 36*, 727–747.

Middlehurst, R. (1995). Leadership and professionals: Comparative frameworks. *Tertiary Education and Management, 1*(2), 120–130.

Miller, P. S., & Kerr, G. A. (2002). Conceptualizing excellence: Past, present, and future. *Journal of Applied Sport Psychology, 14*, 140–153.

Pate, R. R., Trost, S. G., Levin, S., & Dowda, M. (2010). Sports participation and health related behaviors among US youth. *Archives of Pediatric and Adolescent Medicine, 154*, 904–911.

Pedersen, S., & Seidman, E. (2004). Team sports achievement and self-esteem development among urban adolescent girls. *Psychology of Women Quarterly, 28*, 412–422.

Rhodes, T. (2002). The "risk environment": A framework for understanding and reducing drug-related harm. Commentary. *International Journal of Drug Policy, 13*, 85–94.

Ryerson, E. (1847). *Report of a system of public elementary instruction for Upper Canada.* Montreal: Lovell & Gibson.

Sabo, D., Miller, K., Farrell, M., Melnick, M., & Barnes, G. (1999). High school athletic participation, sexual behavior, and adolescent pregnancy: A regional study. *Journal of Adolescent Health, 25*, 207–216.

Schein, E. H. (1991). What is culture? In P. Frost, F. Moore, M. R. Louis, C. Lundberg, & J. Martin (Eds.), *Reframing organizational culture* (pp. 242–253). Thousand Oaks, CA: Sage.

Slutzky, C. B., & Simpkins, S. D. (2009). The link between children's sport participation and self-esteem: Exploring the mediating role of sport self-concept. *Psychology of Sport and Exercise, 10*, 381–389.

Steiner, H., McQuivey, R., Pavelski, R., Pitts, T., & Kraemer, H. C. (2000). High school student athletes: Mental and physical health associations with sports participation. *Clinical Pediatrics, 39*, 161–166.

Stirling, A. E. (2009). Definition and constituents of maltreatment in sport: Establishing a conceptual framework for research practitioners. *British Journal of Sports Medicine, 43*, 1091–1099.

Stirling, A. E. (2011). Initiating and sustaining emotional abuse in the coach–athlete relationship: Athletes', parents', and coaches' reflections. Unpublished doctoral dissertation, University of Toronto, Toronto, Ontario, Canada.

Stirling, A. E., & Kerr, G. A. (2007). Elite female swimmers' experiences of emotional abuse across time. *Journal of Emotional Abuse, 7*, 89–113.

Stirling, A. E., & Kerr, G. A. (2008). Defining and categorizing emotional abuse in sport. *European Journal of Sport Science, 8*, 173–181.

Stirling, A. E., & Kerr, G. A. (2009). Abused athletes' perceptions of the coach–athlete relationship. *Sport in Society, 12*, 227–239.

Stirling, A. E., & Kerr, G. A. (2010). Sport psychology consultants as agents of child protection. *Journal of Applied Sport Psychology, 22*, 305–319.

Stirling, A. E., & Kerr, G. (2013). The perceived effects of elite athletes' experiences of emotional abuse in the coach–athlete relationship. *International Journal of Sport and Exercise Psychology, 11*(1), 1–14.

Stirling, A. E., & Kerr, G. (2014). Initiating and sustaining emotional abuse in the coach–athlete relationship: An ecological transactional model of vulnerability. *Journal of Aggression, Maltreatment & Trauma, 23*(2), 116–135.

Stirling, A. E., Kerr, G. A., & Cruz, L. C. (2012). An evaluation of Canada's National Coaching Certification Program's "Make Ethical Decisions" coach education module. *International Journal of Coaching Science, 6*(2), 45–60.

Stirling, A. E., Bridges, E., Cruz, E. L., & Mountjoy, M. (2011). Canadian Academy of Sport and Exercise Medicine position statement: Abuse, harassment, and bullying in sport. *Clinical Journal of Sport Medicine, 21*, 385–391.

Taliaferro, L. A., Rienzo, B. A., & Donovan, K. A. (2010). Relationships between youth sport participation and selected health risk behaviors from 1999 to 2007. *Journal of School Health, 80*, 399–410.

Tomlinson, A., & Yorganci, I. (1997). Male coach/female athlete relations: Gender and power relations in competitive sport. *Journal of Sport and Social Issues, 21*, 134–155.

Townley, B. (2008). *Reason's neglect: Rationality and organizing.* Oxford: Oxford University Press.

3   A post-structuralist approach to hazing in sport

Jennifer J. Waldron

In October of 2011, parents of a 15-year-old hockey player in Canada described the hazing their son had endured. Specifically, their son had to compete in a dance-off, where he was forced to dance sexily and remove his clothes (CBC News, 2011). Because he lost, he then had to endure *Tug* – a hazing ritual where a water bottle carrier was tied to his scrotum. This incident is an example of a hazing event that *rookies*, or the new members of a sport team, often experience. Other reported hazing practices include tattooing, whippings with weight belts, shaving of genital hair, circling of areas of fat on the body, and even sodomizing teammates (Bryshun & Young, 1999; Campo, Poulos, & Sipple, 2005; Waldron & Kowalski, 2009; Waldron, Lynn, & Krane, 2010).

Unfortunately, these practices are common in the sport environment. National data sets from the United States report that approximately 75% of collegiate student-athletes (Allan & Madden, 2008; Hoover, 1999) and approximately 50% of high school students (Hoover & Pollard, 2000; Madden & Allan, 2008) experience hazing. Hazing has been defined as:

> Any humiliating, degrading, abusive, or dangerous behavior expected of a junior-ranking athlete by a more senior teammate, which does not contribute to either the athlete's positive development, but is required to be *accepted* as part of a team, regardless of the junior-ranking athlete's willingness to participate. This includes, but is not limited to, any activity, no matter how traditional or seemingly benign, that sets apart or alienates any team member based on class, number of years on team, or athletic ability.
>
> (Crow & MacIntosh, 2009, p. 449)

The above definition acknowledges that, unlike individuals in other environments, such as fraternities and sororities, hazed athletes are already members of the team, selected by the coach at try-outs. Thus, when rookies experience hazing on a sport team, they have already demonstrated they are qualified to participate on the team. Hazing becomes a way for the older veterans to persuade younger members, often through pain infliction, to conform to the social roles and appropriate behaviors of the team (Sabo, 2004). Experiencing and remaining silent about hazing experiences transforms an individual's identity from an outsider of the team to an insider or a *real* member of the team.

The questions researchers have been attempting to answer are why do rookie members of the team allow themselves to be hazed, and why do team members not question or challenge these hazing practices more often. The majority of past research has focused on a hierarchical power relationship between veterans and rookies (Bryshun, 1997; Holman, 2004; Stuart, 2012; Waldron & Kowalski, 2009). That is, hazing is a symptom of the values of and the power relationships in the sport environment. As a *total institution* (Atkinson & Young, 2008; Goffman, 1961), similar to the military or prison, sport is an enclosed social system where individuals are compelled to adhere to specific codes of behavior by means of constant monitoring. The primary outcome of these institutions and behavioral practices is to control the life of the individuals in the institutions through the complete infusion of values, beliefs, and behaviors (Goffman, 1961). Therefore, past research has characterized hazing as a tool of power and domination that veterans use on rookies (Bryshun, 1997; Holman, 2004; Stuart, 2012; Waldron & Kowalski, 2009).

Within the institution of sport, many athletes discuss the importance of hazing to team cohesion (Allan & Madden, 2008; Bryshun, 1997; Waldron & Kowalski, 2009; Waldron et al., 2010). Somehow, experiencing and enduring pain or violence as a group during hazing is supposed to create a sense of belonging among rookies who experience it together (Baumeister & Leary, 1995). Hazing is a resocialization process where the shared struggling and suffering supposedly lead to camaraderie and loyalty among members (Pershing, 2006). Similarly, it is common for athletes who have been hazed to report that the experience of pain infliction or degradation resulted in deeper relationships and a closer team (Allan & Madden, 2008; Bryshun, 1997; Waldron & Kowalski, 2009). There is a perception that hazing is an adaptive act that builds cohesion and unity, yet hazing is a coercive act forcing athletes to conform to the norms of the team in degrading and harmful ways.

Although there is the belief that hazing leads to increased team cohesion, there is some research suggesting otherwise. Researchers have shown that hazing deters the development of team cohesion (Van Raalte, Cornelius, Linder, & Brewer, 2007), and some intercollegiate athletes interviewed by Waldron and Kowalski (2009) admitted they experienced decreased team cohesion after enduring hazing. These athletes revealed that hazing created distance between veterans and rookies, which was detrimental to the performance of the team. Indeed, there is an illusion of team bonding via hazing, but the bonding is based on a perpetrator fearing detection or a victim's fear of retaliation (Stuart, 2012). Even if there are cases where hazing builds team cohesion, the severe psychological and/or physical consequences of hazing are often detrimental to the well-being of athletes.

Another aspect of the total institution of sport is that athletes must maintain complicit silence about hazing acts. Even if athletes do not agree with the hazing behaviors, many of them will not recount such behaviors to officials. For instance, 60% of collegiate athletes stated that they would not report hazing (Hoover, 1999), and 95% of college students who were hazed did not report their experiences to campus officials (Allan & Madden, 2008). The power structure of the team is maintained as rookies are unwilling to report acts of humiliation and violence (Stuart, 2012). Because, in this framework, rookies have little to no power on the team, they do not believe they can report these acts. To report these acts would show weakness, which is deplored in an environment of hegemonic masculinity.

Overall, past research has focused on the hierarchical nature of hazing, where veterans have the power and rookies have none (Bryshun, 1997; Holman, 2004; Stuart, 2012; Waldron & Kowalski, 2009). Although this work has provided great insight into hazing practices, the researchers have had difficulty explaining the many contradictions embedded in the hazing experiences and discussions, which are linked to the (re)production of power. Given that past research has been unable to reconcile the contradictions of hazing, additional insight about hazing may be gained by exploring hazing from a post-structuralist perspective, where being an athlete and hazing is constructed within our language use and becomes the taken-for-granted knowledge (McGannon & Mauws, 2002). Within this framework, power is neither hierarchical nor held by certain groups, such as veteran team members, but rather power is relational and dynamic (Ashton, Price, Kirk, & Penney, 2012). Indeed, "what the poststructuralist inquiries make clear is that what is domination and exploitation in the eyes of some is the way things were meant to be in the eyes of others" (McGannon & Mauws, 2002, p. 76). In this manner, a post-structuralist approach to hazing can account for the many contradictions that occur. Therefore, the purpose of this chapter is to illustrate how a post-structural framework can be applied to our understanding of hazing in sport. First, post-structuralism will be explained, and then post-structuralism will be applied to hazing in sport. Lastly, three case studies will be presented in order to illustrate how other researchers and practitioners could use post-structuralism in their hazing work.

Critical approach

In this chapter, I frame hazing from a post-structuralist perspective, which highlights that one's self or one's identity is created and situated within daily language and discourse (McGannon & Mauws, 2002). Discourses "are resources that people draw upon to explain and/or give meaning to who they are and what they experience; discourses also actively shape, enable, and/or constrain behavioral practices" (McGannon & Busanich, 2010, p. 217). In this chapter the discourse of hazing refers to the statements we make and the language we use about hazing, which help to construct the meaning and understanding of hazing. These discourses, then, produce and reproduce what we believe to be true (Weedon, 1997) about hazing.

Post-structuralist theorists assert that each of us is a product of discourse (Foucault, 1982; Weedon, 1997). Discourses are a set of resources or ways of thinking and speaking that provide us with conditions of possibility (Foucault, 1982). By accessing these conditions of possibility, we actively participate in and make choices with regards to the creation and understanding of our identity

(Weedon, 1997). Some discourses provide a significant number of conditions of possibility or ways of thinking and speaking, with further implications for behaviour (McGannon & Mauws, 2002; McGannon & Spence, 2010). For example, there are numerous ways to think and speak about gender. Women and men can be strong and tough or empathetic and caring or assertive and passive. By negotiating these conditions of possibility at particular times, we create identities that are changing, fluid, complex, and at times contradictory (Ashton et al., 2012).

On the other hand, some discourses, such as the dominant discourse of what constitutes a committed athlete in organized and competitive sport, which I will call the discourse of athlete as tough, are more limiting. That is, the language and behavioral practices of an athlete, such as playing through pain, winning at all costs, and being tough (Coakley, 2009), are rigid and inflexible. Because institutions, such as the media, as well as individuals consistently refer to real athletes playing through pain or doing anything to win, this discourse becomes the taken-for-granted of what it means to be a "real" athlete. Moreover, language use and thought both reflect and inform our identity at a particular time and a particular place (Ashton et al., 2012; McGannon & Busanich, 2010; McGannon & Spence, 2010). The media, coaches, and teammates may draw upon a discourse that constructs real athletes as tough and able to ignore pain. When constructing one's athletic identity within the foregoing discourse, the result is athletes tell themselves they are showing toughness during hazing experiences.

Another occasion on which our identities are constructed and made fluid is when we participate in discourses from particular positions, called sites of subjectivity (Weedon, 1997). For example, most athletes draw upon the discourse of athlete as tough in order to construct their self-identity of athlete. Within the discourse of athlete as tough, athletes may occupy the subject position of veteran (longest-standing member of the team), auxiliary teammate (member with two to four years on the team), or rookie (new member of the team). Although all athletes are constrained and shaped by the language and values of being an athlete, one's subject position will result in a particular (1) interpretation of the language of others, (2) thinking pattern, and (3) experience on the sport team (McGannon & Mauws, 2002; McGannon & Spence, 2010). That is, depending upon the discourse, veterans will use language and engage in particular behaviors not available to those who occupy the rookie position within that same discourse. Within the dominant discourse of athlete as tough, committed, and playing through the pain, veterans' thinking "I have to put rookies in their place so they don't get too arrogant" becomes an acceptable and taken-for-granted reason to haze, and also follows the expectation of that subject position. Being a veteran and refusing to haze the rookies may also result in accusative thoughts to the self or accusative language by teammates (e.g., being too soft or too weak), the belief being that the veteran should fulfil their role on the team.

Finally, post-structuralist theorists argue that power is based on relations between individuals, and that the use of particular discourses maintains these relationships of power (Focault, 1982; McGannon & Busanich, 2010; McGannon

& Spence, 2010); that is, language is the means by which power is defined and contested. Power is not linear; rather, it is dynamic, reciprocal, and based on context (Ashton et al., 2012). There is not a set group who is responsible for producing or controlling the language and understanding of a phenomenon (Pringle, 2005), such as hazing. In other words, veterans, auxiliary teammates, and rookies all help structure the hazing experience: hazing would not exist if the rookies and the auxiliary team-mates, as well as the veterans, did not draw upon and support the discourse.

Ultimately, post-structuralism can be condensed into three major tenets (McGannon & Busanich, 2010; McGannon & Mauws, 2002). First, the self and our subject position is a creation of language and discourse. Second, focusing on the language and discourse of a phenomenon is essential to understanding the beliefs and reality of an individual. Third, relationships of power result in some beliefs and some knowledge being more accepted and endorsed than others. Applying these three tenets to hazing on sport teams, when a hazing experience is communicated as a fun evening of team bonding in order to become a *real* member of the team, rookies hear this language and it becomes what is believed to be true. Thus, they willingly participate in the hazing in order to fulfill the duty and display the necessary attributes of being an athlete, even if they do not agree with or experience harm as a result of the hazing.

Application of post-structuralism to hazing

Within a post-structuralist framework, it is important to focus on the taken-for-granted words people use as they account for and talk about hazing. The established and consistently used words we use to discuss athletes need to be examined in terms of identity construction (McGannon & Mauws, 2002; McGannon & Spence, 2010) as it relates to being an athlete or not being an athlete in organized and competitive sport. Athletes' identities are not predetermined and housed somewhere within the mind, but are instead constructed from different types of language or discourses. Thus, with a greater number of possibilities to define themselves as athletes through different types of language and discourse, athletes' construction of identity could emerge in numerous ways (McGannon & Mauws, 2002). Yet the discourse of athlete as tough, committed, and playing through the pain within organized and competitive sport is quite limited, so that there are fewer ways in which to identify as an athlete, resulting in the majority of athletes identifying and behaving similarly.

The dominant discourse of athlete as tough, committed, and playing through the pain emerges within the context of the male-defined and male-dominated institution of sport (Anderson, 2008). Moreover, the dominant discourse of athlete as tough and committed includes *loving* the game, *achieving* perfection, *playing* through pain, and *pursuing* success without question (Hughes & Coakley, 1991). That is, the language about *real, successful* athletes includes such characteristics as tough, aggressive, dominant, competitive, and emotionally detached (Atkinson & Young, 2008). As this limited discourse about being an athlete is circulated in society, individuals situate themselves within this discourse in order to identify as an athlete. Often we hear about the *tough* athletes who are willing to put their bodies on the line for sport, but rarely do we hear about athletes properly healing their bodies; indeed, when we do, it is often in a negative light. These words (e.g., tough, aggressive, pursuing success without question), insofar as they contribute to the formation of a particular identity, encourage or discourage certain behaviors, such as hazing. This dominant meaning of athlete created through language use thus becomes common sense. In other words, we come to believe and take for granted the dominant discourse that athletes have to embody loving the game, achieving perfection, playing through pain, and pursuing success without question.

Pertaining to hazing, such post-structuralist ideas as discourse and identity help us to understand why athletes are compelled to engage in acts of hazing and remain silent about their experiences, even when they do not want to participate or when harm occurs. Additionally, post-structuralist theorists assert that although people do have agency and choice, their choices are not infinite (McGannon & Mauws, 2002). That is, rookies and veterans do have power and choice about hazing; however, their choices are limited by the discourses they adhere to when shaping their identity. Specifically, rookies and veterans are limited by their subject position within the dominant discourse of athlete when making decisions about hazing incidents.

To be an accepted member of the team, individuals have to *prove* that they have positioned themselves correctly within the discourse of athlete as tough and committed. Therefore, within sport, hazing is constructed as a means for older players to persuade younger members to conform to the social roles and appropriate behaviors of the team based on the dominant discourse of being an athlete (e.g., tough, aggressive, pursue success without question). By surviving hazing, athletes *prove* they are valuable teammates by displaying absolute commitment to their sport and meet the expectations of their teammates, such as persevering when confronted by fear, discomfort, or pressure (Coakley, 2009). Through language, hazing is constructed as a way for rookies to demonstrate loyalty, commitment, and the willingness to take one for the team (Allan, 2004; Bryshun & Young, 1999; Kirby & Wintrup, 2002), regardless of the embarrassment or danger it entails. When this occurs, athletes are able to claim team membership and uphold their athletic identities.

The discourse of athlete as tough and committed includes particular roles and duties suited to rookies, veterans, and auxiliary team members that structure an athletic team. Statements and notions within this discourse and language help to construct what constitutes a *veteran, auxiliary teammate,* or *rookie,* and what is considered proper *veteran, auxiliary teammate,* or *rookie* behavior. For veterans, this means they paid their dues on the team and have proved they can adhere to what it means to be an athlete (e.g., playing through pain, loving the game). Within this discourse, veterans are also encouraged to test new members of the team to ensure they are committed to team values, and thus through this language appear to have greater status and power over other teammates. Claims such as "some of it [hazing] is good, I think, to keep the pecking order in line . . . you can't have freshmen being above [seniors] on the chain" (Waldron & Kowalski, 2009, p. 297) or "I think people [haze as] ... a social thing. Like a social acceptance into the group" (Waldron & Kowalski, 2009, p. 298) are an acceptable reason to haze rookies because to do otherwise would breach the expectations of a veteran within this discourse. Veterans are thus successfully fulfilling their roles within the athletic team, and are more likely to experience fulfillment, when these particular attributes and duties are attained.

Auxiliary teammates are those members of the team who are no longer rookies, but have not reached the status of veteran. On a high school or college team, these players are usually the sophomores or juniors. Within the discourse of athlete as tough and committed, auxiliary teammates have already proven their conformity to the team norms by surviving hazing in the past. Auxiliary members are typically bystanders to the hazing incidents, meaning they are present during the incidents but are not actively doing the hazing. In this position, auxiliary teammates will experience satisfaction when they encourage veterans during the hazing, or at least keep quiet about it.

Rookies are viewed as having to pay their dues to become an accepted member of the team. For example, rookies may have different clothes or different practice gear, may be called *dogmeat* by coaches and veterans, or may be forced to carry practice equipment. And, although some rookies may have power due to their greater athletic skills compared to the veterans, they still need to defer to the supposed expertise of veteran team members for social acceptance. Within this discourse, rookies often construct hazing as fun and something that naturally happens on sport teams. For example, one athlete claimed that hazing "is fun to watch and it's even ... fun to be a part of, too," while another shared "every young freshmen goes through [hazing], I might as well go through it. And by the time I'm a senior, I'm gonna be able to do it to the other freshmen" (Waldron & Kowalski, 2009, pp. 296–297). Rookies are best fulfilling their position, and implicitly their identities as athletes, through demonstration of their commitment to the team. In turn, athletes are more likely to experience personal fulfillment when these attributes are realized.

When it comes to hazing, rookies habitually utter phrases to themselves and to teammates that justify hazing, such as "hazing is harmless fun or a rite of passage." Additionally, rookies engage in these hazing incidents because within the dominant discourse of being a tough and committed athlete, they must succumb to hazing to become a real teammate. In short, the need to be accepted as an athlete and teammate takes precedence over avoiding humiliating and degrading experiences. Because of the particular discourse of athlete that frames their experiences, rookies correctly understand themselves to be responsible for needing to experience hazing, and thus they engage in the behaviors. Choice occurs, but within the limits of the discourse of athlete and their position as rookie.

Because language and discourse use is critical to our identity, it is also important to understand the variations of language regarding hazing. Two major discourses, *hazing as harmless fun* and *hazing as violence*, further anchor the spectrum of hazing behaviors (Waldron, Heisterkamp, & Aspleaf, 2012). These anchors include fairly consistent hazing beliefs and behaviors. That is, most athletes would characterize hazing as harmless fun and playful jokes that do not cause harm. These incidents may include singing in public or shaving the heads of rookies. On the other end of the spectrum is hazing as violence. Most athletes would also construct hazing as violence in a consistent manner to include events of torture and extremely distressing experiences. In turn, rookies experience severe mental or physical pain through experiences such as alcohol poisoning or rape/sodomy, and in some instances death due to homicide or suicide.

In the middle of the spectrum are hazing behaviors that are often perceived in contradictory ways. Here, some athletes in some circumstances would consider these behaviors to be harmless fun; however, other athletes in the same circumstances or the same athletes in different circumstances would consider the behaviors to be violent. The middle of the hazing spectrum includes such degrading and abusive practices as transporting athletes to unfamiliar locations, and urinating on them in the shower. Also included in the middle of the hazing spectrum are practices causing physical or emotional injury, such as paddling or enduring harsh weather conditions without proper clothing. The middle of the spectrum, then, becomes a site of contradiction and fluidity within an athlete and among athletes, which can be understood through a post-structuralist framework. In order to further illustrate how to apply a post-structuralist framework to *hazing as harmless fun*, *hazing as violence*, and *hazing contradictions*, case studies will be used in the following sections.

Hazing as harmless fun

Take, for example, the following hazing incident, which took place in the fall of 2012. During the New York Giants (National Football League) training camp, a hazing event occurred that went viral via social media (Fuel Internet Marketing, 2012). Jason Pierre-Paul, a veteran, dumped Prince Amukamara, a rookie, head first into a cold tub and used explicit language with his teammates (i.e., auxiliaries), many of whom were watching and encouraging the antics. Stepping out of the cold water, Amukamara appeared upset. Because the video went viral, much media coverage was devoted to this incident, with the veteran (Pierre-Paul), the rookie (Amukamara), and teammates publicly responding to the incident. Pierre-Paul noted that, although he understood how Amukamara could have been injured, the incident was all fun and games and he would never hurt one of his teammates (Youngmisuk, 2012). In the same story, Amukamara shared that the event was how teammates get along and showed their love for each other. He continued that if the event was personal or threatening, he would have stopped it. Finally, many auxiliary players noted that the event was simple horseplay, a tradition, and a rite of passage that new players accepted as a way to become one of the guys (Youngmisuk, 2012).

Although Amukamara, through being thrown head first into a shallow tub, could have been injured and looked upset, the language he used to describe this hazing incident to the media (re)produced the knowledge that hazing is

(1) harmless fun with no intent to actually hurt teammates, (2) a form of team cohesion, and (3) a rite of passage. Being positioned as a rookie within the dominant discourse of athlete as tough and committed, Amukamara utters the proper phrases about hazing that then re-enact the knowledge and belief that hazing is harmless fun and a rite of passage. Although likely unaware of what he was doing, Amukamara reproduced hazing as harmless fun when his response, to being asked about the message the video portrayed to kids, was that these horseplay situations can be taken too far, with the risk of injury, so kids should just know not to take it too far (Foss, 2012). Through his language, Amukamara condoned hazing as long as no one was hurt, which continues to produce the notion that hazing is fun and harmless unless there is visible injury or damage.

Moreover, other people, including veterans, auxiliary teammates, and coaches, are positioned within the same discourse, and thus reinforced the way that Amukamara was thinking, speaking, and behaving. Pierre-Paul constructed his identity as veteran on the team, and thus was able to order or force rookies to do things they may not have wanted to do, such as be thrown into the cold-water tub. The auxiliary teammates also constructed their identities in this discourse, by willingly participating in the hazing, and by cheering the veterans on and tweeting the video for the world to view. By being positioned within the dominant discourse of athlete, hazing was encouraged, which then constructed and reinforced the identity of the rookies, veterans, and auxiliary teammates.

Another important piece of this case study is that the athletes never used the language of hazing or bullying in association with the incident. When asked whether the cold tub incident was hazing or bullying, Amukamara replied no to both (Foss, 2012). Moreover, another player said that the incident was not bullying but rather a display of the culture of the locker room (Youngmisuk, 2012). This language is consistent with the many interviews I have conducted with athletes who refuse to use the term *hazing* to describe their experiences (Waldron & Kowalski, 2009; Waldron et al., 2010) and with the language use of media journalists (Nuwer, 2004). Because the discourse of hazing as harmless initiation has become intertwined with the dominant discourse of athlete, it has become expected and acceptable for athletes to engage in fun horseplay. By labeling their experiences as *harmless* initiation rituals, athletes create the discourse that hazing acts are only those *really and obviously* abusive experiences. Thus, athletes deliberately refuse to call these acts hazing because that would suggest they were breaching the conventions of being an athlete and being a good teammate.

A post-structuralist framework assumes that athletes have a choice, although it may be limited by identity and the subject position taken up within particular discourses, as to whether or not to engage in hazing (McGannon & Mauws, 2002; McGannon & Spence, 2010). In the present case, Amukamara asserted his power or agency in the situation by participating in the hazing and showing his teammates that he was tough enough to survive the incident, as well as willing to take a joke. Moreover, he asserted in his media interviews that he could have used his power to stop the acts if they had become too threatening. Indeed, other rookies have decided to display their agency by not participating in the hazing. For example, in an earlier hazing incident from the NFL, Des Bryant, a rookie, refused to carry the football pads of the veteran members of the team (Watkins, 2010). Not only did many teammates and the media find this breach of expectation unacceptable, but also there were consequences to Des Bryant's decision: he was forced to pay a dinner bill of $54,896 for his teammates (Watkins, 2010).

Hazing as violence

Another hazing case came to the attention of the media in 2003. During an overnight preseason training camp, three perpetrators (i.e., veteran members) of the Mepham High School football team sodomized and attacked at least three victims (i.e., rookies; Wahl & Wertheim, 2003). As the attacks were happening, auxiliary teammates reportedly encouraged the perpetrators or silently watched in horror, yet all of them kept silent about the incident. The football team at Mepham High School had a history of hazing, with some of the perpetrators in this incident having suffered assaults as rookies (Leung, 2009). When the victims could no longer hide the injuries they had sustained, details about the hazing were slowly revealed. As happens, the victims' identities became known, and they were taunted by classmates with *football fag*, *broomstick boy*, or *butt pirate*, while teammates remained silent about the incident (Wahl & Wertheim, 2003). The football season was canceled, two coaches lost their teaching and coaching jobs, and the three perpetrators were eventually charged as juveniles. Two were sentenced to four months in juvenile facilities and one received probation (Leung, 2009). In response to this hazing, while many newspapers promoted a zero-tolerance approach to such acts, many in the town did not think that the whole football team should be punished for the behavior of three veterans (Wahl & Wertheim, 2003).

Although this hazing incident is much more severe and violent than being thrown in a cold-water tub, there are similarities to how the athletes positioned themselves as veterans, auxiliary teammates, or rookies within the dominant discourse of athlete as tough and committed. Rather than reiterate all the similarities between the two hazing incidents from a post-structuralist perspective, I will focus on three aspects of this abusive incident: the change in language from veterans and rookies to perpetrators and victims, the role of the auxiliary teammates, and the consequences when the victims finally discussed the incident.

In the discourse of *hazing as harmless fun*, the language used to identify specific team positions is veteran and rookie. When hazing is constructed as violence, the language used to describe subject positions changes to perpetrator and victim. This change in language produces the knowledge that someone has committed a crime, and that someone has suffered mistreatment or an injury. In other words, the perpetrators have done something wrong and the victims have been hurt. These word choices, then, (re)create a very different representation of hazing. Here, hazing is harmful, violent, dangerous, and worthy of criminal charges, which should be avoided.

The hazing incident at Mepham High School also highlights the subject position of auxiliary teammates within the dominant discourse of athlete. Although victims were being sodomized, multiple times, by perpetrators, the auxiliary members not only did not stop the incident but also reportedly encouraged the perpetrators. Moreover, the auxiliary teammates remained quiet after returning from the team camp, and many remained silent even when the victims came forward about the hazing (Wahl & Wertheim, 2003). In this situation, the auxiliary teammates situated themselves within the discourse of athlete, and identified as athlete rather than identifying as a moral, ethical individual who would stop or speak out against the abusive acts. By behaving in the expected manner of an athlete (i.e., not speaking out), the auxiliary teammates displayed their power by positioning themselves correctly within the discourse of athlete, and likely experienced some fulfillment because of it. The thought, speech, and behavior of the auxiliary teammates were also reinforced by town members, who believed that the auxiliary teammates did not bear any responsibility for the incident, and that therefore they should not have been punished via the canceling of the football season. These behaviors (re)produced the knowledge that, even when hazing is violent and harmful, it is the duty of auxiliary teammates to uphold the complicit silence about the acts if they want to continue to identify as an athlete.

Finally, the above incident also (re)created the belief that within the dominant discourse of athlete as committed (e.g., being tough, willing to do anything to be a team member, sustaining pain), those rookies who want to identify as committed athletes better remain silent about any serious harm or injury they experience. First, the victims reluctantly came forward about the abusive hazing when medical help was needed due to injuries that were not healing. Again, in this incident, rookies had power to act; however, this power was limited by the discourse in which they situated themselves. Similar to the auxiliary teammates, the rookies' identity of athlete, based on the rigid, dominant language of athlete, was the priority; therefore, the rookies behaved in a manner (e.g., accepted the sodomy and remained quiet) that was expected of their role as rookies. If the discourse of athlete were more flexible, or if the rookies were to use a different identity, then it is likely they would have greater conditions of possibility to act, and could display their power in alternative ways. Second, when the details of the hazing were revealed, the rookies were verbally abused through emasculating taunts by classmates. This language reinforced the belief that rookies who want to identify as athletes better remain silent about any serious harm or injury they experience. These repeated and consistent discourses about athlete and hazing become the taken-for-granted meaning of what it means to be an athlete and hazing.

Hazing contradiction

Within the discourses of *hazing as harmless fun* and *hazing as violence* there are many inconsistent and contradictory beliefs, values, and behaviors. Specifically, athletes with whom I have spoken claim that the veterans would never harm one of their teammates in a violent manner, that they would stop the hazing act if the rookies wanted, and that the incidents where hazing is violent are *messed up* (Kowalski & Waldron, 2010; Waldron & Kowalski, 2009; Waldron et al., 2010). Yet we know from the media and interviews with other athletes that athletes are often injured and harmed during hazing incidents, and that it does not appear as though rookies have a choice as to whether or not to engage in the hazing. Hearing the statements of athletes can draw attention to the contradictory nature of hazing. One athlete stated, "some of the guys probably didn't agree with [hazing], but you know, just went along with it just because that's the way it was with the [club soccer] team" (Waldron & Kowalski, 2009, p. 297). Another athlete reported that:

> If it [hazing] is just somethin' that, you know for that instant, you were uncomfortable with, that might be the best to let it go. But if it's something that, you know, constantly makes you uncomfortable then I think it would be best to go and get it taken care of no matter, well if it didn't make things worse with the teammates.
>
> (Waldron & Kowalski, 2009, p. 299)

One athlete observed that "Obviously when someone gets humiliated or problems arise from it . . . I think if it really starts to bother the person who is getting picked on, probably then it would be called hazing" (Waldron & Kowalski, 2009, p. 298); yet, later in the same interview, they stated that it was difficult to know when someone was hurt by the hazing.

To make sense of these contradictions, it is important to return to the major tenets of post-structuralism. Specifically, to understand the beliefs and reality of athletes, we have to understand the language and discourse of being an athlete and hazing (McGannon & Busanich, 2010; McGannon & Spence, 2010). Due to relations of power, constructing hazing as harmless fun becomes the acceptable belief about hazing. These relations of power are based on (1) constructing and identifying oneself within the dominant discourse of athlete as committed (i.e., tough, aggressive, play through pain) over other identities, especially when among teammates, (2) the belief that rookies have to be tough, and (3) the belief that veterans have to challenge the rookies.

When athletes identify themselves within the dominant discourse of athlete as committed (i.e., tough, aggressive, playing through pain), it shapes their beliefs and behaviors, and creates relations of power. Because the dominant discourse of athlete is rigid and inflexible, it follows that athletes assume it to be common sense that they have to experience hazing, and will then behave in the expected manner. When an athlete identifies themself with the dominant discourse of athlete as committed, it shapes their perceptions, knowledge, and behavior. For example, most athletes would be appalled if, in order to board a bus, they had to be whipped with a weight belt by the bus driver or perform fellatio on a banana. Further, many athletes would press criminal charges against the driver. While the acts themselves would not be out of place for athletes in the context of the locker room, the context of the bus setting is different. In this setting, most athletes are not identifying as an athlete, so the behavior is found unacceptable and even criminal. However, in the athletic context, when the athletic identity is a priority and athletes are embedded in the dominant discourse of athlete, most athletes will endure these behaviors as expected and accepted.

The language used to identify as an athlete is so effective in creating the belief that hazing is harmless fun that rookies often do not believe that the hazing acts are dominating, exploitative, and violent. Language use surrounding athletes is that they need to be tough and strong. Within such language or discourse use, rookies understand they are being tested on these characteristics via hazing. So, even when the hazing acts are violent or turn violent, rookies may be so engrossed in the identity of athlete and the discourse that the hazing is harmless fun that they cannot access the knowledge or belief that harm and violence are being done to them. Although interviewed athletes have reported that veterans would stop the hazing if it appeared that rookies were uncomfortable or were bothered (Waldron & Kowalski, 2009), it is likely that most rookies would not show these emotions because it would be counter to the dominant discourse of athlete. In other words, rookies often show their power in hazing situations by demonstrating how tough, how fun, and how unbreakable they are. In this manner, even when they are uncomfortable with the hazing, they express their agency by surviving the hazing and being able to identify as an accepted member of the team. As one athlete stated, "I didn't mind going through that shit for one night, 'cause now I'm a [team-member]" (Bryshun, 1997, p. 94).

Moreover, hazing situations can easily escalate. When rookies are experiencing harm or injury and do not show it, veterans may decide they can increase the intensity of the hazing. Again, veterans are positioned within the dominant discourse of athlete and believe they have to test and challenge rookies through hazing. The majority of athletes I have interviewed revealed that, as veterans, they would never cross the line to harm the rookies: veterans want to challenge the athletes without causing excessive harm. Yet, most athletes reveal that the determination of harm lies with the rookies and not the veterans. If rookies, from their subject position, refuse to show weakness and harm, then it becomes difficult for veterans to display their agency by stopping or changing the hazing act. In an incident where both rookies and veterans displayed power, Bryshun (1997) reported that the seven rookies of a male hockey team refused to engage in the Elephant Walk (i.e., holding the genitals of the teammate behind), and so the veterans just made the rookies drink more. Moreover, athletes have revealed that veterans would likely seek to punish the rookie who decided to forgo hazing (Bryshun, 1997; Waldron & Kowalski, 2009; Waldron et al., 2010). After a rookie refused to sing in public, veterans stuffed his football helmet and cleats full of excrement, making him late for practice (Bryshun, 1997). Veterans will often pursue the rookie who refuses to engage in the hazing until the veterans believe the rookie has been challenged sufficiently.

Counter to the majority of past research, which focused on hierarchical power relations between veteran and rookie, this chapter explores hazing within the context of post-structuralism. Theoretically, while athletes' behaviors are their own, these individual decisions and behaviors are made within a number of broader discourses (McGannon & Busanich, 2010; McGannon & Spence, 2010). Here, the dominant discourse of athlete and the discourse of hazing influence the decisions athletes make regarding their engagement in hazing on a sport team. The choices and behaviors of veterans, auxiliary teammates, and rookies regarding hazing are not due to something lacking within them, but are due to the internalization of the dominant discourse of athlete and related power relations (McGannon & Busanich, 2010). Because athletes tend to position themselves within different discourses, their speech, thought, and behaviors concerning hazing are often contradictory.

Conclusion

Within a post-structuralist framework, McGannon and Mauws (2002) argued that changes in behavior result from helping individuals realize how discourses, including their language use, contribute to the circumstance. That is, athletes have to be made aware of how their daily conversations and language use about hazing and being an athlete contribute to their hazing experiences. Having conversations with athletes about hazing, then, can raise their awareness. For example, such statements as "Hazing is about abuse of power and control over others" and "Hazing can hurt team trust, respect, and unity" (Allan & DeAngelis, 2004, p. 76) can be starting points for a team discussion. These dialogues can be a technique to help bring awareness to the taken-for-granted notions of hazing.

Moreover, teammates, coaches, and administrators also need to expand their language use so that there is a wider range of discursive possibilities from which athletes can identify. For instance, in a courageous letter to the editor, a group of male athletes from Andover Academy in Massachusetts called for a change to the athletic culture on their high school campus (Olkowski et al., 2013). Although focused on gender issues on campus, these male athletes challenged individuals in the athletic context to brainstorm new and constructive ways to develop team cohesion and team bonding. This is one example of how athletes can start a conversation about what it means to be an athlete, hopefully thereby providing all athletes with a greater number of ways to think, speak, and act.

Broader educational efforts can also be used to help people become aware of and change the discourse of athlete and hazing. For example, Waldron (2012) presented a social norms workshop to prevent hazing. This workshop encouraged athletes and coaches to reflect on and discuss team norms, the purpose of hazing behaviors, and why they should feel responsible for working towards a solution. Discourses of athlete, of hazing as harmless fun, and of hazing as violence are explored during the workshop. As with my interviews with athletes, I have found that contradictory language emerges from these workshops. Through activities and discussions, athletes gain an awareness that it is possible to resist the dominant discourse of athlete and hazing. Because hazing does not occur in isolation, it is also critical that the workshops contain discussions acknowledging and challenging the role of various institutions and broader *societal* practices in influencing individual hazing behaviors. In the end, with workshops and other strategies, it is hopeful that researchers, coaches, administrators, teachers, and others can use a post-structuralist perspective to expand the discourse of athlete and promote beneficial and prideful rituals on sport teams.

References

Allan, E. J. (2004). Hazing and gender: Analyzing the obvious. In H. Nuwer (Ed.), *The hazing reader* (pp. 275–294). Bloomington, IN: Indiana University Press.

Allan, E. J., & DeAngelis, G. (2004). Hazing, masculinity, and collision sports: (Un)becoming heroes. In J. Johnson & M. Holman (Eds.), *Making the team: Inside the world of sport initiations and hazing* (pp. 61–82). Toronto: Canadian Scholars Press.

Allan, E. J., & Madden, M. (2008). *Hazing in view: College students at risk. Initial findings from the National Study of Student Hazing.* Retrieved from University of Maine website: www.umaine.edu/hazingstudy/hazing_in_view_web.pdf.

Anderson, E. (2008). "I used to think women were weak": Orthodox masculinity, gender segregation and sport. *Sociological Forum, 23*, 257–280.

Ashton, M., Price, S., Kirk, S. F. L., & Penney, T. (2012). More than meets the eye: Feminist poststructuralism as a lens toward understanding obesity. *Journal of Advanced Nursing, 68*, 1187–1194.

Atkinson, M., & Young, K. (2008). *Deviance and social control in sport.* Champaign, IL: Human Kinetics.

Baumeister, R. F., & Leary, M. R. (1995). The need to belong: Desire for interpersonal attachments as a fundamental human motivation. *Psychological Bulletin, 117*, 497–529.

Bryshun, J. (1997). Hazing in sport: An exploratory study of veteran/rookie relations. Unpublished master's thesis, University of Calgary, Calgary, Alberta. Retrieved from http://dspace.ucalgary.ca/bitstream/1880/26954/1/24577Bryshun.pdf.

Bryshun, J., & Young, K. (1999). Sport-related hazing: An inquiry into male and female involvement. In P. White & K. Young (Eds.), *Sport and gender in Canada* (pp. 269–292). Ontario: Oxford University Press.

Campo, S., Poulos, G., & Sipple, J. W. (2005). Prevalence and profiling: Hazing among college students and points of intervention. *American Journal of Health Behavior, 29*, 137–149.

CBC News. (2011, October 26). Bottles tied to genitals in Manitoba hockey hazing. *CBC News.* Retrieved from http://www.cbc.ca/news/canada/manitoba/story/2011/10/26/mb-neepawa-hockey-hazing.html.

Coakley, J. (2009). *Sports in society: Issues and controversies* (10th ed.). Boston: McGraw-Hill.

Crow, R., & MacIntosh, E. W. (2009). Conceptualizing a meaningful definition of hazing in sport. *European Sport Management Quarterly, 9*, 433–451.

Foss, M. (2012, August 21). Amukamara says JPP wasn't being a bully. *USA Today.* Retrieved from http://content.usatoday.com/communities/thehuddle/post/2012/08/prince-amukamara-speaks-out-about-giants-hazing/1#.Ub85f_nvjTo.

Foucault, M. (1982). The subject and power. *Critical Inquiry, 8*, 777–795. Retrieved from http://www.jstor.org/stable/1343197.

Fuel Internet Marketing. [OnlineFuel]. (2012, August 18). *NY Giants Prince Amukamara thrown in coldtub by JPP* [video file]. Retrieved from http://www.youtube.com/watch?v=UT5w8eldAiU.

Goffman, E. (1961). *Asylums: Essays on the social situation of mental patients and other inmates.* Chicago: Aldine.

Holman, M. (2004). A search for theoretical understanding of hazing practices in athletics. In J. Johnson & M. Holman (Eds.), *Making the team: Inside the world of sport initiations and hazing* (pp. 50–60). Toronto: Canadian Scholar's Press.

Hoover, N. (1999). *National survey: Initiation rites and athletics for NCAA sports teams.* Retrieved from http://www.alfred.edu/news/html/hazing_study_99.html.

Hoover, N. C., & Pollard, N. J. (2000). *Initiation rites in American high schools: A national survey.* Retrieved from http://www.alfred.edu/news/html/hazing_study.html.

Hughes, R., & Coakley, J. (1991). Positive deviance among athletes: The implications of overconformity to the sport ethic. *Sociology of Sport Journal, 8*, 307–325.

Kirby, S. L., & Wintrup, G. (2002). Running the gauntlet: An examination of initiation/hazing and sexual abuse in sport. In C. Brackenridge & K. Fasting (Eds.), *Sexual harassment and abuse in sport: International research and policy perspectives* (pp. 65–90). London: Whiting & Birch.

Kowalski, C. L., & Waldron, J. J. (2010). Looking the other way: Athletes' perceptions of coaches' responses to hazing. *International Journal of Sports Science & Coaching, 5*, 87–100.

Leung, R. (2009, February 11). Dangerous minds. *Forty Eight Hours.* Retrieved from http://www.cbsnews.com/8301-18559_162-611479.html.

Madden, M., & Allan, E. J. (2008). *Hazing in view: High school students at risk.* Retrieved from University of Maine website: http://www.hazingstudy.org/publications/hs_hazing_summary.pdf.

McGannon, K. R., & Busanich, R. (2010). Rethinking subjectivity in sport and exercise psychology: A feminist post-structuralist perspective on women's embodied physical activity. In T. V. Ryba, R. J. Schinke, & G. Tenenbaum (Eds.), *The cultural turn in sport psychology* (pp. 203–230). Morgantown, WV: Fitness Information Technology.

McGannon, K. R., & Mauws, M. K. (2002). Exploring the exercise adherence problem: An integration of ethnomethodological and poststructuralist perspectives. *Sociology of Sport Journal, 19*, 67–89.

McGannon, K. R., & Spence, J. C. (2010). Speaking of the self and physical activity participation: What discursive psychology can tell us about an old problem. *Qualitative Research in Sport and Exercise, 2*, 17–38.

Nuwer, F. (2004). How sportswriters contribute to a hazing culture in athletics. In J. Johnson & M. Holman (Eds.), *Making the team: Inside the world of sport initiations and hazing* (pp. 118–131). Toronto: Canadian Scholar's Press.

Olkowski, T., Bello, B., Crane, D., Demeulenaere, A., Ellis, E., Fehnel, S., . . . Wang, J. (2013, May 31). Letter to the editor. *Thephillipianonline.* Retrieved from http://www.phillipian.net/articles/2013/05/30/letter-editor-0.

Pershing, J. L. (2006). Men and women's experiences with hazing in a male-dominated elite military institution. *Men and Masculinities, 8*, 470–492.

Pringle, R. (2005). Masculinities, sport and power: A critical comparison of Gramsican and Foucauldian inspired theoretical tools. *Journal of Sport and Social Issues, 29*, 256–278.

Sabo, D. (2004). The politics of sport injury: Hierarchy, power, and the pain principle. In K. Young (Ed.), *Sporting bodies, damaged selves: Sociological studies of sports-related injury* (pp. 59–80). Boston: Elsevier.

Stuart, S. P. (2012). Warriors, machismo, and jockstraps: Sexually exploitative athletic hazing and Title IX in the public school locker room. *Western New England Law Review.* Retrieved from http://scholar.valpo.edu/cgi/viewcontent.cgi?article=1075&context=law_fac_pubs.

Van Raalte, J. L., Cornelius, A. E., Linder, D. E., & Brewer, B. W. (2007). The relationship between hazing and team cohesion. *The Journal of Sport Behavior, 30,* 491–507.

Wahl, G., & Wertheim, L. J. (2003, December 22). A rite gone terribly wrong. *Sports Illustrated.* Retrieved from http://sportsillustrated.cnn.com/vault/article/magazine/MAG1030931/.

Waldron, J. J. (2012). A social norms approach to hazing prevention workshops. *Journal of Sport Psychology in Action, 3,* 1–9.

Waldron, J. J., & Kowalski, C. L. (2009). Crossing the line: Rites of passage, team aspects, and ambiguity of hazing. *Research Quarterly for Exercise and Sport, 80,* 291–302.

Waldron, J. J., Heisterkamp, A., & Aspleaf, S. (2012, November). The activity sponsor's guide on how to prevent hazing: Leading and responding with solutions. Unpublished manuscript, University of Northern Iowa, Cedar Falls, Iowa.

Waldron, J. J., Lynn, Q., & Krane, V. (2010). Duct tape, icy hot, & paddles: Male athlete hazing narratives. *Sport, Education, and Society, 16,* 111–125.

Watkins, C. (2010, September 29). Roy Williams pays back Dez Bryant. *ESPN Dallas/Fort Worth.* Retrieved from http://sports.espn.go.com/dallas/nfl/news/story?id=5626300.

Weedon, C. (1997). *Feminist practice and poststructuralist theory* (2nd ed.). Oxford: Blackwell.

Youngmisuk, O. (2012, August 21). Tom Coughlin unhappy with incident. *ESPN New York.* Retrieved from http://espn.go.com/new-york/nfl/story/_/id/8285739/tom-coughlin-says-new-york-giants-ice-tub-incident-inappropriate.

4   Gender nonconformity, sex variation, and sport

Vikki Krane

> Basketball player . . . College junior . . . Ranked No. 1 nationally in blocked shots (5.2), No. 2 in field goal percentage (.611) and No. 6 in scoring (23.4) . . . First NCAA player to score more than 2,000 points with 500 blocked shots . . . ESPN.com National Player of the Year . . . AP and USBWA Player of the Year . . . Wooden Award, Naismith Trophy, and Wade Trophy Recipient . . . Big 12 Player of the Year . . . NCAA Final Four Most Outstanding Player . . . WBCA Defensive Player of the Year . . . AP All-American (unanimous).[1]
> (baylorbears.com, 2013; Brittney-Griner.com, 2013)

Even the most casual fan of US college basketball would recognize the outstanding nature of this sport resume (the awards are for conference and national level achievements). Add in height of 6'8", a wing span of 88 inches (7'4"), a 9'2" standing one-arm reach, and a size 17 shoe (baylorbears.com, 2013). What possible negative critique could come to such a storied and stellar player? Now imagine that this basketball player is female. Brittney Griner's imposing size, deep voice, and sporting dominance has been met with wanton scrutiny – over her gender. Social media has been abuzz with such callous comments as:

> "Why is Brittney Griner so good at basketball? Because she's actually a man."
> "Britney Griner looks like a straight she-man!"
> "Britney Griner does not count as a female athlete."
> "Britney Griner has a penis."
> "Britney Griner pees standing up."
> (Dixon, 2012; Floyd, 2012)

Our society has defined male–female, girl–boy, masculine–feminine as categorical opposites. You are one or the other. This is referred to as the binary categorization of sex and gender (Kane, 1995; Theberge, 1998; Travers, 2006). When people are deemed to cross into oppositional territory – when it is difficult to identify one's sex or gender, or when a male is too feminine or a female is too masculine – dissonance occurs. This dissonance often leads to questions, condemnation, and criticism. This reaction seems to be especially pronounced in sport, where there are boys' and girls' leagues, men's and women's teams, and even variations of sports specific to male and female athletes (e.g., softball and baseball, hockey and ringette). Athletes like Brittney Griner face prejudice because their appearance differs from what is expected of people of their sex. Other athletes cannot or do not want to fit into these predesignated sex and gender categorizations. Many gender nonconforming or sex variant athletes face bias and exclusion in sport. In this chapter, I apply a critical transfeminist perspective to explore the interplay among sex, gender, and fair play, as well as present a critical approach to inclusion in sport. Using examples of policies purported to be inclusive of gender nonconforming and sex variant athletes, I highlight how these policies reproduce common stereotypes and misconceptions surrounding sex, gender, athletic bodies, and sport.

A critical framework for understanding gender nonconformity and sex variation

My approach to understanding gender nonconformity and sex variance is grounded in feminist cultural studies and transfeminist perspectives. Feminist cultural studies scholars explore how common, everyday activities reinforce power hierarchies in society, particularly those related to gender (Birrell, 2000; Hall, 1996; Krane, 2001). From this perspective, gender is considered "socially and culturally constructed because demeanour and behaviour is governed by social expectations and does not reflect innate distinctions between female and male" (Krane & Symons, 2014). There are a myriad of common practices that reinforce the notion that males will be masculine and females will be feminine, which has led to differential treatment of females and males in sport. For example, it is taken for granted that boys will be athletic and want to play sports rather than dance. As such, many boys do not even consider dance as an activity option. Similarly, that girls will want to play softball rather than baseball simply is expected. Further, power is main-tained through hegemonic acceptance of these customary practices, which are so widely accepted that they are taken as *truth*. For example, historically, the belief that females lacked the strength and stamina necessary for sport led to few opportunities for them to participate in sport and, hence, their lack of ability compared to males. Today, the media continues to reinforce the superiority of men's sport (e.g., through greater coverage of men's sport and the objectification of female athletes) (Duncan, 2006). As such, lower expectations and less value continue to be placed on sport for girls, due to the hegemonic belief that males are better athletes.

Sport is rife with gendered expectations that influence everything from who gets to play certain sports (e.g., Travers, 2011), how we separate girls from and boys, and who receives the most resources to support participation (Messner, 2002). Decisions on these matters follow long-held, hegemonic beliefs that simply are accepted by the people in power (i.e., those who distribute the resources). These hegemonic beliefs about gender and sport are so engrained in the fabric of our social life that they seem natural and often go unquestioned. Through the lens of feminist cultural studies, I question the effects of ordinary, commonplace actions grounded in assumptions about gender.

I also draw on Scott-Dixon's (2006a, 2006b) and Enke's (2012a) conceptualizations of *transfeminism*, a multidisciplinary blend of feminism and transgender studies. Transfeminism, as applied here, critiques the binary conceptualizations of sex and gender and recognizes their impermanent and evolving nature. Transfeminism leads to questioning the emphasis on anatomy as a criterion for social organization. Rather, I recognize and appreciate the complexity of sex and gender and of lived experiences with sex and gender. By taking a transfeminist stance, one honors sex and gender variation and privileges self-defined identity (Nagoshi & Brzuzy, 2010). Transfeminism also embraces a "broad and rich anti-oppression mandate" (Scott-Dixon, 2006b, p. 239) that links transprejudice with all other forms of oppression.

Before delving further into the critique of sex and gender, it is important to clearly distinguish among the various terms that will be used throughout this discussion. Although often conflated, sex and gender are distinct concepts. *Sex* refers to one's biological, hormonal, chromosomal, physiological, and anatomical make-up that categorizes people as males and females. *Gender* is culturally and socially constructed; it is based on social expectations and categorizes people as masculine or feminine. A critical approach to understanding sex and gender focuses on a critique of the dominant binary understanding of them (cf. Cromwell, 2006; Enke, 2012a). For example, the very foundation of sport is grounded in the assumption that there are inherent differences between male bodies and female bodies. This essential view of bodies presumes strength, size, and ability distinctions as naturally occurring; that is, we are born into these bodies that are male or female, and male bodies are better suited to sport than female bodies. This assumption permeates almost all the rules and decisions that have led to a separation between males and females in sport. Concomitant with the sex division in sport is the expectation that females are feminine and males are masculine. Feminine people are demure, dependent, soft, weak, sensitive, and compliant (Choi, 2000). Characteristics corresponding with masculinity (e.g., competitive, independent, strong, and aggressive) are aligned with sporting success, which further reinforces the assumption that male bodies make better sporting bodies than female bodies (Travers, 2006).

However, what happens when bodies and their associated characteristics do not align with these binary categories? This is where we see dissonance, discrimination, and exclusion, and this is what many transgender, transsexual, and intersex athletes face. In the Brittney Griner example, she is taller, has a deeper voice, and is more talented than what is expected of female athletes; the result is that narrow-minded people refer to her as a man. I use the term *gender nonconforming* to refer to individuals "whose gender identity, role, or expression differs from what is normative for their assigned sex in a given culture and historical period" (Coleman et al., 2011). Some gender nonconforming athletes may identify as female or male (sex), yet are read by others as atypical. Other gender nonconforming athletes intentionally subvert gendered expectations (e.g., Travers, 2006).

People who are *transgender* have a gender identity that is not consistent with their physical sex assigned at birth and a gender expression that differs from conventional expectations associated with the assigned sex (Enke, 2012b). An individual's *gender identity* reflects an internal sense of being female, male, transgender, or something else; this personal construal may or may not align with one's physical body (i.e., sex) (Enke, 2012b). How someone presents themselves visibly to others is *gender expression*, which is portrayed through, for example, hair style, attire, physical movements, and mannerisms (Enke, 2012b). Some transgender people may prefer to be recognized as a gender different from their physical sex. Others may identify as *genderqueer*, in which their gender is flexible or fluid, and these people may not identify as male or female (Krane & Symons, 2014). *Transsexuals* are individuals who physically change their bodies to align with their gender identity (Krane & Symons, 2014). These changes often occur through hormone therapy that alters their body chemistry. Some transsexual people will undergo components of, or complete, sex reassignment surgery (SRS), leading to permanent changes so that their genitalia and/or breasts resemble the desired gender. The term *trans* may be used "as an umbrella term that suggests many forms of gender boundary crossing, whether in terms of behaviour, self-presentation, or identity" (Scott-Dixon, 2006c, p. 247).

While we tend to think of sex as only female or male, *intersex* people are born with internal or external genitalia, hormonal and chromosomal make-up, and/or internal reproductive organs that are inconsistent with one sex. That is, they may have a combination of male and female physical characteristics or ambiguous sex characteristics (Looy & Bouma, 2005). Just as sex and gender are socially constructed, so too is intersex. As a society, we have come to expect that certain physical characteristics define one as female or male. This social agreement is framed in medical research and scientific literature that clearly delineates what is to be considered physically male and physically female. Medical authority also dictates what is *abnormal*. As Fausto-Sterling (2000) long has purported, the system of two binary sex categories is insufficient for describing the range of naturally occurring possibilities. The term *variations in sex development* situates intersex and transgender persons within the broad range of possible physicalities and identities (Lee, Houk, Ahmed, & Hughs, 2006). Such an approach is consistent with Krane and Barak's (2012) metaphor of a prism (see Figure 4.1) to describe the range of sex and gender. As they expressed:

> While a prism may radiate obvious lines of color, the spectrum of colors also bleed into one another and can become less distinct. When considering gender identity, sometimes sex and gender are aligned recognizably and in socially expected manners (e.g., feminine females and masculine males). Yet, as seen in the prism, a wide array of outcomes can emerge, which cannot be predicted or prescribed.

(p. 39)

Considering sex and gender as a prism invites inclusion by recognizing the myriad variations and possibilities. Some identities are easily recognized, similar to the

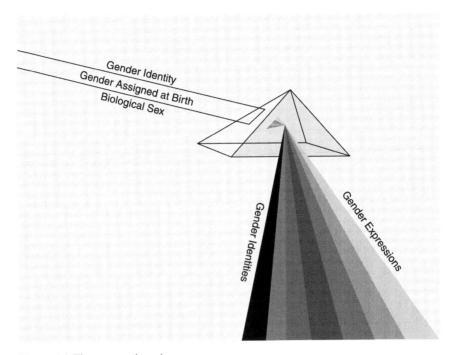

Figure 4.1 The sex–gender prism.

Source: modified from Krane and Barak (2012).

primary colors in the prism. Other gender expressions may be less common, but are not less natural or valued, much like the areas of the prism where the colors blend together. The image of a rainbow infers a vibrancy emerging from its entirety. Applied to sport, each sport team draws its strength through the inclusion and acceptance of all members. Everyone has a place, no matter how unique one may be. Thus, while athletes like Brittney Griner may be unique, they also are respected and even admired.

Landmark sport policies

Contemporary sport has begun recognizing sex and gender variations and is acknowledging that transgender, transsexual, and intersex athletes are participating; it also is grappling with how best to include these athletes in ways that ensure fairness for all participants. As a whole, such rules regarding transgender, transsexual, and intersex inclusion are grounded in binary assumptions about sex and gender. Current policy often reflects cultural and social expectations about sex and gender more than contemporary scientific understandings of sporting bodies. As such, the institution of sport reproduces hegemonic standards grounded in the presumption that male sporting bodies are always superior to female bodies (Cavanagh & Sykes, 2006). Because female identified transgender, transsexual, and intersex athletes often mistakenly are perceived to have a masculine advantage, they also are confronted with naïve accusations and intolerant restrictions.

In their attempts to be inclusive, the International Olympic Committee (IOC) and the National Collegiate Athletics Association (NCAA; the governing body of US college sport) have taken the lead in creating policy regarding sex variant and gender nonconforming athletes. As many sport organizations look to their processes as models, it is important to carefully critique the standards they set. In 2003, the IOC approved the Stockholm consensus, which allows transsexual athletes to compete in Olympic events if they have had complete sex reassignment surgery, they can show legal recognition of the assigned sex, and they can verify that they have been on hormone therapy for "a sufficient length of time to minimize gender-related advantages in sport," or what was determined two years after gonadectomy (sex reassignment surgery) (IOC, 2003).

On the surface, this policy was ground-breaking in that it provided an opportunity for transsexual athletes to participate in Olympic sport. At the same time, it overlooked a large segment of the trans athlete population. Most obviously, only athletes who have had complete sex reassignment surgery (SRS) are eligible for Olympic competition. This mandate raises a number of issues. SRS includes the removal of the uterus and ovaries (in some bodies), the construction of a vagina or penis, changes to breast size, and in some cases cosmetic surgery. The need for breast and genital surgeries to support athletic eligibility is questionable. Such a mandate does not take into consideration that some trans individuals may take exogenous hormones (i.e., those from outside the body, not naturally produced in the body), yet do not choose to have any surgery. Other trans people may have only breast surgery and not genital surgery. Further, genital surgery is highly invasive and complex (Bowman & Goldberg, 2006). SRS may entail multiple surgeries as well as a lengthy rehabilitation period. While breast and genital surgeries are not related to athletic advantage, what they do achieve is creating bodies that are consistent with appearance expectations for male and female athletes. In effect, the IOC policy reinforces binary assumptions about gender as only those individuals whose bodies adhere to the expectation that males have penises and females have breasts and vaginas are allowed to participate.

The NCAA has taken a different approach to the inclusion of trans athletes. Unlike the Olympic policy, the NCAA (2011) does not mandate surgery; instead, this policy focuses on athletes' use of exogenous hormones. Consistent with their policy, a trans female (male-to-female; MTF) on testosterone suppression medication can continue to compete on a men's team. After one year of testosterone suppression treatment, she is eligible to compete on a women's team. For a trans male (female-to-male; FTM) athlete, once he begins hormone therapy (i.e., taking testosterone), he is eligible to compete only on men's teams. Such an approach appears logical as research supports that bodily changes, which may affect athletic performance, will occur. Female-to-male trans athletes taking exogenous testosterone will experience increased muscle mass and upper body strength, a redistribution of body fat (from hips and buttocks to the abdomen), stoppage of menses, voice changes, and hair growth changes (Dahl, Feldman, Goldberg, & Jaberi, 2006). These changes typically will occur within the first year of hormone therapy. For male-to-female individuals, within one year of hormone therapy, there is decreased muscle mass and decreased upper body strength, redistribution of body fat in female body patterns, breast growth, and decrease in bone mineral content and bone density (Dahl et al., 2006; Lapauw et al., 2008).

The NCAA policy also recognizes that not all transgender athletes will choose to make physical changes to their bodies. In fact, some transgender athletes will delay beginning hormone therapy so as not to interfere with athletic eligibility. When considering college sport in the United States, for example, athletes have only 4–5 years of eligibility. Changing one's hormonal balance may impact strength and balance, and, given that it may take a year for these changes to stabilize, hormone therapy could interrupt eligibility or athletic capability. The NCAA (2011) policy also states that a trans male (FTM) athlete who is not taking testosterone is eligible to compete on either a men's or a women's team, whereas a trans female (MTF) athlete not on hormone treatments may compete only on a men's team. In these cases, the athlete may change appearance to be consistent with gender identity; however, no bodily changes occur.

It is important to recognize that this policy still is steeped in the assumption that male bodies make better athletic bodies, as it prohibits MTF athletes from joining a female team. This perspective ignores MTF athletes' gender identity and disallows self-selection of gender. While many male athletes may have a size and strength advantage over many female athletes, this is not an absolute certainty. Instead, this stance reinforces the hegemonic social expectation that males naturally are better athletes than females. This policy also does not take into consideration the specific sport. For example, in rowing there are weight categories to match rowers based on size. In gymnastics or synchronized swimming, size alone may not be an advantage. In some situations, there may not be reason to disallow a male-bodied athlete with a female gender identity from competing on a women's team. Although seemingly a realistic alternative to the IOC Stockholm consensus, the NCAA policy continues to reproduce problematic narratives surrounding gender in sport; transgender athletes are provided access to sport participation, yet assumptions of male superiority prevent complete access.

More recently, the IOC (2011) has considered the participation of intersex athletes, more specifically women with elevated testosterone levels. Referred to as hyperandrogenism, these female athletes have atypically high levels of androgens (i.e., testosterone). The IOC guidelines include:

> A female recognised in law should be eligible to compete in female competitions provided that she has androgen levels below the male range (as shown by the serum concentration of testosterone) or, if within the male range, she has an androgen resistance such that she derives no competitive advantage from such levels.
>
> (IOC, 2011)

One goal of these regulations is to guarantee fairness (IOC, 2011), which in elite sport historically has been focused on ensuring that males do not interlope in female competition and fraudulently defeat the women. Between the 1960s and the 1990s, all women in Olympic or Olympic-qualifying events were sex tested. Today, international sport no longer mandates sex testing of all females. However, according to current IOC policy (2012), "An Expert Panel shall be appointed to evaluate a *suspected* case of female hyperandrogenism" (emphasis added). In other words, women who appear *too masculine* still can be mandated to undergo sex testing to ensure fair competition, and females who are *too masculine* can be deemed ineligible for female competition. Given the binary sex categorization of elite athletes, a woman athlete with "excessive amounts of testosterone" by default is considered a male.

Poignantly, simply recognizing that intersex individuals exist confirms that not all bodies neatly fit into the binary categories of female or male. Yet sport leaders in the IOC continue to adhere to long-standing hegemonic assumptions about testosterone and sex as the IOC policy presumes that sex can be objectively determined based solely on testosterone levels. As Karkazis, Jordan-Young, Davis, and Camporesi (2012) frankly stated, "sex is *always* complex. There are many biological markers of sex but none is decisive; that is, none is actually present in *all* people labeled male or female" (p. 6, emphasis in original). Previous attempts at sex-testing elite female athletes have shown the complications inherent in attempting to confer femaleness or classify all female bodies based on a single attribute (e.g., Heggie, 2010). Although aimed at safeguarding female competition, and purporting to uncover a few gender frauds,[2] more often these sex tests "caught" and scapegoated intersex women (Karkazis et al., 2012).

Early sex tests examined Barr bodies, which revealed the chromosomal make-up of the female athletes. This test detected the presence of a second X chromosome and, based on the assumption that all female bodies have XX chromosomes and all male bodies have an XY chromosomal make-up, identified female bodies. In 1992, the Barr test was replaced with the polymerase chain reaction (PCR) test, which identified the presence of a Y chromosome. As history shows, both tests were problematic (Heggie, 2010; Tucker & Collins, 2010). Important to understand in this discussion is the wide array of chromosomal irregularities that may occur in the human body. For example, females with Turner syndrome have only one X chromosome (XO) and males with Klinefelter syndrome have an extra X chromosome (XXY) (Tucker & Collins, 2010). Women with androgen insensitivity (AIS) will have an XY karyotype, yet their bodies are unable to respond to or use testosterone. Still, when athletes *failed* their sex test, they were disqualified from competition, and many of the disqualified women had AIS, which conferred no athletic advantage.

Knowing this history problematizes the 2012 IOC Regulations on Female Hyperandrogenism; that a large part of this policy is based on the *suspicion* of having hyperandrogenism leading to required sex tests is especially disconcerting. Consider what may lead to such suspicion: highly developed musculature, a masculine appearance or demeanor, deep voice, exceptional performance, or generally appearing inconsistent with Western ideals of femininity. In other words, suspicion is grounded in social constructions of binary sex and gender; female sexed athletes should have feminine characteristics. Since the end of mandated sex testing (in 1999), any female athlete whose gender was questioned typically was indicted based on their musculature and other masculine-perceived characteristics (e.g., Caster Semenya of South Africa, Santhi Soundarajan of India). Conspicuously, as Kauer and Krane (2012) pointed out, "in recent years, the only athletes whose gender has been questioned publicly have been athletes of color from poor, rural towns in countries with lower human development indexes" (p. 13).[3] As Olympic policy has left the door open to the seeking out and interrogation of "suspicious" females, what is declared as an acceptable female body is constructed within intersections of nation, race, class, sexuality, and gender (Kauer & Krane, 2012).

What constitutes fair play in sport?

As noted, policies surrounding gender nonconforming and sex variant athletes were established largely to maintain a level playing field. Sport is predicated on the concept of *fair play* (cf. Reeser, 2005; Sullivan, 2011). It is a meritocracy; the rules assume that everyone who participates has an equal opportunity to become skilled and successful. In fact, many league and association rules are aimed at creating this level playing field. We see this as sport teams are separated based on age, weight, size, ability, or sex. These regulations are aimed at ensuring that all participants compete equally and justly – creating fair play. In particular, separating athletes based on sex is so endemic that it rarely is questioned. However, when transgender, transsexual, and intersex athletes appear, it becomes obvious that some rules also are exclusionary, leading us to ask the questions what is fair play and fair play for whom?

Historically, fair play has been determined by sport ruling bodies, typically populated by those who benefit from the rules. For example, early rules regarding amateurism presumably were enacted to maintain the purity of sport and respect for the intrinsic values of sport; yet they effectively kept "amateur" competition as an opportunity only for the social elite (Loland, 2002). When considering sport for gender nonconforming and sex variant athletes, fair play rests on social constructions of sex, gender, and sporting bodies. Nonconformity with socially accepted gender expression or sex presentation still is considered deviant, leading to the policing of bodies in the name of fair play.

The IOC overtly frames its policy decisions regarding trans and intersex athletes within the hegemonic narrative of fair play. As stated in the policy about hyperandrogenism, rules are needed to "guarantee the fairness and integrity of female competitions for all female athletes" (IOC, 2011). These beliefs about fair play rest on the assumption that testosterone alone represents an unfair advantage for some female athletes. Conventional wisdom presumes that the reason many male athletes are bigger and stronger than many female athletes is because they have higher levels of endogenous testosterone (i.e., that which naturally occurs in the body). However, does this same logic apply when comparing female athletes to other female athletes? Bioethicist Katarina Karkazis and her colleagues (2012) presented medical evidence that questions common assumptions about the role of testosterone in athletic performance. As they stated, "*there is no evidence showing that successful athletes have higher testosterone levels than less successful athletes*" (p. 8, emphasis in original). Yet IOC policy infers testosterone is *the* deciding factor in performance differences among female athletes. Karkazis et al. countered this assumption with the fact that there is a disproportionate number of women with complete androgen insensitivity syndrome (CAIS) who have become elite athletes. Women with CAIS are unable to utilize the high levels of testosterone produced by their bodies (Tucker & Collins, 2010). Seemingly against the odds, some women with CAIS gain the musculature, strength, and endurance needed as world-class athletes. This fact begs the question *how*? How are athletes who cannot process testosterone able to be so successful? We must consider what else influences athletic ability.

Truly, elite athletes are exceptional; they have exceptional physicality, mental toughness, strength, and abilities. Their bodies, minds, and capabilities are outside the norm. To unravel what enables elite athletes to perform at exceptional levels, we must consider a wide array of skeletal, physiological, genetic, and even financial and regional characteristics. If we agree that one relatively rare variation is akin to an unfair advantage, where should we stop? Following the logic of the IOC and testosterone testing, should athletes who have any *unfair* athletic advantage be monitored or banned? Consider, for example, sprinters with a high percentage of fast-twitch muscle fibers, basketball players of exceptional height, swimmers whose elbows hyperextend, or gymnasts with a low center of gravity and hyperflexibility. All of these are naturally occurring characteristics, just as are levels of endogenous testosterone, but there are no regulations about any of these other characteristics. Yet, it is worth repeating, the only naturally occurring bodily variation that is banned from elite competition is atypically high testosterone in females. Considering that athletes legally may, for example, have lasik surgery to enhance their vision or use hypoxic air machines to enhance the oxygen carrying capacity of their blood, the rationale for testing hyperandrogenic women seems *unfair*.

Curiously overlooked when monitoring testosterone levels is *intent*. Often, discussion about trans and intersex athletes becomes conflated with doping; both ingesting exogenous testosterone and having high levels of endogenous testosterone are perceived to confer an unfair advantage in the same manner as does taking steroids (Lucas-Carr & Krane, 2011; Teetzel, 2006). However, transsexuals taking testosterone to balance their gender identity and physicality reflects completely different motives from taking testosterone to gain a sporting advantage (not to mention the widely differing amounts used in relation to the different motives). The emphasis on athletes' (so-called masculine) appearance, and the fact that accusations disproportionately are aimed at non-Western women of color, leads to further questioning of the legitimacy of the IOC policies. As Nyong'o (2010) expressed, "we should contest the essentialist conviction that bodies must have a stable sex that presents itself in appropriate dress, voice, attitude, and performance, and that anybody who does not must by definition be engaged in deception" (p. 98).

One interpretation of the IOC policies is that they are as much about protecting Western ideals regarding masculinity and femininity as they are about sport performance and fair play. That trans athletes must undergo surgery that only affects appearance and *masculinized* intersex female athletes can face mandated sex tests supports such a conclusion. Further, allowing *suspiciously masculine* women to be reported and subsequently tested increases the policing of how women perform gender, a historically contentious issue in women's sport. In an environment where exceptional athleticism should be celebrated, such policies perpetuate heteronormativity and heighten homonegativism and transprejudice. Fear of accusations that one is not truly a woman summons up images of lesbian-baiting and can cause women to feel compelled to present an appropriately feminine appearance to avoid suspicion (cf. Kauer & Krane, 2006).

Patently absent across much discussion surrounding the IOC policies is consideration of what is in the best interest of the transsexual, transgender, or intersex athlete. When considering the question of fair play for whom, it appears that the IOC has favored athletes who meet social expectations associated with their sex and gender. Like all other competitors, sex variant and gender nonconforming athletes have dedicated themselves to the extraordinary training necessary to become elite. And, similar to many other elite athletes, they have overcome challenging circumstances. It is time to reframe the discussion to privilege inclusion and celebrate the wide range of athletic bodies.

Conclusion: towards an ethics of inclusion

The predominant approach guiding policy about transsexual, transgender, and intersex athletes in elite sport has been to develop criteria they must meet in order to participate. Such an approach places an undue burden on the athlete to prove eligibility. It also frames athletes with nonconforming gender or sex variation as *other*. Such labeling has serious implications, often leading to misunderstanding and/or prejudice. Because of these consequences, these athletes face many challenges and barriers in their pursuit of sport participation. Although framed as being inclusive, policing transsexual, transgender, and intersex bodies will not lead to greater inclusion or more welcoming climates. Guided by a transfeminist approach, in this section I embrace a compassionate inclusion that prioritizes the dignity of all athletes.

Compassionate inclusion begins with questioning and countering the taken-for-granted narrative grounded in the social construction of the binary sex and gender categories. This transfeminist approach privileges self-naming and self-categorization over appearance. In such an environment, policing of athlete bodies is replaced with a celebration of accomplishments. As Ross, Barak, and Krane (2013) expressed, "if strength, muscularity, and athleticism can be disentangled from gendered notions, then athletic individuals simply can be appreciated for their talent and expertise." Truly, gender and sex inclusive sport will move away from binary assumptions and create space for non-conforming athletes.

In a recent report, the Canadian Centre for Ethics in Sport (CEES, 2012) took the unique stance of emphasizing that fair play should be aimed at the trans and intersex athletes, not the protection of *normal* athletes (i.e., sex and gender con-forming athletes). The primary perspective of this report privileges the sentiment that "fairness dictates a preference for inclusion" (p. 9). Exclusion, distrust, and suspicion have far more damaging social and psychological outcomes than inclu-sion. Although anecdotal, reports that Caster Semenya,[4] after her suspicious appearance led to mandated sex tests that were leaked to the press, was suicidal and emotionally distraught (CBC Sports, 2009) reveal the high stakes of policing trans and intersex athletic bodies. Gender nonconforming youth often are the target of bullying, name calling, physical assaults, and rejection by peers and family (Greytak, Kosciw, & Diaz, 2009; Roberts, Rosario, Slopen, Calzo, & Austin, 2013). This treatment can lead to decreased self-esteem, and increased stress, depression, and suicide ideation or attempt (Russell, Ryan, Toomey, Diaz, & Sanchez, 2011). Continued policing of athletic bodies will support hegemonic assumptions that lead to prejudice due to gender nonconformity. Decision-makers in sport should be ethically bound to protect all athletes from harassment, which may occur as sport is reconfigured as embracing inclusion.

A transfeminist approach embraces the CEES (2012) emphasis on respect, dignity, and inclusion that can "secure the most human outcomes for everyone involved" (p. 10). Recognizing, and celebrating, sex and gender diversity will benefit all athletes. Removing the stigma surrounding *masculine-appearing* or *suspicious* female athletes will allow them to focus their energies on performing at their best. Such an approach not only relieves trans and intersex athletes of a heavy burden, but also would remove fear of suspicion from any highly muscular, high performing athletes (i.e., most elite female athletes). Rather than focus on filtering out sex and gender cheaters, sport can "instead 'welcome in' athletes across the whole spectrum of diversity, including gender self-identification" (CEES, 2012, p. 25). Reframing policy to focus on inclusion will be more constructive for everyone and is consistent with NCAA, Olympic, and most sport program ideals of equity and non-discrimination.

Attempting to fit all athletes into a binary system of sex and gender does not work. Socially constructed notions of sex and gender are historically, socially, and culturally bound. As such, today's description of male/female and masculine/feminine likely will differ from future viewpoints. The athletes who fall outside these illusory binaries have been burdened with forcing themselves into a box or choosing not to compete. Even when some gender nonconforming athletes describe themselves as female or male, which may or may not fit neatly into binary categorizations, great scrutiny ensues. A compassionate approach recog-nizes the empowerment of the self-expression of gender identity. The whole dialogue surrounding trans and intersex athletes can be reframed to highlight their experiences. In spite of the stigma and prejudice that gender nonconforming and sex variant athletes face, they defy social norms and are resilient and successful in their rise to elite levels of sport (Krane & Barak, 2012). These athletes should be celebrated, not censored.

What a transfeminist perspective teaches us is the need to consider the broad social and cultural issues surrounding policy and decisions regarding inclusion and exclusion. While tackling the complexities of sex and gender is challenging, we also should consider the intersections of race, nation, social class, and sexuality as we move forward. At the center of any debate should be the well-being of all athletes. A goal of empowering each athlete to compete without prejudice leads us to question common taken-for-granted assumptions and truths people hold – including policy-makers – about sex and gender in sport. It also can lead us towards privileging inclusion without imposing narrow Western, heteronormative expectations on elite athletes.

Notes

1 This list of awards includes the top honors awarded by a number of US national associations: National Collegiate Athletic Association (NCAA), the US Basketball Writers Association (USBWA), the Women's Basketball Coaches Association (WBCA) and the Associate Press (AP). The Wooden Award, Naismith Trophy, and Wade Trophy are presented by other sport groups all bestowing player of the year honors.
2 The veracity of these cases is meticulously critiqued by historian of science Vanessa Heggie (2010).
3 HDI is a statistic used by the United Nations that combines economic indices, education, and life expectancy to rank countries (United Nations, 2011).
4 For a more complete discussion of Caster Semenya, see Schultz (2011) and Cooky, Dycus, and Dworkin (2013).

References

Baylorbears.com (2013). Women's basketball website. Retrieved from http://www.baylorbears.com/sports/w-baskbl/mtt/griner_brittney00.html.

Birrell, S. (2000). Feminist theories for sport. In J. Coakley & E. Dunning (Eds.), *Handbook of sports studies* (pp. 61–76). Thousand Oaks, CA: Sage.

Bowman, C., & Goldberg, J. M. (2006). Care of the patient undergoing sex reassignment surgery. *International Journal of Transgenderism, 9*, 135–165.

Brittney-Griner.com (2013). Basketball phenom Brittney Griner. Retrieved from http://www.brittney-griner.com.

Canadian Centre for Ethics in Sport (CCES) (2012). Sport in transition: Making sport in Canada more responsible for gender inclusivity. Ottawa, Ontario. Retrieved from http://www.cces.ca/files/pdfs/CCES-PAPER-SportInTransition-E.pdf.

Cavanagh, S., & Sykes, H. (2006). Transsexual bodies at the Olympics: The International Olympic Policy on transsexual athletes at the Athens Summer Games. *Body and Society, 12*, 75–102.

CBC Sports (2009, September 17). Runner Semenya under suicide watch: Report. Retrieved from http://www.cbc.ca/sports/amateur/story/2009/09/17/sp-amateur-semenya-watch.html.

Choi, P. Y. L. (2000). *Femininity and the physically active woman*. London: Routledge.

Coleman, E., Bockting, W., Botzer, M., Cohen-Kettenis, P., DeCuypere, G., Feldman, J., . . . Zucker, K. (2011). Standards of care for the health of transsexual, transgender, and gender-nonconforming people, version 7. *International Journal of Transgenderism, 13*, 165–232.

Cooky, C., Dycus, R., & Dworkin, S. L. (2013). "What makes a woman a woman?" versus "Our First Lady of Sport": A comparative analysis of the United States and the South African media coverage of Caster Semenya. *Journal of Sport & Social Issues, 37*, 31–57.

Cromwell, J. (2006). Queering the binaries: Transsituated identities, bodies, and sexualities. In S. Stryker & S. Whittle (Eds.), *The transgender studies reader* (pp. 509–520). New York: Routledge.

Dahl, M., Feldman, J. L., Goldberg, J. M., & Jaberi, A. (2006). Physical aspects of transgender endocrine therapy. *International Journal of Transgenderism, 9*, 111–134.

Dixon, R. (2012, April 5). Brittney Griner called a man because she is athletic. Retrieved from http://www.clutchmagonline.com/2012/04/brittney-griner-called-a-man-because-she-is-athletic/.

Duncan, M. C. (2006). Gender warriors in sport: Women and the media. In A. A. Raney & J. Bryant (Eds.), *Handbook of sports and media* (pp. 247–269). New York, NY: Taylor & Francis.

Enke, A. F. (2012a). Introduction: Transfeminist perspectives. In A. Enke (Ed.), *Transfeminist persectives: In and beyond transgender and gender studies* (pp. 1–15). Philadelphia: Temple University Press.

Enke, A. F. (2012b). Note on terms and concepts. In A. Enke (Ed.), *Transfeminist perspectives: In and beyond transgender and gender studies* (pp. 16–20). Philadelphia: Temple University Press.

Fausto-Sterling, A. (2000). *Sexing the body: Gender politics and the construction of sexuality*. New York, NY: Basic Books.

Floyd, B. (2012, July 11). Every time Brittney Griner is on TV, this happens. Retrieved from http://www.sbnation.com/ncaa-basketball/2012/7/11/3153845/brittney-griner-espys-tweets.

Greytak, E. A., Kosciw, J. G., & Diaz, E. M. (2009). *Harsh realities: The experiences of transgender youth in our nation's schools*. New York, NY: GLSEN. Retrieved from http://www.glsen.org/binary-data/GLSEN_ATTACHMENTS/file/000/001/1375-1.pdf.

Hall, M. A. (1996). *Feminism and sporting bodies*. Champaign, IL: Human Kinetics.

Heggie, V. (2010). Testing sex and gender in sports: Reinventing, reimagining, and reconstructing histories. *Endeavour, 34*, 157–163.

IOC (2003). Statement of the Stockholm consensus on sex reassignment in sports. Retrieved from http://www.olympic.org/Documents/Reports/EN/en_report_905.pdf.

IOC (2011). IOC addresses eligibility of female athletes with hyperandrogenism. Retrieved from http://www.olympic.org/content/press-release/ioc-addresses-eligibility-of-female-athletes-with-hyperandrogenism.

IOC (2012, June 22). IOC regulations on female hyperandrogenism: Games of the XXX Olympiad in London, 2012. Retrieved from http://www.olympic.org/Documents/Commissions_PDFfiles/Medical_commission/2012-06-22-IOC-Regulations-on-Female-Hyperandrogenism-eng.pdf.

Kane, M. J. (1995). Resistance/transformation of the oppositional binary: Exposing sport as a continuum. *Journal of Sport and Social Issues, 19*(2), 191–218.

Karkazis, K., Jordan-Young, R., Davis, G., & Camporesi, S. (2012). Out of bounds? A critique of the new policies on hyperandrogenism in elite female athletes. *American Journal of Bioethics, 12*(7), 3–16.

Kauer, K. J., & Krane, V. (2006). "Scary dykes" and "feminine queens": Stereotypes and female collegiate athletes. *Women in Sport & Physical Activity Journal, 15*(1), 43–55.

Kauer, K. J., & Krane, V. (2012). Heteronormative landscapes: Exploring sexuality through tales of elite women athletes. *Psychology of Women Section Review, 14*(2), 10–19.

Krane, V. (2001). One lesbian feminist epistemology: Integrating feminist standpoint, queer theory, and feminist cultural studies. *The Sport Psychologist, 15*, 401–411.

Krane, V., & Barak, K. S. (2012). Current events and teachable moments: Creating dialog about transgender and intersex athletes. *Journal of Physical Education, Recreation, and Dance, 83*(4), 38–42.

Krane, V., & Symons, C. (2014). Gender and sexual orientation. In A. Papaioannou & D. Hackfort (Eds.), *Fundamental concepts in sport and exercise psychology* (pp. 119–135). Abingdon, UK: Taylor & Francis.

Lapauw, B., Taes, Y., Simoens, S., Van Caenegem, E., Weyers, S., Goemaere, S., . . . T'Sjoen, G. G. (2008). Body composition, volumetric and areal bone parameters in male-to-female transsexual persons. *Bone, 43*, 1016–1021.

Lee, P. A., Houk, C. P., Ahmed, S. F., & Hughs, I. A. (2006). Consensus statement on management of intersex disorders. *Pediatrics, 118*, e488–e500.

Loland, S. (2002). *Fair play in sport: A moral norm system*. Abingdon, UK: Routledge.

Looy, H., & Bouma III, H. (2005). The nature of gender: Gender identity in persons who are intersexed or transgendered. *Journal of Psychology & Theology, 33*, 166–178.

Lucas-Carr, C. B., & Krane, V. (2011). What is the T in LGBT? Supporting transgender athletes via sport psychology. *The Sport Psychologist, 4*, 532–548.

Messner, M. A. (2002). *Taking the field: Women, men, and sports*. Minneapolis: University of Minnesota Press.

Nagoshi, J., & Brzuzy, S. (2010). Transgender theory: Embodying research and practice. *Journal of Women & Social Work, 25*, 431–447.

NCAA (2011). NCAA inclusion of transgender student-athletes. Retrieved from http://www.uh.edu/lgbt/docs/Transgender_Handbook_2011_Final.pdf.

Nyong'o, T. (2010). The unforgivable transgression of being Caster Semenya. *Women & Performance: A Journal of Feminist Theory, 20*, 95–100.

Reeser, J. C. (2005). Gender identity and sport: Is the playing field level? *British Journal of Sports Medicine, 39*, 695–699.

Roberts, A., Rosario, M., Slopen, N., Calzo, J., & Austin, S. B. (2013). Childhood gender nonconformity, bullying victimization, and depressive symptoms across adolescence and early adulthood: An 11-year longitudinal study. *Journal of the American Academy of Child & Adolescent Psychiatry, 52*, 143–152.

Ross, S. R., Barak, K. S., & Krane, V. (2013). Out of focus: Sport media, women athletes, and media literacy. In L. Azzarito and D. Kirk (Eds.), *Pedagogies, physical culture and visual methods* (pp. 115–130). London: Routledge.

Russell, S. T., Ryan, C., Toomey, R. B., Diaz, R. M., & Sanchez, J. (2011). Lesbian, gay, bisexual, and transgender adolescent school victimization: Implications for young adult health and adjustment. *Journal of School Health, 81*, 223–230.

Schultz, J. (2011). Caster Semenya and the "question of too": Sex testing in elite women's sport and the issue of advantage. *Quest, 63*, 228–243.

Scott-Dixon, K. (2006a). Introduction: Trans/forming feminisms. In K. Scott-Dixon (Ed.), *Trans/forming feminisms: Trans-feminist voices speak out* (pp. 11–33). Toronto: Sumach.

Scott-Dixon, K. (2006b). Conclusion: Towards transfeminisms. In K. Scott-Dixon (Ed.), *Trans/forming feminisms: Trans-feminist voices speak out* (pp. 235–241). Toronto: Sumach.

Scott-Dixon, K. (2006c). Glossary. In K. Scott-Dixon (Ed.), *Trans/forming feminisms: Trans-feminist voices speak out* (pp. 246–249). Toronto: Sumach.

Sullivan, C. F. (2011). Gender verification and gender policies in elite sport: Eligibility and "fair play". *Journal of Sport & Social Issues, 35*, 400–419.

Teetzel, S. (2006). On transgendered athletes, fairness and doping: An international challenge. *Sport in Society, 9*, 227–251.

Theberge, N. (1998). "Same sport, different gender": A consideration of binary gender logic and the sport continuum in the case of ice hockey. *Journal of Sport and Social Issues, 22*, 183–198.

Travers, A. (2006). Queering sport: Lesbian softball leagues and the transgender challenge. *International Review for the Sociology of Sport, 41*, 431–446.

Travers, A. (2011). Women's ski jumping, the 2010 Olympic games, and the deafening silence of sex segregation, whiteness, and wealth. *Journal of Sport & Social Issues, 35*, 126–145.

Tucker, R., & Collins, M. (2010). The science of sex verification and athletic performance. *International Journal of Sports Physiology and Performance, 5*, 127–139.

United Nations (2011). Human Development Index. *Human Development Reports*. Retrieved from http://hdr.undp.org/en/statistics/hdi/.

5 "The dark side" and beyond

Narrative inquiry in professional golf

Kitrina Douglas and David Carless

Introduction

For more than a decade we have been conducting research into the life experiences of professional women golfers. The work began as Kitrina's doctoral research, initially focusing on motivation and persistence in women on the European golf tour (Douglas, 2004). We have subsequently published developments of this work in various journals (e.g., Carless & Douglas, 2009; Douglas, 2009; Douglas & Carless, 2006, 2009a, 2009b, 2012a, 2012b; Sparkes & Douglas, 2007). From early on we have been aware that the stories we represent often tend towards what some describe as the dark side of sport (Gilbourne & Andersen, 2011, p. xi). This is evident through a number of participants recounting troubling experiences, such as depression, sexual abuse, emotional isolation, and self-harm.

When we share our research with students in lectures, they sometimes describe feeling shocked, surprised, saddened, or depressed at the insights they gain into life in professional sport. Students describe how it is not only the kinds of trauma listed above that prompt these responses, but also how some participants talk about their day-to-day life. We hear similar responses from colleagues when we present our research at academic conferences. Coaches, too, regularly express surprise, disbelief, disappointment, or sadness at the experiences recounted by highly successful professional golfers. In our research with coaches (Douglas & Carless, 2008), after hearing how one multiple tournament winner played for her father rather than herself, one coach responded: "I would have thought that it would be difficult to be successful if you were not playing for your own enjoyment" (p. 38). In response to sport performance becoming the overriding focus in life, another coach responded: "Feel very sad for this athlete. This would be the ideal candidate for the loony bin! Have to give them praise for their dedication but at what costs to their long term 'life?'" (p. 38).

These responses suggest to us that professional athletes' stories of their lives do not align with the *expectations* and/or *assumptions* held by many students, academics, and coaches. In other words, the experiences recounted by the women in our research contrast or conflict with public understandings of what life in professional sport is like. Our aim in this chapter is to consider why this might be and how this situation could have developed. To do so, we turn to our narrative research with professional women golfers.

Narrative research in professional golf

Our work is part of an emerging tradition in sport and exercise psychology, which has seen narrative approaches used across a number of contexts, including spinal cord injury (e.g., Smith & Sparkes, 2002), eating practices (e.g., Papathomas & Lavallee, 2006), flow (e.g., Sparkes & Partington, 2003), and aging (e.g., Phoenix & Smith, 2011). The research we draw on here relates to longitudinal life history research over 10 years with eight women professional golfers who were members of the European Tour. Six of the women were multiple winners on the European Tour and would be considered by any criteria to be among the most successful golfers in the world (Georgi, Leanne, Christiana, Kandy, Hannah, and Debbie). In contrast to these women were two participants who had not won an event (Annabel and Berni). Because they are well known for their achievements, we have not published their ages as this could jeopardize anonymity.

Central to the research is Kitrina's relationship with the participants and her own involvement in professional golf. As a multiple winner on the European Tour, Kitrina is an *insider* to professional golf culture. Insider status raises a host of complex and ethically challenging methodological issues, which we have explored elsewhere (see Douglas, 2012; Douglas & Carless, 2012a, 2012b). However, it also provided two benefits for this research. First, Kitrina has her own embodied experiences to draw upon, gained through 20 years of international golf (see Douglas, 2009). Second, from a feminist perspective, the types of research relationships Kitrina developed with participants during her playing career and through the research deepen and enrich what can be known through the research process (see Etherington, 2004).

Narrative as a critical methodology

As Smith and Sparkes (2009) point out, it is "difficult to give a single and clear-cut definition of narrative, or draw a precise boundary around its meaning" (p. 2), because various definitions exist in the literature. For some, narrative research is about gathering and analyzing stories told by an individual that are seem as presenting "an inner reality to the outside world" (Lieblich, Tuval-Mashiach, & Zilber, 1998, p. 7). Here, a person's story is assumed to portray 'how life actually is' for that person. Others might utilize similar stories, but would see any individual's story as a construction that draws upon narrative "building blocks available in their common culture, above and beyond their individual experience" (Lieblich et al., 1998, pp. 8–9). Through this social constructionist perspective, stories are understood as being *social artifacts* that tell us as much about the culture surrounding the teller as they do about the 'inner reality' of the teller. In Smith's (2007, p. 391) terms: "The context, setting, audience, the particular situated purpose of a story, tellability, and the narrative resources available to tellers frame *what* might be said and *how* it can be narrated." From this perspective, in addition to providing insights into how a person's life 'actually is,' an individual's story offers clues regarding how her or his life has been constructed (i.e., shaped or constrained) by the surrounding culture, the social mores that permit or prohibit talking about certain experiences or events, and shared language conventions that influence what can and cannot be put into words.[1]

Two further issues add complexity to the storytelling process. First, a storyteller requires an audience or witness who will hear and acknowledge the story; second, they also require someone who will provide testimony (Frank, 1995). The researcher is one individual (among many) who is potentially called to give testimony to personal stories, as participants rely on us to listen without foreclosing or finalizing their stories. We then have the responsibility to 'amplify' their story through relating it to others. A researcher's ability to hear, however, is in turn dependent on (and potentially restricted by) her/his *horizon of interest* (Gadamer, 1975) – the implicit understanding of what is relevant. This is shaped and constrained by the researcher's biographical particulars, history, embodied ideological knowing, assumptions, and openness to the story's logic. All these issues have the potential to influence the kind of stories an individual may share at any particular time.

In this chapter, we utilize a social constructionist critical awareness regarding the nature of personal stories and the storytelling process to consider the following questions: why might it be that the stories women professional golfers share about their lives contest what others expect? How could this situation have come to be? What sociocultural factors shape (1) the stories athletes *tell* (and don't tell) of their lives, and (2) how these stories are *heard* (or not heard) by those within sport culture? We explore these questions by focussing on examples of two particular kinds of stories that we see as typically *excluded* or *silenced* in most public discourse around elite sport. These relate to (1) stories of playfulness and joy, and (2) stories of vulnerability. Through our exploration we illuminate some of the relationships between life as *lived*, life as *storied*, and life as *understood by others* within the particular context of professional golf. Central to all this, we suggest, is the role of elite sport culture in shaping and constraining representations of athletes' lives.

Stories of playfulness and joy

The first type of silenced story is captured in the question, 'Where has the joy gone?' By this we mean where – within elite and professional sport – are the stories that make sport sound like it is ludic, playful, creative, and joyous? The picture that emerges from research across sport shows the involvement of young people – novice athletes – often revolves around playful and creative activity. Then, athletes who make it to the top enter a phase of sport involvement that becomes increasingly storied as 'work' – disciplined, policed, planned, structured, and deliberate, progressively including more formal instruction and training (see Côté & Hay, 2002; Ericsson, Krampe, & Tesch-Römer, 1993; Salmela, 1994; Wylleman & Lavallee, 2003). Is it the case, therefore, that by the time an athlete reaches the professional level an inevitable consequence is that all the fun has gone from *playing* sport and the athlete is left with a mundane 'job' of sport being about income generation? The enduring public narrative in the UK around the 2012 Olympic Games, for example, seems to have been that the gold medals won made the hard work and sacrifice worth it, rather than the four preceding years were fun and the medals were the icing on the cake.

Looking through our interview transcripts and field notes, we can see that participants' stories of their early lives in golf often portray carefree, light-hearted, independent, and creative selves. They appeared less aware of how each was 'supposed' to story training and competition. Yet even at a young age, these stories and actions were often in tension with sport culture. For example, Leanne described how she and her partner, in an international match as amateurs, re-enacted a *Monty Python* comedy sketch as they walked between shots down the fairway.[2] They were reprimanded by their national governing body even though they won the event – they weren't supposed to be laughing and joking while competing. During a National Coaching Session Kandy recalled visiting the boys' dorm at night and 'playing games.' She too was reprimanded. Georgi recalled how her parents 'sent her to Coventry'[3] because they perceived she was 'just enjoying herself' and not 'trying hard enough' to win an event. We don't have in golf, for example, training programs for coaches that suggest young people be allowed to make up games during competitions, at training sessions, or when they are supposed to be sleeping. Instead, we have rules and regulation to punish those who do.

Moments in some women's stories of their professional career drift towards the contours of a performance narrative, in which professional sport is storied as 'work' where the purpose is to win events and earn money (Douglas & Carless, 2006). The following illustration is taken from an interview with Kandy:

> The day I played badly, or the tournaments I played badly, it was not like, I am not good enough or I am bad. No, I have less money. It was part of the job. For me it was "Well, I am pro." I don't know, if you are a butcher you have to cut meat.
>
> (Douglas & Carless, 2006, p. 22)

Here, playing golf professionally is clearly storied as work – like any other job, metaphorically she *cuts meat*. The following excerpt has a similar tone. It is drawn from a section of an interview where Debbie was talking about the place of money in her golf career:

Kitrina: Your bottom line is the money?
Debbie: Yeah, of course it is. You don't go out there for fun do you?
Kitrina: Do you judge whether you are successful or not by how much money you earn?
Debbie: Mmmm, yeah! Oh, sorry, *of course it is*! *You* know! *You* won eight times! What's the matter with you? Of course it's for the money.

Here, Debbie explicitly makes the point that the purpose of professional sport is to earn money, not to have fun. This extract is revealing because it demonstrates an assumption that all professionals (Kitrina included) are the same in this regard. Here, then, a single story (in this case *you don't play professional sport for fun*) silences alternative stories. Debbie's question to Kitrina ("What's the matter with you?") suggests Debbie believes that there is something 'wrong' with an individual who doesn't accept that "it's for the money." As a tournament winner, Debbie seems to think Kitrina *should know better*. This exchange illustrates how a singular story risks becoming totalitarian: Debbie asserts that Kitrina (and, by implication, all professionals) align with her in this storyline, regardless of whether Kitrina's (or other tournament professionals') stories actually align with it or not.

Yet other narratives were also evident in participants' stories of their lives as professionals. These stories had more in common with participants' stories of their early lives in golf, portraying a sense of creativity, playfulness, or joy. When storying her own life, Kitrina, for example, demonstrates that in the process of enhancing sport performance a tour player *can* be creative and playful, perhaps by making up songs and playing games (Douglas, 2009, 2012). The following is an example of a cricket 'game' developed during golf practice:

> Nathan pulled out the big tournament bag as well as a bag of balls and with the remains of the baguette wandered over to an empty range. Carefully placing the bag down with its flattest surface facing down the range so that it formed "the stumps", he took a club from the bag in readiness to defend his wicket. She wandered 20 yards away humming a song switched off in mid-flow with the engine and emptied 10 balls. Adopting a sideways stance, Nathan took a step forward making an imaginary swipe at a ball with a cricket swing, then, in front of the bag he patted down a few uneven patches of grass and awaited delivery of the first ball. It arrived like a guided missile chipped on target, but he anticipated its flight and before the ball connected with the waiting bag he swung forward and took the rising ball flush on face of the club, THWACK!
> "Nice hit!" she shouted, watching the ball fly overhead.
> "That's a six!" he shouted down the wicket through a huge grin and raised arm . . . and so the game progressed.
> (Douglas, 2009, pp. 185–186)

Other players too countered the narrative plot of the dominant work and performance stories. Annabel, in the following quotes, talks very unspectacularly about her simple enjoyment of playing and practicing golf, first as an amateur and then after turning professional:

> It was just a nice sport to go and play. I used to just cycle after school to the golf club and play golf until dark, cycle home. Go to sleep, get up, go to school, cycle to the golf club, play golf and live up at the golf club in the summer holidays. I just enjoyed it. It was something I was just totally into and I enjoyed and it wasn't a chore or anything . . . When the Ladies European

Tour came to places like Kingswood, which was about an hour from home, I used to go and watch people like you [*laughs*] and I just thought it looked great.

It's just being outside ... the golf course is my office, the practice ground is my office, rather than four walls, a ceiling and a floor, looking at a computer all day. So I feel very lucky, very privileged to have done that. It is nice to go up in the evenings to have a practice for two or three hours.

For Annabel, two or three hours on the practice ground are not storied as work, a chore, or a sacrifice, and she doesn't story sacrifice or dedication (although others may story her in this way). Rather, three hours outside in the evening is *a privilege*. When she storied "watching" tour players at an event near her home, what she saw (in the sense of what was inspiring to her) wasn't wins, trophies, or money, but rather something that "looked great." While some players story sport at the top as work, difficult, and therefore they have to be serious, others show having fun and winning can coexist and are not mutually exclusive (see Douglas, 2004, 2009, 2012).

Therberge (1987, p. 389) suggested there "is little question" that life on tour "is demanding and difficult." What makes it difficult *for Therberge* is that women golfers have to play golf and practice nearly every day. Yet the 'thing' that Therberge cites as demanding is the very thing through which Annabel – and other tour players too – experiences joy. In his ethnography of the Ladies' Professional Golf Tour, Todd Crosset (1995) believed it was necessary to *omit* much of what was fun, colorful, and dramatic about women's golf because *his* interest was social structures. In light of examples like these, is it any surprise that dominant (outsider) understandings about life in elite sport fail to align with many athletes' experience?

In answer to our question *Where has the joy gone?* we suggest that playfulness and creativity are still present in many elite athletes' sport experiences. Yet within the dominant performance narrative, the story goes: professional sport is (and must be) *work not fun* (Douglas & Carless, 2006). This monologue undermines the believability of any and all alternative stories. As a result, why would an athlete share personal stories of joy and creativity if they are unlikely to be believed or respected?

Stories of vulnerability

A second way others have sometimes responded to our research is with surprise, disappointment, or sadness on the basis of the *vulnerability* revealed or portrayed in golfers' stories. These individuals, it seems, typically did not expect to hear that successful athletes could, for example, be adversely affected – sometimes in severe ways – by their careers in golf. Many expected *successful* golfers to be immune to psychosocial challenges or difficulties. "These are *winners*, yet here they are telling stories of problems and vulnerability," seems to be the sentiment underlying this surprise. We have witnessed a variety of stories in which highly successful athletes reveal what might be considered some form of vulnerability. Each of the extracts in this section illustrates what we see as a form of vulnerability that is experienced through a lack of *narrative alignment* (McLeod, 1997) – or 'fit' – between the narrator's embodied experience and her own story or a cultural story in which she is immersed.[4]

A first and perhaps most obvious example portrays psychological or mental health difficulties as being the result of periods of poor form or disappointing results. At these times, our interpretation would be that the teller's concrete experience of not winning (or performing to expectations) is in tension with the culturally dominant performance narrative. Georgi provided an example, describing her response to 'missing the cut' (i.e., failing to score well enough to enter the final round of an event):

> When I missed those cuts I felt dreadful about myself. I was letting everybody down and myself. I had no self-esteem, everything just went, totally. I was distraught. What do you do? You know, you feel lower and lower about yourself. It was just a nightmare. Huge. I think I just lost all my confidence in one round of golf.
>
> (Douglas & Carless, 2006, p. 20)

Here, a catastrophic loss of self-esteem is portrayed as resulting from one poor performance. This objective event had the psychological consequence of leaving Georgi feeling vulnerable and profoundly uncertain about her worth. Of all possible stories of vulnerability, this kind of story is most likely to be shared publicly because it is to be expected within the plot of the performance narrative, where sport and self are taken to be closely intertwined (Douglas & Carless, 2006).

Other women shared stories that reveal vulnerabilities that are rarely heard in public discourse because they are not expected within the performance plot. The following examples all express a degree of personal vulnerability (such as emotional trauma, self-doubt, regret, loneliness) that arose through a conflict or tension with the dominant stories of elite sport:

> I used to hate that, going away. As soon as I was away I wanted to be home [*laughs*]. So it just doesn't work, well, it didn't work for me.
>   *Kitrina: When you are away, what do you feel? How do you know you want to be at home?*
>   Don't know, just something within. You just miss someone. You just want to be back. Soon as you leave the house, soon as I left the house, I didn't really want to go. (Annabel)

> Lucy was small and it is very tough to go away, nights were very hard, you know, when you are back alone at the hotel and you know that you've got the

kid at home. The first two or three years, really, really tough [*pause*]. You are alone, crying, depressed, thinking "Fucking golf!" and "Fucking everything!"

(Kandy; Carless & Douglas, 2009, p. 60)

I think the fact that I haven't been married or I haven't had any relationships or stuff like that, you know, that is something that I will always wonder about, whether I failed at.

(Christiana; Carless & Douglas, 2009, p. 58)

I didn't want my baby. I resented him because my golf career was over. I'd care for him, I wouldn't want to hurt him or anything, but I blamed him for my golf—I felt I was out of the environment I knew and I felt lost. I tried to hide it. I couldn't cope. I wouldn't talk . . . I didn't think I could make any contribution to life.

(Debbie; Douglas & Carless, 2009a, p. 222)

We suggest that across all these excerpts women's stories reveal a sense of sacrificing elements of a relational narrative and self (Douglas & Carless, 2006) to conform to the demands of the performance narrative. Vulnerability arises, in these examples, *despite* success in performance terms. The tension is between women's behaviors (which here favor golf and achieving performance outcomes) and a broader relational narrative and/or self outside sport. The vulnerability arises, then, through sacrificing relationships in favor of actions that fit the script of the performance narrative.

Leanne's words provide some insight into why these kinds of stories of vulnerability are not voiced more often in elite sport culture: "No-one ever asked how I was, it was all about my golf, 'how did you score?', 'where did you finish?' No-one ever asked how I was" (Douglas & Carless, 2006, p. 23). This excerpt is telling because it provides an illustration of what we see as a general disinterest (within sport culture) in stories that are not directly or indirectly about performance. Leanne's account portrays the captain, selectors, and media as interested only in stories about winning – not about Leanne's well-being. Kandy, too, articulated a similar scenario when she said: "No-one ever asked about my daughter or how I was coping. The media only wanted good news. My problems did not interest them at all" (Douglas & Carless, 2006, p. 21). For Kandy, it seems acknowledgment of her vulnerability might validate her decision to leave her daughter (which transgresses expectations of being 'a good mother').

Several women's stories portray various ways in which sport culture – embodied by coaches, managers, selectors, journalists, sport media, family members, and sport psychologists – routinely, systematically, and perhaps subconsciously steers away from stories of vulnerability. This may take the form of failing to invite, support, hear, or take seriously these kinds of stories. As a result, stories of vulnerability are largely absent in elite sport culture. Instead, sport culture abounds with stories of 'mental toughness' (e.g., Crust & Clough, 2011), 'strength' (e.g., Disch & Kane, 1996), 'resilience' (e.g., Wadey & Hanton, in press), and 'competitiveness' (see Messner et al., 1999). It is a culture in which war metaphors are frequently used and, 'when needed,' it is accepted that sports people can be excessively aggressive to be a 'winner' (e.g., Anderson, 2009). We suggest that the absence of vulnerable stories among elite and professional athletes has less to do with the 'reality' of life in sport requiring 'toughness' and 'resilience' than it does with the preference or affinity of many people in sport for stories that portray athletes as *invulnerable* – whether this be tough, resilient, strong, or heroic.

Narrative theory as a critical lens

Our aim with this chapter was to illuminate some of the relationships between life as *lived* and life as *storied*, to reveal how sport culture silences some stories and promotes others. We suggested that although stories are built on concrete events, we also consider them to be social artifacts that typically tell us as much about the culture surrounding the teller as they do about the teller herself. We are thus provoked to consider the political dimension of stories and their wider implications. Frank (2010, p. 167) considers stories *tools* that "may be best understood by what they are able to do." Using this metaphor, we would like to reflect on *what* the stories shared earlier may be *doing* for the teller, and what they achieve in sport culture.

By telling tales about life being hard and the 'bottom line' being money, Kandy and Debbie, as female athletes, are able to align themselves with stories that are valued in the culture they are part of – specifically, to act (in storied form at least) and talk *like a man in a man's world*. Playing golf, when it's a business, is serious, and sport becomes serious when it is storied as "more important" (Georgi tells us) than relationships, when it "becomes your whole life" (Douglas & Carless, 2006). When women tell these stories they begin to challenge the way women and women's sport have historically been undervalued, trivialized, sexualized, and depoliticized (Bruce, 1998; Edwards, 1999). Although the sporting landscape may be changing and becoming less sexist, the small number of female coaches at the top of sport and the generally lower levels of funding for women's sports compared with men's are indications of how entrenched the culture of sport (and therefore many people's expectations) remains (Gault, 2011; Norman, 2010). Each week, women tour players play in pro-ams with (almost always male) sponsors, facing questions like: "What does your husband think of you being away each week?" The story of sport being work, a way to earn a living, goes some way to justifying what they do under the terms of a culturally accepted narrative.

On the other hand, asking 'Where has the joy gone?' creates space for other stories to be heard. For those women who don't want to be 'like a man,' who don't want to 'dominate,' to be overly competitive, to use war metaphors, to 'trample the opposition,' or to 'collect scalps' on 'a march to victory,' creating a story about practice being an opportunity to write poetry and songs, to laugh, to enjoy close communion with a lover, or to enjoy a sunset provides them with a means of asserting their values. Stories about valuing the creative, exploratory, and joyful dimensions of movement resist the dictum of the culturally dominant 'win, win, win' story.

Telling culturally transgressive stories – about, for example, practice being playful/joyful or one's vulnerabilities – is a dangerous tactic for women within a culture that values work and toughness. It is not surprising that these stories were elicited in a private, supportive, caring interview situation (see Douglas & Carless, 2012a, 2012b). That these women shared sensitive and problematic stories suggests that the 'work' these stories achieved in the interview was perhaps to reclaim identities that had for the most part been hidden, silenced, or suppressed.

We also should reflect on the part played by *our* (and by that we mean the community of sport researchers, scholars, and educators) collective story; that is, how *we* write and story athletes' lives and the work *our* stories achieve in the hands of those who use them. Research exploring elite sport seldom reaches elite athletes directly, but is more often used by funding agencies, governing organizations, performance directors, and coaches to achieve particular ends. For Denison (2007), recent years have seen athletes become less autonomous while their time and practice habits have become increasingly managed by coaches. Yet coaches and performance directors "never discuss how training spaces can begin to function as confining places, or as a way for coaches to control and impose order on athletes" (Denison, 2007, p. 374). It is worrying that the body of literature we (i.e., the wider community of researchers, scholars, and educators) are creating seems to be resulting in a story that contributes to athletes having less autonomy over their lives and fewer opportunities to do things differently.

Stories – set loose by a teller – align with different narrative plots and grand narratives. Some of the stories told here align with the performance narrative – a story that sees self-worth tied to winning and achievement, a story about hard work, sacrifice, and dedication, where life in sport is a "roller coaster" and retirement like "losing a limb" (Douglas & Carless, 2006). As we suggested earlier, these stories tend to be preferred by coaches, and, in the hands of a coach who wants more control, this narrative map provides perfect examples of athletes who have 'given everything' for their sport and succeeded. Other stories told above align with the relational narrative, where connection, and being with and for others, is integral. Still other stories align with the discovery narrative, where life and sport are landscapes to be explored and discovered for the pleasure of discovering them. Aligning with a particular narrative type can provide social esteem; in different avenues it is not only 'winners' but also 'explorers' that have been narrated as heroes (Amelia Mary Earhart, Jacques-Yves Cousteau, and Sir Edmund Hillary come to mind). As such, these stories have the potential to create valued social identities and thus provide something positive to a storyteller. Yet in sport *one* story seems too often to map the road and language for success – to the point where it has become accepted as *the* route to success. It is this that troubles us, because in doing so it becomes a monologue. For Frank (2010, p. 198), a monologue is "speech that is single voiced" as opposed to dialogical speech, which recognizes and invites conversation from differing positions. Monological speech does not respond to alternative ways to story one's experiences, but rather closes down other ways to story life – "it asserts rather than engages" (p. 198).

Critical narrative inquiry prompts us to consider: is the dominant story so dominating that it has become dangerous for an athlete to reveal an alternative story? In the hands of a performance director who says, "This is what I want and value," it would take a brave (or naïve or stupid) athlete (who relies on these people for funding and selection) to say they have different values or wish to story *their* life in a *different* way. This perspective has revealed more clearly to us that there are many different (sometimes subtle) ways in which stories are silenced. When we conduct research it is therefore important that, first, we bear witness to the work that stories do on behalf of the teller. From this position, we are better able to give testimony to alternative ways of being in sport, give consideration to political influences on our research, and become more aware of the *stories that hold us captive*. Without some degree of reflexivity, we are likely to (perhaps unwittingly) ignore, silence, or devalue alternative stories that call for witnesses and testimony, simply because we are ourselves held captive by a different way of storying life.

Thoughts on future research

The kind of critical narrative methodology we have utilized here could usefully be employed in future research to expand, interrogate, and develop the practical and theoretical interpretations we have proposed. Among a wealth of possibilities, we suggest that future research might address three particular points. First, there is much to gain by exploring the stories and experiences of athletes from diverse sports. Our initial work has focused on women's golf, and we have begun to develop this work by exploring the experiences of athletes in such sports as rugby union, cricket, track and field athletics, rowing, hockey, swimming, and judo (Carless & Douglas, 2012, 2013a, 2013b). But what stories are told by athletes in, say, such aesthetic sports as diving, skating, or synchronized swimming? How do the experiences of those in these very different sporting modalities align with or challenge the interpretations we have offered?

Second, the processes underlying young people's socialization and enculturation into particular story types represent a potentially fruitful line of research (Gottzén & Kremer-Sadlik, 2012) by which to expand our understanding of how significant others in young people's lives (e.g., PE teachers, coaches, parents, teammates, public figures) shape the adoption or rejection of the performance script. Finally, as we have demonstrated elsewhere (Douglas & Carless, 2009b, 2012a, 2012b), the relationship between researcher/s and participant/s is central to the kind of critical narrative scholarship we advocate. Connectedness, reciprocity, longitudinal involvement, reflexivity, and a feminist ethic of care constitute just some of the qualities that researchers will require if they are to be entrusted with counter-cultural stories, and if they are to be able to hear, witness, and respond to those stories. Without developing researchers who embody these qualities, it seems unlikely that athletes will feel suitably empowered to share personal stories that transgress the status quo.

Notes

1 Brackenridge (2001) has shown that sport governing bodies are reluctant to admit to abuse in their sports, and, as a result, silence, dismiss, or trivialize stories of rape and abuse as being exaggerated, unlikely, or impossible to substantiate. Second, an individual who has been raped is aware of how stories of rape and abuse are received and written in news media, and that the culture of sport can be hostile. Added to these fears, the experiences of rape and abuse are at best difficult and sometimes impossible to story. In contrast, social mores invite, accept, and promote stories about winning, and athletes are supported in creating, telling, and sharing stories of success.

2 A sketch known as "The Ministry of Silly Walks," in which characters demonstrate a series of comic walking styles in an effort to gain recognition by the fictitious ministry.

3 Being 'sent to Coventry' references events in the English Civil War to describe the action of ignoring or ostracizing someone.

4 Our aim with these extracts has been to reveal different types of vulnerability among women tour players and to show how vulnerability relates to more than just performance concerns. We have provided analysis and interpretations of each of these in full elsewhere and, given space restrictions, have not repeated them here. Please see Douglas and Carless (2009a, 2009b) for discussion of Debbie and Berni; Carless and Douglas (2009) for discussion of Kandy and Christiana; and Douglas and Carless (2006) for an exploration of the three different narrative types. For a fuller description of how narrative types can restrict individual stories, see Frank (1995).

References

Anderson, E. (2009). *Inclusive masculinity*. Abingdon, UK: Routledge.

Brackenridge, C. H. (2001). *Spoilsports: Understanding and preventing sexual exploitation in sport*. London: Routledge.

Bruce, T. (1998). Audience frustration and pleasure: *Women* viewers confront televised *women's* basketball. *Journal of Sport and Social Issues, 22*, 373–397.

Carless, D., & Douglas, K. (2009). "We haven't got a seat on the bus for you" or "All the seats are mine": Narratives and career transition in professional golf. *Qualitative Research in Sport and Exercise, 1*, 51–66.

Carless, D., & Douglas, K. (2012). Stories of success: Cultural narratives and personal stories of elite and professional athletes. *Reflective Practice, 13*, 387–398.

Carless, D., & Douglas, K. (2013a). "In the boat" but "selling myself short": Stories, narratives, and identity development in elite sport. *The Sport Psychologist, 27*, 27–39.

Carless, D., & Douglas, K. (2013b). Living, resisting, and playing the part of athlete: Narrative tensions in elite sport. *Psychology of Sport and Exercise, 14*, 701–708.

Côté, J., & Hay, J. (2002). Children's involvement in sport: A developmental perspective. In J. M. Silva & D. E. Stevens (Eds.), *Psychological foundations of sport* (pp. 484–502). Boston: Allyn & Bacon.

Crosset, T. W. (1995). *Outsiders in the clubhouse: The world of women's professional golf*. New York: Suny.

76 Kitrina Douglas and David Carless

Crust, L., & Clough, P. (2011). Developing mental toughness: From research to practice. *Journal of Sport Psychology in Action, 2*, 21–32.

Denison, J. (2007). Social theory for coaches: A Foucauldian reading of one athlete's poor performance. *International Journal of Sports Science & Coaching, 2*, 369–383.

Disch, L., & Kane, M. (1996). When a looker is really a bitch: Lisa Olson, sport, and the heterosexual matrix. *Signs, 21*, 278–308.

Douglas, K. (2004). *What's the drive in golf: Motivation and persistence in women professional tournament golfers.* Doctoral dissertation, University of Bristol.

Douglas, K. (2009). Storying my self: Negotiating a relational identity in professional sport. *Qualitative Research in Sport and Exercise, 1*, 176–190.

Douglas, K. (2012). Signals and signs. *Qualitative Inquiry, 18*, 525–532.

Douglas, K., & Carless, D. (2006). Performance, discovery, and relational narratives among women professional tournament golfers. *Women in Sport and Physical Activity Journal, 15*, 14–27.

Douglas, K., & Carless, D. (2008). Using stories in coach education. *International Journal of Sports Science and Coaching, 3*, 33–49.

Douglas, K., & Carless, D. (2009a). Abandoning the performance narrative: Two women's stories of transition from professional golf. *Journal of Applied Sport Psychology, 21*, 213–230.

Douglas, K., & Carless, D. (2009b). Exploring taboo issues in professional sport through a fictional approach. *Reflective Practice, 10*, 311–323.

Douglas, K., & Carless, D. (2012a). Membership, golf and a story about Anna and me: Reflections on research in elite sport. *Qualitative Methods in Psychology Bulletin, 13*, 27–35.

Douglas, K., & Carless, D. (2012b). Taboo tales in elite sport: Relationships, ethics, and witnessing. *Psychology of Women Section Review, 14*, 50–56.

Edwards, J. (1999). The black female athlete and the politics of (in)visibility. *New Political Economy, 4*, 278–282.

Ericsson, K. A., Krampe, R. T., & Tesch-Römer, C. (1993). The role of deliberate practice in the acquisition of expert performance. *Psychological Review, 100*, 363–406.

Etherington, K. (2004). *Becoming a reflexive researcher: Using our selves in research.* London: Jessica Kingsley Publishers.

Frank, A. W. (1995). *The wounded storyteller.* Chicago: University of Chicago Press.

Frank, A. W. (2010) *Letting stories breathe: A socio-narratology.* Chicago: University of Chicago Press.

Gadamer, H. G. (1975). *Truth and method.* New York: Seabury.

Gault, N. (2011). *Big deal: The case for commercial investment in women's sport.* UK Commission on the Future of Women's Sport. Retrieved from http://www.wsff.org.uk/system/1/assets/files/000/000/287/287/2badaa5f0/original/Big_Deal_report.pdf.

Gilbourne, D., & Andersen, M. (2011). *Critical essays in applied sport psychology.* Champaign, IL: Human Kinetics.

Gottzén, L., & Kremer-Sadlik, T. (2012). Expectations, fatherhood and youth sports: A balancing act between care and expectations. *Gender & Society, 26*, 639–664.

Lieblich, A., Tuval-Mashiach, R., & Zilber, T. (1998). *Narrative research: Reading, analysis and interpretation.* London: Sage.

McLeod, J. (1997). *Narrative and psychotherapy.* London: Sage.

Messner, M., Hunt, D., Dunbar, M., Perry, C., Lapp, J., & Miller, P. (1999). *Boys to men: Sports media. Messages about masculinity: A national poll of children, focus groups, and content analysis of sports programs and commercials.* Oakland, CA: Children Now.

Norman, L. (2010). Feeling second best: Elite women coaches' experiences. *Sociology of Sport Journal, 27*, 89–104.

Papathomas, A., & Lavallee, D. (2006). A life history analysis of a male athlete with an eating disorder. *Journal of Loss and Trauma, 11*, 143–179.

Phoenix, C., & Smith, B. (2011). Telling a (good?) counterstory of aging: Natural bodybuilding meets the narrative of decline. *Journal of Gerontology Series B: Psychological Sciences and Social Sciences, 66B*(5), 628–639.

Salmela, J. H. (1994). Phases and transitions across sport careers. In D. Hackfort (Ed.), *Psycho-social issues and interventions in elite sports* (pp. 11–28). Frankfurt: Lang.

Smith, B. (2007). The state of the art in narrative inquiry: Some reflections. *Narrative Inquiry, 17*, 391–398.

Smith, B., & Sparkes, A. C. (2002). Men, sport, spinal cord injury, and the construction of coherence: Narrative practice in action. *Qualitative Research, 2*, 143–171.

Smith, B., & Sparkes, A. C. (2009). Narrative inquiry in sport and exercise psychology: What can it mean, and why might we do it? *Psychology of Sport and Exercise, 10*, 1–11.

Sparkes, A. C., & Douglas, K. (2007). Making the case for poetic representations: An example in action. *The Sport Psychologist, 21*, 170–189.

Sparkes, A. C., & Partington, S. (2003). Narrative practice and its potential contribution to sport psychology: The example of flow. *The Sport Psychologist, 17*, 292–317.

Therberge, N. (1987). Sport and women's empowerment. *Women's Studies International Forum, 10*, 387–393.

Wadey, R., & Hanton, S. (in press). Psychology of sport injury: Resilience and thriving. In F. G. O'Conner & R. Wilder (Eds.), *Running medicine*. New York: McGraw-Hill.

Wylleman, P., & Lavallee, D. (2003). A developmental perspective on transitions faced by athletes. In M. Weiss (Ed.), *Developmental sport psychology* (pp. 507–527). Morgantown, WV: Fitness Information Technology.

6   Ultraempowering women

A feminist analysis of the ultramarathoning culture

Cindra S. Kamphoff and Kelsey Timm

For many people, running a marathon is the ultimate in physical endurance, but for a small subculture of runners, 26.2 miles is only the beginning. More people are running ultramarathons, which are races longer than the traditional marathon distance of 26.2 miles. Interest in ultramarathoning has increased dramatically in the last several years. In 2013, for example, there were as many as 760 ultramarathon races worldwide (Godden, 2013). The growth is also evident in the number of 100-mile races in North America: in 1998 there were only 21 100-mile races, whereas by 2013, 115 100-mile races were taking place in North America (Godden, 2013; Hoffman & Fogard, 2011). While not as popular as the traditional marathon, the number of ultra races has tripled since the 1980s, and has spiked in the last few years (Medinger, 2009; Milroy, 2001).

In general, the growth in ultramarathoning can be attributed to the increased interest in long distance running, as well as the fitness boom that occurred in the late 1970s and 1980s (Hanold, 2010). Hanold argued that long distance running became popular through the media, which helped to construct it as a sporting activity for anyone that wanted to improve their physical fitness and well-being. The more recent growth of the ultramarathon has been attributed to Christopher McDougall's (2009) national bestseller, *Born to Run*, in which McDougall followed a group of Tarahumara Indians and Americans as they trained for and ran a 50-mile race.

Given this recent growth of interest in the sport, there is still a notably large difference in participation rates of women and men in ultramarathoning. Hoffman, Ong, and Wang (2010) reported that there were virtually no women participating in the 100-mile ultramarathon race in North America in the late 1970s and early 1980s (their report began in 1977). In the early 1980s, few women raced in ultra events because women were not allowed to compete in distance events internationally, including the Olympic Games (Hanold, 2010; Martin & Gynn, 2000). When women were first allowed to compete in ultramarathons in the 1980s, only 4% of entrants were female (Milroy, 2001). Through the 1990s, participation of women increased to 10% as the popularity of ultras continued to grow, but even in 2008 women still accounted for only about 27% of participants in ultramarathon races (Medinger, 2009).

Less than one-third of all ultramarathon participants are women, yet the experience of training and running an ultramarathon has proven to be empowering for the women who participate. In fact, running an ultramarathon has been described as life-changing and transformative, while the culture has been described as inclusive of all types of people and bodies (Hanold, 2010; Harris, Kamphoff, & Armentrout, 2013). A critical lens is needed to place women's experiences at the center and examine the uniqueness of their experiences in the ultramarathoning culture. Therefore, the purpose of this chapter is to examine the culture of ultramarathoning using a feminist standpoint approach to understand women's experiences from their perspective or standpoint, place women's experiences at the center, and highlight women's experiences that are often overlooked. This chapter starts with a description of the feminist standpoint approach used to guide this chapter, and then describes four themes related to women's experiences in ultramarathoning while providing a critical analysis of their experiences.

The critical approach used

Feminist standpoint theorists suggest that in order to understand women's experiences you must hear from the women themselves (Harding, 2000; Hartsock, 2000). The feminist standpoint approach purposefully brings women's experiences to the fore because they are often ignored in sport, and specifically within the culture of ultramarathoning. Sport and physical activity in general has historically been organized around the needs and experiences of men. Hall (1996) argued that sport is anti-feminist because the focus has traditionally been on men's experiences and perspectives. Long distance running, including marathoning and ultramarathoning, has historically been defined and described as a men's event because there is generally a lack of women in the sport, and most of the written information on long distance running has focused on men's experiences (Martin & Gynn, 2000). Women were forbidden from participating in the ancient Olympics, for example, because they were not allowed to view men competing in the nude, and were also viewed as second-class citizens. The punishment was so harsh that if a woman did spectate at the Games, she could face execution (Lovett, 1997). In the modern era of sport, there were no women's marathon races in the Olympics until 1984 (Lovett, 1997; Martin & Gynn, 2000). The physiology of the women's body was seen as a barrier to women's participation. There was a belief that women were not physically capable of running long distances, as well as a general belief (not medically supported) that a woman's uterus would fall out if she was to run a marathon or longer (Longman, 1996).

Using a feminist standpoint approach means that women's experiences are placed at the center. Similarly, feminist research is conducted *for* women, not *on* women. Research *on* women typically judges women against male standards, and does not involve careful examination of social institutions that structure our society, or consider how the experience or research can better women's lives (Klein, 1983; Thompson, 1992). In contrast, feminist research brings women's experiences to the fore with the intention of bettering the lives of the women involved and showcasing how women can be and are empowered (Klein, 1983; Thompson, 1992). The interpretation of the problem should be complex and involve a process of "peeling off the labels" to understand the whole experience, and the researcher must not view the experience as simple or straightforward (Van Den Bergh, 1989).

Given the history of women's long distance events, and that women were completely absent from long distance running until the 1970s, a feminist stand-point approach is important in that it allows us to gain the perspective of the women involved, and to bring women's experiences to the forefront of the analy-sis. Due to several calls for feminist analyses of sport (Birrell & Cole, 1994; Birrell & Theberge, 1994; Hall, 1996; Messner & Sabo, 1990), the complexities of sport as both a constraining and a liberating experience for women have been recognized. As seen in the history of women's distance running, sport has been a constraining experience for women given that they weren't supported or accepted in long distance running events until the late 1970s or early 1980s. Women are in a unique position from which to understand the division within sport and long distance running. It seems appropriate to begin to understand the women's stand-point and their individual stories to better understand the "social conditions that construct such groups" (Hill Collins, 2000, p. 43). Similarly, Krane (2001) proposed that in order to understand the experiences of those that are oppressed and marginalized within society, the analysis must begin "from the perspective or situation of a particular social group" (p. 403).

Hence, the intention of this chapter is to explore the experiences of female ultramarathoners and the culture of ultramarathoning using a feminist standpoint approach. The approach is important because, as demonstrated, sport and long distance running has been described as a male domain. At the same time, research-ers have indicated that running long distance events can be a liberating experience for women. They are able to push their bodies, experience personal fulfill-ment, and accomplish something that few women have (Harris et al., 2013). The following section draws on other studies, including Hanold (2010) and a research study in which we (Harris et al., 2013) interviewed 13 female ultramarathoners (average age of 41) about their experiences training for and running ultramara-thons. Using a feminist standpoint approach, the chapter focuses on four aspects of ultramarathons: (1) why women participate in ultramarathons; (2) ultraempower-ing for women; (3) pain, discomfort, and pushing the body; and (4) a supportive community for women.

Why do women participate in ultramarathons?

Unlike marathons, which typically take place on the road, ultramarathons are run off the beaten path, on remote trails through forests, up and down mountains, or across deserts. Common race distances are 50 kilometers, 50 miles, 100 kilometers, and 100 miles, but could include races over 100 miles (Dillon, 2004). Longer races are often held in stages over several days, such as the Relentless Ultramarathon in Great Britain in which runners cover 1,500 miles in 29 days, averaging about 50 miles a day (Ultra Running Ltd., 2013). Other ultramarathon races take place for a specific amount of time, such as 6, 12, 24, or 48 hours, and these races typically take place on a short circuit, such as a track, a 1-kilometer loop, or a short trail that is a few miles long (Dillon, 2004). The Badgerland 12- and 24-hour races in Wisconsin, for example, are run on a track, with participants reaching distances of up to 137 miles (Dillon, 2004). These short circuit timed events allow the runners to talk to and support one another throughout the event; they also provide a convenience factor, since the runners are always near an aid station, as well as friends and family.

Women have specifically indicated that the adventure of ultramarathons is one of the main reasons why they participate (Harris et al., 2013). Participants can expect to be challenged by extreme cold and heat and daunting elevation changes, in addition to the common trail-race hazards of uneven paths, wildlife encounters, and the difficulty of running in the dark. Both men and women who sign up for the popular Western States 100 are warned of the possibility of heat stroke, hypothermia, altitude sickness, injuries from falling and wildlife, muscular cell death, and renal shutdown (Dudney, 2008). Many ultradistance runners also report experiencing muscle cramps, nausea and vomiting, blisters, vision problems, and even hallucinations during their races (Harris et al., 2013; Hoffman & Fogard, 2011).

As to why women choose to put their bodies through these grueling events, they cite several reasons. Many runners are looking for the extra challenge beyond a marathon as the marathon distance becomes increasingly popular (Benyo, 2009). Pushing the body just to see how far it can go is also a popular reason for competing in ultramarathons (Hanold, 2010). Breaking through new barriers and completing these races give participants a sense of achievement, accomplishment, personal growth, and empowerment (Harris et al., 2013; Hughes, Case, Stuempfle, & Evans, 2003). Some do it for the scenery and the chance to get away from the pavement, some believe the longer distances are easier on the body, and others prefer the less competitive atmosphere and the supportive community (Harris et al., 2013; Shea, 2004).

Ultraempowering for women

Few women run ultramarathons, and completing the challenge of an ultramarathon motivates them to continue to run ultras. Given that few women participate in ultramarathons, this creates a feeling of pride and improved self-confidence. For example, one female ultramarathoner said, "There are so few women that can run an ultramarathon. When you can run an ultra, people really respect you. Even the male runners, they'll be impressed that a woman is gonna accomplish the same distance as them" (Harris et al., 2013, p. 19). This quote points to the gendered nature of ultramarathons, and more broadly the gendered nature of sport. Men are expected to be bigger, faster, and stronger than women, and when women demonstrate that they can run with the men, people are surprised and the women are respected for running the long distance. It is surprising that women are able to run with the men. And when women show that they can run with the men, respect follows, which leads to the empowerment of women as they run ultramarathons. Women have the opportunity to finish ahead of the men, and although the atmosphere of ultramarathon races is less competitive than traditional marathons, women notice when other women are winning and beating the men, which empowers them to continue (Hanold, 2010; Harris et al., 2013).

Other women have described the experience of training for and completing an ultramarathon as "transformative," while some have described themselves as a "new me" after they have trained for an ultramarathon and been a part of the culture. Women report that ultramarathoning taught them about themselves and improved their confidence and inner strength. For example, one woman indicated:

> Ultramarathoning gives you an inner strength that I don't think other sports do. You learn that your mental toughness goes way beyond you, beyond what you've ever imagined. Ultramarathons have taught me that I'm pretty fricken strong. The ultramarathon showed me what I'm made of.
>
> (Harris et al., 2013, p. 20)

This quote demonstrates that many women were surprised at the impact that ultramarathoning had on their lives. They were surprised by the extent of their toughness and strength, as though women are not typically tough and strong. As the quote above suggests, the women recognized that they possessed more fortitude than even they anticipated. Men would likely not be surprised by the toughness and strength because these are typically masculine traits. Physical and mental toughness are not expected in women, however, yet when women displayed these masculine characteristics they felt empowered through ultramarathoning. In particular, the women indicated that this empowerment was specific to the ultramarathon, as opposed to other sports or activites.

Women ultramarathoners have also stated that the skills they learned in ultramarathoning, those that pushed them to persevere and continue running, are transferable to everyday life. Women, for example, have reported that they are able to take on challenges in life outside of ultramarathoning and tackle them in the same way as they do the race – by breaking them down into smaller segments in order to not be overwhelmed (Harris et al., 2013). Other women have described starting ultrarunning as a "pivotal point in their life," with the confidence received from ultramarathoning transferring to other areas of their lives. The key change the women describe is that their confidence in themselves has been enhanced because they are able to run a distance that the majority of people cannot. They push their minds and bodies in ways that other people cannot imagine, and the sense of accomplishment they experience from ultramarathoning is life changing.

The sense of seeking achievement and accomplishment keeps the women going, and the ability to push their bodies is empowering for women ultramarathoners. Krissty Moehl, a top ranked ultramarathoner, said, "Pushing your physical limits, putting yourself to an unknown challenge is personally inspiring"

(Powell, 2011, p. 25). The accomplishment of pushing their body through discomfort is consistent with other studies on women runners, including Appleby and Fisher's (2009) study where they applied a critical feminist perspective. They found that women's perception of discomfort and pain changed after having children, which empowered them to believe they could keep going. Similarly, one woman in our research project said, "You have to work harder in ultramarathoning, so the sense of accomplishment is even more rewarding. Not only did I beat the distance but I've beat the challenges to get there." Many women ultramarathoners discover that their bodies are capable of doing more than they had expected, which is empowering for the women involved. Many women, for example, never imagined that their bodies could run a distance over the marathon distance (26.2 miles), and to experience their bodies feeling strong and powerful was more than they expected before they started ultramarathoning. Conquering the fear and challenges of the ultramarathon can be exhilarating and satisfying for the women. For example, one woman said, "There's a real sense of satisfaction . . . doing something so difficult, something that you know most of the population thinks is just crazy" (Harris et al., 2013, p. 18). Hence, accomplishing an ultramarathon empowered the women to keep running ultras regardless of the perceptions of being crazy or doing something women typically do not do.

An additional reason why women experience empowerment from training for and completing the ultramarathon is because of the personal time they are able to dedicate to themselves. Very often, women ultramarathoners are balancing other roles as mothers, wives, and employees, and ultramarathoning allows them to appreciate the time alone for themselves. For example, one woman said, "[Running ultras is] something that you can do all for yourself and all by yourself . . . it's one of the most uplifting things that I do in my life," while another said, "It makes you feel good, feel like you're more than just an accountant. I'm a runner. I'm an ultramarathoner. It's my thing, it's my time" (Harris et al., 2013, p. 13). Many of the women felt that personal time on the trails was motivational because running allowed them to break away from their daily stresses and reconnect with their thoughts and emotions. This time and freedom provided these women with empowerment – empowerment to do something for themselves, including to relieve their stress in their own way or "run by myself most of the time for myself" (Harris et al., 2013). Finding time to focus on themselves was empowering for women ultramarathoners, as if they had not experienced this freedom before they began running ultramarathons. They discussed "finding time for themselves" as unique, as if it were a rare experience for women in general. These quotes also reveal that the women felt they must justify their sports interests to others, a feeling that a male ultramarathoner may not experience. Similarly, several of these quotes reveal an undertone of guilt for devoting time to oneself that a male ultramarathoner may not experience. This guilt undertone has been discussed by such scholars as Appleby and Fisher (2009) and McGannon and Schinke (2013). The runners and physically active women in their studies experienced guilt when choosing to run because being a "good mom" meant placing their children's needs over their own. Similar standards do not exist for a "good dad," meaning it is more acceptable for men to spend time by themselves to train for an ultra than mothers.

Previous research has revealed that "fast bodies" have been the type of bodies that count in distance running (Hanold, 2010), yet ultramarathons are empowering for women because all bodies are accepted, which makes the women feel accepted within the ultramarathoning community and culture. All women "fit" in the ultramarathoning community. Chase (2008), for example, stated that only fast runners count as "marathoners," while Smith (1998) provided evidence that "joggers" have less status in the distance running community. Yet with the emphasis placed on finishing in an ultramarathon race (as compared to winning), a different type of body emerges and a broader view of what counts as a running body is apparent in ultramarathoning. Indeed, all of the participants in Hanold's (2010) study of women ultramarathoners claimed that there was no ideal body in ultramarathoning. One participant, for example, stated that "there are so many different body types. There are short people, tall people, people who are heavier or people who are tall and thin. Still all doing the same and doing really well" (Hanold, 2010, p. 168). The culture of ultramarathoning, in general, reflects a feminist culture and community. All types of women (and men) are accepted, including fast, slower, fit, and unfit. Ultramarathoners are also willing to help other runners improve, which reflects a feminist culture of community and empowerment.

Women may feel more accepted in the ultramarathoning culture given that all types of bodies are accepted; hence, they are empowered to be themselves and feel comfortable in their body, regardless of the look. One of the participants in Hanold's study, for example, discussed a new awareness of the ideal body and how ultramarathoning has allowed her to accept her body. She said:

> I know what kind of energy goes into not to have body fat, and that is not worth it. It can ruin your life ... [ultrarunning has helped] totally and absolutely because rather than my body being something that in the past I've targeted almost with hate in a way that a lot of people with other eating disorders would, blaming all their problems on their body, my body's changed from a vehicle of something that I hate to something that helps me get to amazing places.
>
> (Hanold, 2010, p. 171)

Ultramarathoning can change the women involved. They feel empowered because they accomplish a feat that many other men and women have not and cannot. The women have learned to push their bodies through discomfort despite the circumstances or situations they cannot control. They find "me time" through ultramarathoning. Furthermore, ultramarathoning is empowering in a gendered way. The women were surprised by their toughness and strength, and others were surprised when they ran with the men, suggesting that women are not expected to be able to do so. In addition, the women felt they must justify their sports interests to others, and some revealed a guilt undertone for devoting time to themselves to be their best.

Pain, discomfort, and pushing their body

The culture of ultramarathoning emphasizes the idea of being tough, pushing the limits of your body to finish, and not necessarily being the fastest as the definition of success (Hanold, 2010). Long distance running, in general, is typically constructed as demanding, discomforting, with the possibility of injury prevalent. In fact, several authors have provided evidence that long distance runners typically regard pain and discomfort as inevitable when running (Hockey, 2005; Major, 2001; Markula, 2000). For example, Bridel and Rail (2007) observed that identifying as a "runner" included rigorous training that involved injury, pain, and discomfort as frequent and expected components. Similarly, Jaeschke and Sachs (2012) provided a definition of mental toughness as it relates to ultramarathoning, and central to that definition is the ability to transcend physical pain and push oneself beyond perceived physical limitations. Many of the participants in their study stated that the ability to push through or exceed limitations within an ultramarathon was central. For example, one ultramarathoner said that mental toughness was "being able to control, celebrate, and embrace pain as a welcomed reality of life" (p. 54). More specifically, ultramarathoners described the ability to overcome both mental and physical limitations or ignore signals from the mind or body as important to running at your best. In fact, many of the ultramarathoners stated that their ability to ignore messages from their mind and body telling them to stop or quit played an important role in their ability to finish the race. The importance of accepting and embracing discomfort that the women ultramarathoners described is contrary to the typical reaction to discomfort and pain. Most people, when they experience discomfort or pain, would stop engaging in the activity; instead, these women ultrarmarathoners relentlessly continued, regardless of pain and discomfort, in their pursuit of their goal. In fact, they adhered to the sport ethic, of which two of the four components are that athletes accept risks and play through pain to prove to others they will not succumb to the pressure or fear, and that athletes accept no obstacles in the pursuit of the possibilities of their sport (Coakley, 2007; Kenow & Kamphoff, 2013).

In a further account of women ultramarathoners' experiences with pain and discomfort, Hanold (2010) stated that many of the women described their body experiences in terms of pushing the body to its limits, and referred to three distinct types of pain: discomfort, good pain, and bad pain. Both discomfort and good pain were normalized as part of being and becoming an ultramarathoner; the bad pain, however, involved injury where you should know when to stop because you are on the "verge of hurting yourself" (p. 172). Each of the participants Hanold interviewed discussed races they continued despite feeling bad or hurting. The women indicated, in fact, that discomfort and pain were what they signed up for, and that experiencing discomfort and good pain made them feel like they were working hard. Many of the women ultramarathoners in both Hanold's (2010) and

Harris et al.'s (2013) studies stated that discomfort was inevitable, and that if they keep going and pushing they know that a second, third, or fourth wind is possible. For example, one female ultramarathoner said, "It's [running through discomfort] no big deal, you always live. You always come back from it, so don't worry about it" (Hanold, 2010, p. 72). Another female ultramarathoner said:

> They never feel exactly the same one time to another. I mean, it can feel like dying – like this sort of disintegration – like the body's shutting down and it's usually followed by some sort of resurrection, literally, like something outside of yourself, something bigger than yourself comes in and gives you support.
>
> (Hanold, 2010, p. 172)

Yet despite the discomfort, the women kept going and pushing. Given that the majority of the women in this study had experienced the pain of childbirth, it is possible that they understood how to overcome the discomfort. As Appleby and Fisher's (2009) study indicated, giving birth can modify the perceptions of running pain. It is speculated that giving birth can decrease one's perception of pain or increase one's pain tolerance. In fact, several of the participants in Harris et al.'s (2013) study compared ultramarathons to childbirth. One woman, for example, said:

> It is like giving birth when you're in the midst of it, it's just hell and you say to yourself, "I'm never gonna do this again," and "What was I thinking?" Then when you are done, it was such an achievement, and you forget the pain.
>
> (p. 18)

The childbirth metaphor is one that men may not be able to understand, but demonstrates that extreme discomfort is part of the ultramarathoners' experience, and that the experience of childbirth may have given the women a greater ability to overcome the discomfort.

In all of these accounts, women describe pushing through the discomfort and pain as empowering. They embrace the discomfort and pain to improve as an ultramarathoner, but also to experience the rewards after the race. Pushing through the discomfort or "good pain" serves as a way for these women to further empower themselves. They see themselves as winners and runners that persevere despite obstacles. For example, the women in Hanold's (2010) study felt empowered when pushing their limits and finishing the race, and felt good about their bodies and that they could do anything. Hanold argued that running is typically constructed as demanding, arduous, and injury prevalent, and that pushing through discomfort is part of the ultramarathoner's experience.

While pushing their bodies to extremes, many women ultramarathoners experience hallucinations, which provide the women with a sense of adventure and amusement. The hallucinations included seeing nonexistent people, animals, or dresses hanging from the trees. For example, one of the women stated: "Basically your brain has kind of gone to sleep but your eyes are open and you're still capable of seeing your surroundings. It's kind of like you're dream running but you're awake" (Harris et al., 2013). The women have come to expect hallucinations, which, when they occur, they realize are part of extreme running and ultramarathoning. Again, most people would stop running after experiencing a hallucination, yet these women continued because of the strong sense of accomplishment and courage they knew they would experience at the end of the race. The hallucinations represent another component of ultramarathons that they have learned to overcome and embrace. Another woman ultramarathoner said, "I kept thinking I was seeing things like off to the side, like dinosaurs or something, but I knew it was just my mind playing tricks. I never seriously thought 'I'm in danger.'" Hallucinations were described with humor, and instead of seeing them as symbolic of pushing their bodies to the limit, the women approached them with light-heartedness. This light-heartedness is reflective of the ultramarathoning culture, in which one is expected to push one's body to the extreme. It is expected that participants will experience discomfort and fatigue, and, as a result, hallucinations occur.

Similarly, the women expected to put themselves in danger, which included the potential of falling on the trail or encountering such wildlife as bobcats, coyotes, and rattlesnakes, all of which might cause injury. Many of the women in Harris et al.'s (2013) study described the excitement resulting from jumping over roots and rocks, and notably described the adventure of pushing on after the pain of a fall to finish the race. As one woman ultramarathoner observed, "This is typical of a runner . . . Unless a bone is protruding from the skin, you usually just keep going." This quote demonstrates that pain and discomfort can position women as runners, equal in their abilities to men. The women interviewed for Harris et al.'s (2013) study enjoyed jumping over obstacles, running past wildlife, and hallucinating because not knowing what to expect next was a fun adventure for them. Ultramarathoning has allowed the women to push through boundaries. These boundaries include gender boundaries; we'd more likely expect men to love the adventure of ultramarathoning, not women. These women ultramarathoners also pushed the boundaries of discomfort and extreme fatigue, which they experienced in very unique ways, including hallucinations. Furthermore, they weren't afraid to place their bodies at risk of harm, regardless of the possibility of encountering bobcats, coyotes, or rattlesnakes.

A supportive community for women

The ultramarathon community is unique in many ways, and can be differentiated from the traditional marathon community in its lack of competitive atmosphere, its closely knit community, and its camaraderie (Allison, 2001; Massa, 2006; Milroy, 2001). Women have observed that this noncompetitive atmosphere was a significant source of motivation (Harris et al., 2013). This collective approach was attractive to the women because it allowed them to develop friendships and receive support from others. For example, one woman ultramarathoner explained that the ultramarathon community felt like a family, and that she wouldn't have the friendships and relationships she has now if it wasn't for the ultramarathoning community. Another ultramarathoner spoke of the time when countless runners approached her during a race willing to lend her a hand after she had fallen (Harris et al., 2013).

Powell (2011), the author of *Relentless Forward Progress*, a mantra often cited by ultramarathoners to keep themselves moving forward, describes how training for and running ultramarathons connects you with a whole group of friends. He observes that most runners who begin running ultras find a tight-knit but welcoming community that is eager to share the trail with anyone. An ultramarathoner in his book stated, "The training and friends you make in ultrarunning are the real pay offs: the race itself can almost be secondary in importance" (Powell, 2011, p. 23).

Dillon (2004) describes the ultramarathoning culture as not entirely without competitiveness, but observes that runners, and specifically women, tend to help one another more than competitors in other events. The culture of ultramarathoning is less competitive than the culture of the traditional marathon, and this lack of competitiveness creates an openness for runners to help other runners. She describes runners as apt to help other runners on the trail, as having a certain "we're all in this together" mentality, and "like one big happy family" (Dillon, 2004, p. 48), which reflects a feminist culture within ultramarathoning. For example, one ultramarathoner she interviewed said, "Everyone is in pain and suffering on some level; if you see someone who is worse off than you feel at the moment, you're likely to see whether they need help. Stopping for a minute or two to help someone is minuscule in the course of a nine- or 10-hour race" (Dillion, 2004, p. 49). The mentality of the female ultramarathoners seems counter to the conventional competitive practices of athletes, where they are focused on themselves with the goal of winning or beating other runners. This non-traditional form of sport is reflective of a feminist culture, similar to the beginnings of sport for women.

In her historical account of women's participation in sport, Hult (1994) described the feminist culture that key women physical education leaders promoted when women began participating in sport and physical activity in the 1960s. She described this feminist culture as downplaying competition while emphasizing enjoyment and sportsmanship, promoting physical education for *all* rather than a few, experiencing the joy of sport, and preventing exploitation (see also Gill, 2001). The exploitation, commercialism, and overemphasis on winning in the men's programs greatly concerned the leaders of women's sport, who didn't want any of these characteristics in sport played by women. The ultramarathon community reflects these feminist ideals given that women appear to be accepted in the culture, the lack of emphasis on competition and outcome, and emphasis on enjoyment, relationships, and cooperation. The ultramarathoning culture is different from the competitive form of sport that is standard in today's culture. As Hult outlined, this standard form of sport is masculine and male-like. The ultramarathoning community, on the other hand, reflects the feminist ideals of cooperation and support. Furthermore, women have made advancements physically in this cooperative atmosphere, insofar as they are getting faster compared to men. More specifically, researchers have examined the possibility that women tend to perform better than men as distance increases (Bam, Noakes, Juritz, & Dennis, 1997; Neporent, 2004). It appears that, as increasing numbers of women run ultramarathons, they will continue to be a place of empowerment and transformation.

Conclusion

Although only about 27% of all ultramarathoners are women, the women who train for and complete an ultramarathon describe the experience as "transformative" and empowering. They are able to prioritize their own needs and wants, and to enjoy the adventure of the ultramarathon. They feel empowered by the experience of running through discomfort or good pain while accepting the hallucinations and wildlife they might encounter along the way. The ultramarathon community reflects feminist ideals given that women are accepted in the culture and there is less emphasis on competition and outcome, with more importance given to enjoyment, relationships, and cooperation. Given this acceptance of women in the ultra culture, and the empowerment that women experience, the percentage of women ultramarathoners can only grow. Since there has been a lack of research on women's experience of distance running in general, and of ultramarathoning in particular, further research should examine women's experiences in these two sports. More specifically, to advance the research in this area, authors should interview women about their frustrations and the ways in which the ultra community may not be empowering for women. Furthermore, additional research should critically examine ultramarathoning beyond applying the feminist standpoint approach.

References

Allison, D. (2001). Twenty years later: How ultrarunning has changed. *Ultrarunning, May*, 6–11.

Appleby, K. M., & Fisher, L. F. (2009). Running in and out of motherhood: Elite distance runners' experiences of returning to competition after pregnancy. *Women in Sport and Physical Activity Journal, 18*(1), 3–17.

Bam, J., Noakes, T. D., Juritz, J., & Dennis, S. C. (1997). Could women outrun men in ultra marathon races? *Medicine and Science in Sport and Exercise, 29*, 244–247.

Benyo, R. (2009) Well beyond. *Marathon & Beyond, July*, 8–12.

Birrell, S., & Cole, C. L. (Eds.). (1994). *Women, sport, and culture*. Champaign, IL: Human Kinetics.

Birrell, S., & Theberge, N. (1994). Feminist resistance and transformation in sport. In D. M. Costa & S. R. Guthrie (Eds.), *Women and sport: Interdisciplinary perspectives* (pp. 361–376). Champaign, IL: Human Kinetics.

Bridel, W., & Rail, G. (2007). Sport, sexuality, and the production of (resistant) bodies: De-/re-constructing the meanings of gay male marathon corporeality. *Sociology of Sport Journal, 24*, 127–144.

Chase, L. F. (2008). Running big: Clydesdale runners and technologies of the bodies. *Sociology of Sport Journal, 23*, 130–147.

Coakley, J. (2007). *Sports in society: Issues & controversies*. New York, NY: McGraw-Hill.

Dillon, D. (2004). A marathoner's next frontier. *Marathon & Beyond, November*, 41–50.

Dudney, G. (2008). Beyond 26.2 miles. *American Fitness*, 39–41.

Gill, D. L. (2001). Feminist sport psychology: A guide for our journey. *The Sport Psychologist, 15*, 363–372.

Godden, K. (2013) *Ultramarathon running resource*. Retrieved from www.ultramara-thonrunning.com.

Hall, M. A. (1996). *Feminism and sporting bodies: Essays on theory and practice*. Champaign, IL: Human Kinetics.

Hanold, M. T. (2010). Beyond the marathon: (De)construction of female ultrarunning bodies. *Sociology of Sport Journal, 27*, 160–177.

Harding, S. (2000). Comment on Hekman's "Truth and method: Feminist standpoint theory revisited": Whose standpoints need the regime of truth and reality? In C. Allen & J. A. Howard (Eds.), *Provoking feminisms* (pp. 50–57). Chicago: University of Chicago Press.

Harris, A., Kamphoff, C., & Armentrout, S. (2013). Revealing the challenges and motivation experienced by female ultramarathon runners. Under review.

Hartsock, N. (2000). Comment on Hekman's "Truth and method: Feminist standpoint theory revisited": Truth of justice? In C. Allen & J. A. Howard (Eds.), *Provoking feminisms* (pp. 35–42). Chicago: University of Chicago Press.

Hill Collins, P. (2000). Gender, Black feminism, and Black political economy. *The Annals of the American Academy of Political and Social Science, 568*, 41–53.

Hockey, J. (2005). Injured distance runners: A case of identity work as self-help. *Sociology of Sport Journal, 22*, 38–58.

Hoffman, M. D., & Fogard, K. (2011). Factors related to successful completion of a 161-km ultramarathon. *International Journal of Sports Physiology and Performance, 6*, 25–37.

Hoffman, M. D., Ong, J. C., & Wang, G. (2010). Historical analysis of participation in 161-km ultramarathons in North America. *International Journal History of Sport, 27*, 1877–1891.

Hughes, S. L., Case, H. S., Stuempfle, K. J., & Evans, D. S. (2003). Personality profiles of Iditasport ultra-marathon participants. *Journal of Applied Sport Psychology, 15*, 256–261.

Hult, J. (1994). The story of women's athletics: Manipulating a dream 1890–1985. In D. M. Costa & S. R. Guthrie (Eds.), *Women and sport: Interdisciplinary perspectives* (pp. 83–106). Champaign, IL: Human Kinetics.

Jaeschke, A., & Sachs, M. (2012). 100,000 miles closer to a definition of mental toughness: The farther you run, the more the mind dominates. *Marathon & Beyond, Sept/Oct*, 44–67.

Kenow, L. J., & Kamphoff, C. S. (2013). Sociocultural aspects of injury and injury response. In M. Granquist, J. Hamson-Utley, J. Ostrowski, & L. Kenow (Eds.), *Psychosocial strategies for athletic training*. Philadelphia: F.A. Davis Company.

Klein, R. D. (1983). How to do what we want to do: Thoughts about feminist methodology. In G. Bowles & R. Klein (Eds.), *Towards a methodology for feminist research* (pp. 88–104). London: Routledge & Kegan Paul.

Krane, V. (2001). One lesbian feminist epistemology: Integrating feminist standpoint, queer theory, and feminist cultural studies. *The Sport Psychologist, 15*, 401–411.

Longman, J. (1996, June 23). How the women won. *New York Times*. Retrieved from www.nytimes.com.

Lovett, C. (1997). *Olympic marathon: A centennial history of the Games' most storied race*. Westport, CT: Greenwood Publishing Group.

Major, W. F. (2001). The benefits and costs of serious running. *World Leisure Journal, 43*(2), 12–25.

Markula, P. (2000). "I gotta do the marathon": Women's running as a truth-game. *Aethlon, 18*(1/2), 89–106.

Martin, D. E., & Gynn, R. W. H. (2000). *The Olympic marathon: The history and drama of sport's most challenging event*. Champaign, IL: Human Kinetics.

Massa, T. (2006). 1981–2006: A look inside the numbers. *Ultrarunning, May*, 14–15.

McDougall, C. M. (2009). *Born to run: A hidden tribe, superathletes, and the greatest race the world has never seen*. New York: Random House.

McGannon, K. R., & Schinke, R. J. (2013). "My first choice is to work out at work; then I don't feel bad about my kids": A discursive psychological analysis of motherhood and physical activity participation. *Psychology of Sport and Exercise, 14*, 179–188.

Medinger, J. (2009). The year in review. *Ultrarunning, March*, 31–50.

Messner, M., & Sabo, D. (Eds.). (1990). *Sport, men and the gender order*. Champaign, IL: Human Kinetics.

Milroy, A. (2001). Women's ultrarunning since 1981. *Ultrarunning, May*, 19.

Neporent, L. (2004). Are women better in the long run? *Muscle and Fitness Hers, 5*, 73.

Powell, B. (2011). *Relentless forward progress: A guide to running ultramarathons*. Halcottsville, NY: Breakaway Books.

Shea, S. B. (2004). The ultra challenge. *Muscle and Fitness Hers, 5*, 70.

Smith, S. (1998). Athletes, runners, and joggers: Participant-group dynamics in a sport of "individuals." *Sociology of Sport Journal, 15*, 174–192.

Thompson, L. (1992). Feminist methodology for family studies. *Journal of Marriage and the Family, 57*, 847–865.

Ultra Running Ltd. (2013). *Relentless 2013*. Retrieved from http://www.ultrarunningltd. co.uk/relentless.html.

Van Den Bergh, N. (1989). Renaming: Vehicle for empowerment. In J. Penfield (Ed.), *Women and language in transition* (pp. 130–136). Albany, NY: SUNY Press.

Part II

Critiques of the medical model, sport culture and sport research

7   Disability, sport, and impaired bodies

A critical approach

Brett Smith and Marie-Josee Perrier

There is a growing amount of sport psychological research that examines disability and sport. It is, however, extremely rare that this work explicitly adopts and promotes a critical approach. In this chapter, we address this absence by first connecting sport psychology with critical disability studies and, second, by highlighting the potential of the social relational model for developing a critical study of the psychology of disability, sport, and physical activity. We conclude with a series of future directions for continued critical work on the topic of disability, sport, and physical activity.

Before turning to all this, it needs to be acknowledged that because of the absence of critical work on disability within sport psychology we must go into uncharted territory and bring home a set of ideas from outside our field. This was not easy for us. Engaging with ideas outside the field might not be easy either for some readers rooted in sport psychology. But, for us at least, if we do not engage with such ideas there is the real danger that sport psychology falls far behind work being done in other fields on disability and risks producing outdated or pedestrian work. Or, put more positively, as researchers it is our moral imperative to assume the responsibility to grapple with some difficult yet important ideas expressed in different fields in order to productively develop a more nuanced understanding of disability and sport. Many others support this. For instance, as Nisbett (1990) and Mishler (2006) argued, instead of staying inside one's field and possibly being 'blinkered' or intellectually 'stifled' by our traditional ways of knowing, our work can become deeper and more complex through interaction with other researchers from different fields: scientific creativity can be greatly fostered and the work we do with various disabled people enhanced. Please, then, consider taking the plunge with us into critical waters.

Understanding disability: moving beyond the medical model to critical disability studies

Sport psychological research on disability, either knowingly or unknowingly, has often been framed by a medical model understanding of disabled people. The medical model, or what is sometimes referred to as the individual model of disability, defines disability as any lack of ability resulting from an impairment to perform an activity within the range considered normal for a person (Smith & Perrier, in press; Thomas, 2007). Thus, in this model disability is 'caused' by parts of the body that do not work 'properly'. Despite historically being a dominant platform from which to understand disability and position research, the medical model has several inter-related problems.

First, because the medical model relies on bio-physical assumptions of 'normality' to define disability, the socio-cultural forces that play a major part in defining – constructing – what is 'normal' are overlooked. Not only does this mean we are left with biological reductionist explanations of disability and, in turn, a very inadequate conception of disability, but also we leave untouched the very idea of 'normality'. In so doing, there is the risk of perpetuating a 'normal'/'abnormal' binary. There is likewise the danger of reifying 'normality' as something 'natural' rather than as a social construction that acts on and for people in dangerous and 'positive' ways. For instance, in defining disability as any lack of ability resulting from an impairment to perform an activity within the range considered normal, the medical model constructs disabled people as defective (i.e. 'not normal') and others ('the normals') as definitive or superior human beings who can assume authority and exercise power. As Meekosha and Shuttleworth (2009) pointed out:

> How societies divide "normal" and "abnormal" bodies is central to the production and sustenance of what it means to be human in society. It defines access to nations and communities. It determines choice and participation in civic life. It determines what constitutes "rational" men and women and who should have the right to be part of society and who should not.
>
> (p. 65)

A second problem is that within the medical model disability is depicted as inevitably a personal physical tragedy and psychological trauma that should be overcome. Third, the medical model locates the 'problem' of disability squarely within the individual. In so doing, the social world is left under-theorized and unchallenged. Again, then, the danger inherent in this model is that "disability is seen as lying with the disabled person rather than the social world that responds negatively to disability" (Goodley, 2012, p. 313).

Given these problems, where else might sport psychologists turn to better understand the ever more complex nature of disability? How might we position our work differently? One response is to connect with what has come to be known as critical disability studies (CDS). According to Meekosha and Shuttleworth (2009), Shildrick (2012), and Goodley (2013), the word 'critical' in terms of the study of disability denotes a sense of self-reflexivity and rethinking about where we have come from, where we are at, and where we might be going in terms of our conventions, assumptions, and aspirations of research, theory, and activism. They suggest that the emergence of CDS can be put down to a number of recent developments, many of which intertwine and relate. These developments include the influence of disciplines previously on the outskirts, such as critical psychology, entering the field; attempts to challenge the dogmatic tendencies of some theories and theorists through reference to eclecticism and intellectual imagination; work by scholars that throws the spotlight on the community as the place to address issues of social change and well-being; the promotion of praxis (i.e. the intertwining of activism and theory) that appears to go beyond thinking *about* disabled people to engaging *with* disabled people; accounts that show what is possible when impaired and how disability can be affirmative; a shift in theorizing beyond the medical model as well as what is known as the social model; and calls for nuanced analyses of disabled people's experience that investigate culture, the body, impairment, and narrative.

Despite sport psychologists not connecting with CDS, the critical study of disability does, however, hold numerous benefits. For example, CDS carves out a productive space in which we can be reflexive about where we have come from and where we are at present. As part of this, CDS encourages researchers to employ a critical attitude to current dominant beliefs that are often seemingly beyond critique because these beliefs are ostensibly beyond doubt, infused with power, taken for granted, and/or an established structure or theme upon which research and development must operate. But what might a critical attitude look like? Turning our gaze critically back on to a theme we have promoted, and which is an established thematic focus in sport and exercise psychology, consider the example of 'exercise as medicine'.

In recent years, it has become commonplace to believe that sport or exercise *is* medicine, and to promote these activities as such. For example, regularly participating in physical activities like sport or exercise is said to be a cost-effective way to help minimize secondary health conditions that go with impairment (e.g. pressure sores), prevent certain diseases (e.g. coronary artery disease), aid recovery from illness (e.g. depression), and promote positive subjective well-being (e.g. self-esteem). Although we do not dispute such matters, and have contributed to such beliefs (e.g. Perrier, Smith, & Latimer-Cheung, 2013; Smith, 2013a), this does not mean that the exercise–medicine relationship should escape critical scrutiny.

Turning a critical gaze on to the exercise–medicine relationship, we are troubled by the danger of reconstructing disabled people simply in terms of the medical model. The limits of this model were highlighted above. Suffice to say that in talking about sport and exercise as 'medicine' we risk medicalizing disabled people's bodies, neglecting forms of oppression that damage health or well-being, and placing disabled people in the 'expert hands' of medicine rather than respecting that they themselves are the experts as well. There might also be a hidden politics within the very one-sided presentation of the 'evidence' that exercise is medicine. For example, the 'experts' in academia, which include sport and exercise psychologists, can have vested interests in promoting the 'product' of exercise as medicine in order to keep generating grants, swelling their publication output, gaining tenure, and building centers of power. These points might seem ludicrous. However, when we consider that such matters have been observed within other domains, such as in obesity research and the so-called obesity epidemic (e.g., Gard, 2011), it would be naïve, in our own best interests, or intellectually vacuous of us simply to dismiss them.

A related danger of uncritically and un-reflexively promoting exercise as medicine is that we can, implicitly or explicitly, promote what Shilling (2008) described as the health role within a context of neoliberalism. This context is one in which social order is seen as being dependent on individual responsibility: governments are deregulated, social programs are cut and/or privatized, and social problems have to be solved by individual, private solutions. In this context, the disabled body is presented as making demands. Disabled people are required to provide for their own needs while they should simultaneously avoid burdening welfare services, a central tenet of many government agendas as we write. Within a context of neoliberalism, therefore, the health role calls on the individual to be a responsible citizen who must personally take care of his or her own health by doing things like exercising regularly.

Without discounting the benefits to health and well-being that exercising brings, there are several dangers that go with the neoliberal health role. The health role morally depicts those disabled individuals who engage regularly in exercise as the 'good' citizens. But, by corollary, those who do not exercise are 'bad'. The largely inactive or sedentary disabled individual – the 'bad' person – is seen as lacking the inner motivation, mental toughness, or resilience to engage in sport or exercise. It is them, and only them, therefore, that are to blame for their own health problems, for numerous so-called epidemics (e.g. obesity), and for rising costs to our health services. Yet depicted in these ways, the socio-cultural environments or power relations that can restrict what activities people with an impairment can do are ignored. In other words, social or cultural oppression against disabled people – that is, disablism – is brushed under the carpet and the status quo is maintained. Further, as Shilling (2008) argued, the health role can leave disabled people feeling that their bodies are deviant, disgusting, socially unacceptable, and culturally illegitimate, thereby actually damaging their well-being.

Another possible danger of the health role in relation to sport or exercise is that it overlooks the dark side of these activities. Like sport, exercise isn't always good for one's health or well-being. It can be associated with such troubling conditions as eating disorders (e.g. Papathomas & Lavallee, 2010). Finally, but by no means least, the health role introduces the risk of notions of disabled people engaging in sport or exercise for the sake of it – to enjoy themselves, and to experience their physicality in vibrant, disruptive, pleasurable, creative ways – being hijacked by those more interested in controlling bodies for economic, disciplinary, or normalizing reasons. In the health role the pleasures and intrinsic values of playing sport or exercising can be eclipsed by a focus on the instrumental value of being active. This can be detrimental to a disabled person's well-being and motivation to be active across the life course.

Let us be clear. We are not arguing against the benefits that can come with exercising regularly. Nor are we advocating the removal of 'exercise or sport as form of medicine' from the research or policy agenda. Our point is that sport and exercise psychologists need to be critically reflexive about, rather than shy away from, the difficult problems that go with such matters as 'exercise is medicine' if we are to grow as a field, honor the complex psychological worlds we live in, and make a real difference. We need to open up alternative lines of critical inquiry about commonly held beliefs to elucidate issues that will be beneficial to the study of disability and contribute to an expanded understanding of disabled people's place in the world. Such critical reflexivity must of necessity also remain receptive to new theoretical perspectives or models to shed light on the changing structures and meanings that define and restrict emancipation. With this in mind, in what follows we offer one new direction for the consideration of those sport psychologists interested in better understanding disability.

The social relational model

Before we detail the social *relational* model, it is important that we highlight the social model. This is of importance because the former was developed out of the latter, and, as suggested earlier, CDS emerged from a shift in theorizing beyond the social model. As a direct riposte to the medical model, the social model asserts that disability is not caused by impairment but by the social barriers (structural and attitudinal) that people with impairments (physical, sensory, and intellectual) come up against in every arena. In this regard, having and being an impaired body does not equate with disability. Instead, and severing the causal link between the body and disability that the medical model created, disability is a consequence and problem of society. The 'solution', therefore, lies not in cures, therapy, psychological interventions, physical adjustments to the impaired body, and so on. Rather, improvements in disabled people's lives necessitate the sweeping away of social barriers that disable people, and the development of social policies that facilitate full social inclusion and citizenship (Thomas, 2007).

The social model has been impressive. For example, in re-defining disability as an act of exclusion – people are *disabled* by society – the model influenced anti-discrimination legislation in the form of various Disability Discrimination Acts around the globe. As a consequence, although not perfect or always followed, disabled people in numerous countries should by law now have access to gyms, sport clubs, sporting stadiums, and so on. When disabled individuals encounter the social model, the effect can also be revelatory and liberating. Rather than themselves being the 'problem' and the 'solution' traced to their own individual body, disabled people have been enabled by the social model to recognize that society is often the problem and that solutions are to be found there, 'outside' their own bodies. This is exemplified in the following interview account taken from a sport psychology study that examined men's narratives of hope following acquiring spinal cord injuries (SCI) whilst playing sport:

> Hearing people, including non-disabled, talk about their lives, and knowing that it's not me individually, but a societal issue, including the barriers we face, whether that's access to buildings or equal rights for employment, has helped. Knowing that it's not me had a major lift and helped me to change, to

be reborn. It's important, I think, to let our voices be heard and be valued. We can to stick together, which can be hard. But, and I know this isn't for everyone, but for me it feels good knowing that I'm part of something and not alone. The knowledge I've been given by the social view, and disabled people in general, has been tremendously important to me in how I've developed as a person and the ideas I've got now. With their help, it's become a lot easier to resist saying "I do want hope for a cure".

(Smith & Sparkes, 2005, p. 1101)

Under the umbrella of the social model, therefore, very real theoretical, as well as practical, achievements have been made. However, helped significantly by schol-ars within CDS, the social model has in recent years been subject to critical scrutiny. First, it is argued that a world free of all physical barriers is idealistic because the natural environment can limit access (Smith & Perrier, in press). For example, wheelchair users can be restricted climbing rocky mountains. Second, the social model has been criticized for over-socializing the phenomenon of dis-ability (Goodley, 2012; Smith & Perrier, in press; Thomas, 2007). People's lived experiences and the cultural discourses that help constitute disability are ignored in the model. For instance, a women's experience of challenging negative views of disability sport in the media is overlooked. The 'personal is political' (or the 'political is personal') feminist slogan is left unacknowledged and people's 'private' accounts are artificially separated from 'public' issues.

Third, by conceptually separating impairment from disability, the social model has been heavily critiqued for creating another dualism and, in turn, ignoring the body (Hughes & Patterson, 1997; Smith & Perrier, in press; Thomas, 2007). The disability/impairment dualism has been heavily lambasted for treating the impaired body as simply biological: as pre-social, inert, uneffected by cultural discourses, and isolated from people's experiences of being and having an impairment within networks of relations (Hughes & Paterson, 1997). Likewise, because in the social model disability is proposed as having nothing to do with the body, the importance of impairment in people's lives is overlooked. The impaired body as not simply biological but also a social source or location of disablism that is lived is ignored. For instance, by providing ramps to a sporting facility, social barriers are removed for a wheelchair user and thus, in theory, so are disability and disablism. Yet a disabled person's activity may not be restricted by pain alone. When a coach tells them that they cannot participate in sports within the facility because they have a bodily impairment, their activity is likewise restricted, and they are oppressed.

Accordingly, whilst the social model has been impressive, there are failings. Given this, as CDS researchers suggest (Goodley, 2013; Meekosha & Shuttleworth, 2009), what is needed is a shift in theorizing beyond the social model. Where, however, might we go if we are to move beyond the social model? One response is to connect with the social relational model (SRM) as described by Thomas (2007). The SRM builds on the problems with the social model as well as the discontent with the individualist tradition (see Gergen, 2009; Smith, 2013b), in which the individual mind and bounded/autonomous self is considered the fundamental atom of human life. Instead of conceptualizing disability, disablism, or impairment as originating within the individual, the SRM carves out a space of understanding in which these are reconstituted as a manifestation of social relationships. As Thomas argued, the study of disability should:

> engage both with social structure (order) and social agency (action), and should therefore accommodate analyses of social relations and social forces that construct, produce, institutionalize, enact and perform disability and disablism. The *lived experience* of both disablism *and* impairment should have its place, as should theorizations of impairment *per se*.
>
> (2007, pp. 181–182)

The SRM, therefore, foregrounds disability as a social relationship between people and, importantly, expands how we understand *disablism* and *impairment*. Disablism, as extended by Thomas (2007) in the SRM, is "a form of social oppression involving the social imposition of restrictions of activity on people with impairments *and* the socially engendered undermining of their psycho-emotional well-being" (emphasis added; p. 73). Conceptualized this way, the SRM uniquely encompasses and extends disablism by proposing that people can experience several forms of social oppression (i.e. structural disablism *and* indirect or direct psycho-emotional disablism) and that these forms emerge not from the individual's mind but instead out of relationships with structures and human beings. In other words, what differentiates the SRM from other models, and makes this model attractive, is the deliberate inclusion of psycho-emotional disablism and a shift toward identifying this form of social oppression as originating from social relationships with material barriers and other people, not from within the individual. For example, psycho-emotional disablism can involve being stared at by strangers when in the gym, having jokes made about impairment during a football game, seeing denigrating images of impairment in coaching books, or having to deal with intended or unintended hurtful words spoken by others when out training. As exemplified in the work of Smith and Sparkes (2008), Smith (2013a, 2013b), and Sparkes and Smith (2005) with people who acquired a spinal cord injury through playing sport, the effects of such psycho-emotional disablism can be profound. Self-esteem, confidence, and ontological security can be damaged when a spinal cord injured wheelchair user is stared at on the way to the gym. When a stranger, without asking, pushes them up an entrance ramp to a gym, they can be made to feel worthless, useless, of lesser value, and burdensome. In such social interactions, a disabled person's psycho-emotional well-being is not simply undermined. As a result of such undermining, they may avoid the gym altogether in the future. Hence, psycho-emotional disablism can damage well-being as well as place limits on what one *can do* and *can become*.

Complementing disablism, and bringing the body back into analytical focus, the SRM also encompasses impairment by way of what Thomas (2007) termed a non-reductionist materialist ontology of the body that allows *impairments* and *impairment effects* to be critically attended to. By a non-reductionist materialist ontology of the body, Thomas is referring to an understanding of the body as simultaneously biological, lived, social, and cultural. At its simplest, then, in the SRM impairment is a 'biological reality'. It is recognized that this reality – the raw materiality of the body – can *sometimes* directly *affect* what a person does and how they feel. In other words, the impaired body as a biological entity can be held directly responsible for restricting some activities a person can do and, at times, damaging psycho-emotional well-being. When this is the case, when impairment effects are just corporeal, disablism is then absent: social oppression is not engendered because it is the biological 'realness' of having an impaired body that simply affects activity or well-being. That recognized, the picture is often more complicated than this. The reason for this is that the body is more than just biological. It is *also* experienced, socially constructed, and culturally fashioned, thereby making impaired bodies simultaneously biological, lived, social, and cultural.

For example, when a double-amputee track athlete cannot compete in a competition simply because they are experiencing phantom limb pain and feel miserable as a direct consequence, it is the immediacy and obdurate reality of their biological body that restricts activity and damages their psycho-emotional well-being. Accordingly, the presence of phantom limb pain is an effect of impairment that is directly associated with being impaired, but which, in this case, does not constitute disability or oppression: removing all disablist and disabling barriers wouldn't enable the athlete in this scenario to compete or change how they feel. However, the biological reality of bodily impairment and its effects on what one can do, may become, or experience can rarely be decoupled from the experiential, social, and cultural. As noted, impairment and impairment effects are complex bio-lived-social-cultural phenomena. When the athlete in pain tells her coach that she cannot compete, and the coach responds by saying that he does not believe she is in pain – epistemic invalidation (Smith & Sparkes, 2008; Wendell, 1996) – and must then either compete or leave the team, the impaired body becomes the substratum or medium for the social enactment of oppressive practices.

Let us offer one more example of the social relational model in action, and why decoupling the biological reality of the body from the experiential, social, and cultural, is to paint a limited picture of impairment, impairment effects, and disablism. Imagine an able-bodied tennis coach telling a spinal cord injured wheelchair person who wants to be a tennis coach that they cannot become one *because* they are impaired: he or she cannot run around the court or stand to serve, so they should not coach tennis to able-bodied people. Certainly the biological reality of the body does prevent these activities. Yet, the body does not operate within a lived-socio-cultural vacuum. When the coach *imposes upon* the spinal cord injured person what they can do or become *because* of their impairment, and potentially damages their psycho-emotional well-being as a result, he or she is not simply drawing on a set of social and cultural assumptions about what counts as a tennis coach and which bodies should and can coach. The able-bodied coach is also enacting a form of disablism. That is, the effect of the coach interacting with a person who is impaired is oppression. This oppression includes imbalanced personal relationships, social exclusion, and restricted autonomy and opportunities for growth for the spinal cord injured person.

Given the lack of talk in this chapter about 'the mind', 'enhancing performance/ psychology of sporting excellence', or 'changing behavior', at this point a sport psychologist might well ask, 'Why should I care about, connect with, or use the social relational model?' The simple answer is that, as uniquely articulated within the model, disabled individuals live lives shaped by impairment and impairment effects, as well as by the effects of structural and psycho-emotional disablism. To ignore or set these aside is to risk perpetuating – being complicit in – an apolitical, individualistic, neoliberal, disembodied, and simplistic way of knowing disability sport. Put another way, disabled people are undervalued and discriminated against and this cannot be changed simply through the traditional psychological study of 'the mind', 'affect', 'performance', 'excellence', or 'behavior'. Of course, a critic might bemoan that revealing oppression and challenging discrimination is not the job of a sport psychologist. This is a narrow and simple-minded view. It is also one that means we are subtly complicit in the reproduction of oppressive practices and discrimination. Here, then, we return to the ethical imperative of responsibility: what can we – each of us, in our work – do to make a difference?

One possibility is to adopt the character the *parrhesiast* as described by Foucault (2001). The parrhesiast is a particular kind of truth teller. He or she literally speaks 'truth' to power; for example, revealing oppressive practices or bringing topics like diversity, social justice, praxis, and culture to the forefront of major sport psychology conferences that typically relegate such topics to the margins. A second possibility is to adopt the character of the *trickster* (Frank, 2010), who develops the ability to slip out of definitions that seek to limit whatever is defined. For example, when sport psychology is simply defined as the study of the mind or the pursuit of sporting excellence, then we have a limited definition of who a sport psychologist is and can be, along with the kind of work that can and could be done (see also McGannon & Mauws, 2000; McGannon & Spence, 2010). Slipping out of such narrow definitions might mean opening up opportunities to enmesh the psychological study of 'the mind', 'affect', 'performance', 'excellence', 'self', or 'behaviour' with a critical lens that includes a careful analysis of embodied relations and the various forms of oppression disabled people encounter daily. Connecting with the SRM offers fertile ground for doing this.

Indeed, as we have hinted at, the SRM holds several benefits. Without sliding into an individual approach, the SRM honors lived experience, psycho-emotional well-being, disablism, and impaired bodies as simultaneously biological, cultural, and social. When connected to CDS, the SRM carves out a vital space in which we are encouraged to be reflexive about where we have come from and where we are at present. The SRM also encourages those of us within sport psychology to consider where we might go in terms of our conventions, assumptions, and aspirations of research, theory, and activism. In so doing, not only are opportunities created to question taken-for-granted assumptions, pose critical questions about the usefulness of dominant theories of disability, and reassess what we think we know now. There are also great possibilities for us to think differently and expand our ways of knowing so that we can develop more complex and state-of-the-art understandings of disabled sport, as well as enhance how our research can make a difference (Smith & Sparkes, 2012).

Additional future directions: expanding the psychology of disability sport further

In addition to CDS and the SRM, sport psychologists might harness the power of narrative theory and methods to study disability (Smith & Sparkes, 2009; Sparkes & Smith, 2013). Narrative research is needed because, as Hughes and Paterson (1997) stressed, not only is disability experienced in, on, and through the body, but also "impairment is experienced in terms of the personal and cultural narratives that help to constitute its meaning" (p. 335). Thus, if we are to understand disabled people's lives and what it means to have an impaired body, we need to examine the narratives that people draw on and use in various environments (Perrier et al., 2013). These environments might include indoor active rehabilitation centers designed specifically for disabled people to exercise in. Another environment where narratives circulate is the 'blue gym', that is, the natural water-based environment in which people can be physically active (Smith & Sparkes, 2012). With regard to disability, within sport psychology such environments have largely escaped critical attention.

More work is needed that also critically attends to the differing ways in which cultural narratives, as actors, *do* things on and to disabled people, as well as the various ways they themselves, as active human agents, *do* things with narratives, such as resisting in different ways and with differing effects negative views of disability (Phoenix & Smith, 2011). Furthermore, sport and exercise psychologists might start to fill the gap in research that attends to intersectionality (Goodley, 2013; Valentine, 2007). Intersectionality is concerned with attending to the interconnections and contradictions between disability, gender, age, race, sexuality, class, athletic identity, and so on that are fundamental to developing complex understandings of human lives across the life course. Finally, but by no means least, as illustrated in the work by Blodgett, Schinke, Smith, Peltier, and Pheasant (2011) with an Aboriginal community, sport psychology researchers might consider engaging with disability communities through participatory action research and/or cultural research.

Conclusion

Sport psychology is at an exciting juncture. If we are to act in a morally responsible way – and, dare we say it, do what we are paid to do – then we must not simply contemplate ideas within the field of sport psychology. *If* we are to develop further issues that will be beneficial to disabled people's lives, and engage with them to challenge and change oppressive practices, then researchers need also to engage with the risky but exciting challenge of crossing borders into other fields. Such fields have a rich vineyard of approaches, models, theories, lines of inquiry, and ways of being that we might draw on. These include, as we have noted here, a CDS approach, the SRM, narrative inquiry, intersectionality, and community based participatory action research. There are of course many other approaches, models, theories, lines of inquiry, and ways of being that are growing and currently being planted. We hope this chapter has encouraged sport psychologists not just to think more critically about and with disability, but also to cross into other fields and consider, with a critical reflexive attitude, connecting with various ideas that can expand how we understand disability sport.

References

Blodgett, A., Schinke, R., Smith, B., Peltier, D., & Pheasant, C. (2011). Exploring vignettes as a narrative strategy for co-producing the research voices of Aboriginal community members. *Qualitative Inquiry, 17*, 522–553.

Foucault, M. (2001). *Fearless speech*. Edited by J. Pearson. Los Angeles: Semiotext(e).

Frank, A. W. (2010). *Letting stories breathe*. Chicago: University of Chicago Press.

Gard, M. (2011). *The end of the obesity epidemic*. London: Routledge.

Gergen, K. (2009). *Relational being*. Oxford: Oxford University Press.

Goodley, D. (2012). The psychology of disability. In N. Watson, A. Roulstone, & C. Thomas (Eds.), *Routledge handbook to disability studies* (pp. 310–323). London: Routledge.

Goodley, D. (2013). Dis/entangling critical disability studies. *Disability & Society, 28*, 631–644.

Hughes, B., & Paterson, K. (1997). The social model of disability and the disappearing body: Towards a sociology of 'impairment'. *Disability & Society, 12*, 325–340.

McGannon, K. R., & Mauws, M. K. (2000). Discursive psychology: An alternative approach for studying adherence to exercise and physical activity. *Quest, 52*, 148–165.

McGannon, K. R., & Spence, J. C. (2010). Speaking of the self and physical activity participation: What discursive psychology can tell us about an old problem. *Qualitative Research in Sport and Exercise, 2*, 17–38.

Meekosha, H., & Shuttleworth, R. (2009). What's so 'critical' about critical disability studies? *Australian Journal of Human Rights, 15*, 47–75.

Mishler, E. (2006). Foreword. In R. Rapport & P. Wainwright (Eds.), *The self in health and illness* (pp. iv–vii). Oxford: Radcliffe Publishing.

Nisbett, R. E. (1990). The anticreativity letters: Advice from a senior tempter to a junior tempter. *American Psychologist, 45*, 1078–1082.

Papathomas, A., & Lavallee, D. (2010). Athletes' experiences of disordered eating in sport. *Qualitative Research in Sport and Exercise, 2*, 354–370.

Perrier, M.-J., Smith, B., & Latimer-Cheung, A. E. (2013). Narrative environments and the capacity of disability narratives to motivate leisure-time physical activity among individuals with spinal cord injury. *Disability and Rehabilitation, 35*, 2089–2096.

Phoenix, C., & Smith, B. (2011). Telling a (good?) counterstory of aging: Natural bodybuilding meets the narrative of decline. *The Journals of Gerontology Series B: Psychological Sciences and Social Sciences, 66*, 628–639.

Shildrick, M. (2012). Critical disability studies: Rethinking the conventions for the age of postmodernity. In N. Watson, A. Roulstone, & C. Thomas (Eds.), *Routledge handbook to disability studies* (pp. 30–41). London: Routledge.

Shilling, C. (2008). *Changing bodies: Habit, crisis and creativity*. London: Sage.

Smith, B. (2013a). Disability, sport, and men's narratives of health: A qualitative study. *Health Psychology, 32*, 110–119.

Smith, B. (2013b). Sporting spinal cord injuries, social relations, and rehabilitation narratives: An ethnographic creative non-fiction of becoming disabled through sport. *Sociology of Sport Journal, 30*, 132–152.

Smith, B., & Perrier, M.-J. (in press). Understanding disability, sport and exercise: Models and narrative inquiry. In R. Eklund & G. Tenenbaum (Eds.), *Encyclopaedia of sport and exercise psychology*. Champaign, IL: Human Kinetics.

Smith, B., & Sparkes, A. C. (2005). Men, sport, spinal cord injury and narratives of hope. *Social Science & Medicine, 61*, 1095–1105.

Smith, B., & Sparkes, A. C. (2008). Changing bodies, changing narratives and the consequences of tellability: A case study of becoming disabled through sport. *Sociology of Health and Illness, 30*, 217–236.

Smith, B., & Sparkes, A. C. (2009). Narrative analysis and sport and exercise psychology: Understanding lives in diverse ways. *Psychology of Sport and Exercise, 10*(2), 279–288.

Smith, B., & Sparkes, A. C. (2012). Disability, sport and physical activity: A critical review. In N. Watson, A. Roulstone, & C. Thomas (Eds.), *Routledge handbook to disability studies* (pp. 336–347). London: Routledge.

Sparkes, A. C., & Smith, B. (2005). When narratives matter. *Medical Humanities, 31*, 81–88.

Sparkes, A. C., & Smith, B. (2013). *Qualitative research methods in sport, exercise and health: From process to product*. London: Routledge.

Thomas, C. (2007). *Sociologies of disability and illness*. London: Palgrave.

Valentine, G. (2007). Theorising and researching intersectionality: A challenge for feminist geography. *The Professional Geographer, 59*, 10–21.

Wendell, S. (1996). *The rejected body: Feminist philosophical reflections on disability*. London: Routledge.

8 A few good men

Male athlete eating disorders, medical supremacy and the silencing of a sporting minority

Anthony Papathomas

Male athletes are not immune to the weight pressures associated with competitive sport. Consequently, nor are they immune to such disordered eating behaviors and eating disorders as anorexia nervosa and bulimia nervosa (Baum, 2006). In accordance with prevalence rates in the general population (see Hudson, Hiripi, Pope, & Kessler, 2007), fewer male athletes suffer with eating disorders than female athletes; nevertheless, they do still suffer. Male athletes do self-starve, they do binge and purge, and they do experience the mental burden that comes with an obsessive concern with food and weight (Papathomas & Lavallee, 2006). Yet, it remains that the literature is overwhelmingly focused on females. In this chapter I will explore potential reasons as to why male athlete eating disorders is a neglected area of study. I will discuss the possible consequences of this neglect for sport psychologists, coaches and the athletes themselves. Ultimately, I argue that a "few men" is "enough men" when it comes to a rationale for a more concerted research focus in this area. It is a rationale that is strengthened when we consider that the "few men" may actually be more than we think (Smink, van Hoeken, & Hoek, 2012).

My own interest in male athlete eating disorders began when one of my closest friends, a former elite youth soccer player, disclosed he was living with bulimia nervosa. We were studying at college at the time and his confession came after a number of beers at a student bar – telling another guy you have a "female disease" obviously demanded an element of Dutch courage. I'd already started to take an interest in psychology, and specifically sport psychology, so I was aware that men, often those participating in sport, could experience eating disorders; nevertheless, I was still shocked. Here was one of my closest friends, the best player on the soccer team, and the life and soul of every party; yet behind this front, within his "backstage self" (see Goffman, 1990), was a man who often experienced extreme feelings of insecurity, self-doubt and self-loathing. I hadn't ever suspected that Mike was struggling in any way. Nothing taught me more about the capacity for individuals to conceal an eating disorder than this experience. In the weeks, months and years that followed we would often discuss aspects of his illness and muse over the psychological pathologies that resided, to a greater or lesser degree, in every single one of us. I would later conduct a life history study on Mike (see Papathomas & Lavallee, 2006), which served as my master's degree thesis and my first foray into eating disorders research. Carrying out the literature review for this project was both a frustrating and an exhilarating process. I was frustrated that of the masses of academic research out there so little provided insight of the like I had gleaned from just talking to Mike; on the other hand, this was exhilarating as it told me that taking my single case life history approach was the way to go. I still believe this to be the case, but I am not in a majority. For the majority, only medical science can provide a route to a better understanding of eating disorders in sport. In the first half of this chapter I discuss why such a rigid medical scientific stance can be hugely problematic, before arguing the case for alternative forms of research.

Medical supremacy: psychology's scourge?

The study of eating disorders is underpinned by the medical model of scientific research, which is characterized by a focus on causes, symptoms and treatments and the categorization of individuals as either "normal" eaters or "pathological" eaters (Botha, 2009; Busanich & McGannon, 2010). Medical science is grounded in the philosophical principles of positivism, and is duly concerned with explanation, prediction and control (Ponterotto, 2005). The ultimate goal of a positivist science, as well as the more moderate post-positivist position, is to reduce the world to simple cause and effect relationships so that these relationships can be manipulated. Originating within the natural sciences, (post-)positivism is pervasive in psychological study and has dominated eating disorders in sport investigations. For example, an extensive body of work has indicated variables that might *cause* an athlete to develop an eating disorder (e.g. Krentz & Warschburger, 2011). These "risk factor" studies typically involve correlating factors hypothesized to increase eating disorder risk, for example perfectionism or body dissatisfaction, with some measure of eating disorder behavior. The aim of such studies is prevention via control; if onset can then be *predicted*, it can be guarded against through the *manipulation* of the offending causal variable. So, if we are aware that males with high levels of body dissatisfaction are at risk of disordered eating, in theory a practitioner simply works on reducing body dissatisfaction in order to reduce this risk and ultimately prevent the occurrence of an eating disorder. Research-grounded prevention efforts rarely follow such a smooth, linear trail, however, and the promise of cause and effect, certainly where the study of eating disorders in sport is concerned, remains very much a promise. The primary reason why efforts to identify a "cause" have failed is a simple one: an eating disorder is a multi-causal illness. It is widely accepted that psychological, biological, social and cultural influences interact in different ways for different people (Polivy & Herman, 2002), and as such it is difficult to establish concrete rules for effective treatment and prevention.

Not all sport researchers feel comfortable with the medical model, and many express a lack of fulfillment at what it can offer in terms of advancing the understanding of eating disorders in sport (e.g. Busanich & McGannon, 2010; Papathomas & Lavallee, 2012). The experiment itself, the gold standard for a medicalized psychological science and the only way to establish a true *causal factor*, has been severely criticized for ignoring both process and context (Murray & Chamberlain, 1999). A growing number of scholars have therefore questioned the utility of (post-)positivist principles in the study of psychological issues (e.g. Bruner, 1990; Polkinghorne, 1988; Sarbin, 1986). Unlike the natural or biological sciences, psychology does not obviously lend itself to universal laws (Bruner, 1990). Psychological pursuits, such as thoughts, feelings and beliefs, are by their very nature subjective, idiosyncratic and context dependent; accurate prediction is therefore troublesome if not futile. To observe the human psyche outside of its rich cultural milieu is to not really observe the human psyche at all. As early as 1981, Seymour Sarason expressed such a sentiment when he commented that "the substance of psychology cannot be independent of the social order. It is not that it *should* not be but that it *cannot* be" (p. 827). It is posited that this disconnect may be impeding progress within the discipline. Polkinghorne (1988) lamented how the knowledge derived through psychological research bore little relevance to the practical world of his applied practice. More bluntly, and perhaps somewhat controversially, Polkinghorne emphasizes that where medicine can point to conquering polio and smallpox, the great achievements of psychology are less emphatic. To address these limitations, Bruner (1990) has called for a "cultural psychology," one that lets go of its obsessions with causal explanation and tends to socially situated personal meanings and individual interpretations. Building on these early foundations, the cultural sport psychology movement also seeks to develop a meaning focused, highly contextualized understanding of psychological issues (see Ryba, Schinke, & Tenenbaum, 2010; Schinke & Hanrahan, 2009).

The current eating disorders literature, both generally and within sport, remains entrenched in (post-)positivist ideologies. To borrow Bruner's (1990) phrase, it has suffered from a lack of "cultural psychology." Botha (2009) argued that this has led to an aetiological literature base overly concerned with causes, diagnostics and treatment outcomes. Discussing the athlete literature specifically, Papathomas and Lavallee (2012) have argued that this medical focus has led to "a plateauing and unnecessarily narrow body of knowledge" (p. 397). Their critique centers on what they consider to be a lack of methodological diversity within eating disorders in sport research. Within sport and exercise psychology, Busanich and McGannon (2010) concurred, and have aired their concerns at the general lack of sensitivity to the true impact of such broader sociocultural influences as the sporting environment and its interacting constituent parts. Busanich and McGannon go on to state that even when environmental and social issues are addressed (e.g. peer/coach pressures), they are viewed as "distinct and separate from the individual" (p. 386), who is typically viewed as vulnerable to these external influences. Ultimately, the supremacy of medical scientific approaches hinders alternative ways of knowing and limits our understanding of the experiential aspect of eating disorders (Busanich, McGannon, & Schinke, 2012). It is denying any knowledge of eating disorders outside of observable symptomatology. It is failing to account for such existential issues as "inner hurt, despair, hope, grief and moral pain which frequently accompany, and often indeed constitute, the illnesses from which people suffer" (Greenhalgh & Hurwitz, 1999, p. 50). As I will now go on to discuss, this positivist monologue may also present with profound and grave consequences for male athletes' experiences of disordered eating in sport.

A disease of the mind: blaming the victim?

In shunning fully contextualized social and cultural understandings, psychology has constructed eating disorders as an individualized condition – a disease that lives within the mind (Botha, 2009). Accordingly, it is the personal *weaknesses* of *vulnerable* athletes, rather than the intensely pressurized sporting environment athletes inhabit, that is the primary determinant of problematic eating (Busanich et al., 2012). The explosion of studies exploring possible risk factors has been pivotal in communicating this dangerous message. As argued by Papathomas and Lavallee (2012), much risk-factor research "indirectly places responsibility for the illness, somewhat unfairly, at the door of the sufferer" (p. 389). The insinuation is that if the athlete were somehow mentally stronger, more confident, less neurotic, then there would not be a problem. The person with an eating disorder is effectively blamed for its occurrence. Further, such factors as coaching cultures and pressurized sporting environments are consequently rarely studied in their own right, but rather in terms of how they interact with an athlete's individual psychopathology. It is not, therefore, the nature of a coach's comment that is interrogated, but rather the character flaw that leads to an athlete's sensitivity to it. For male athletes, the inherent focus on personal weakness is hurtful and discouraging of support seeking or participation in research studies.

In problematizing the above, I must underline that risk-factor work is not "bad" per se – it is an important line of inquiry – but it is judicious and ethical to consider the real-world consequences of its "person-as-problem" connotations. When it is the individual that is viewed as flawed, symptoms can be aggravated and recovery efforts suppressed (Lock, Epston, & Maisel, 2004). This stunting of recovery occurs because sufferers uncritically accept this dominant and often taken-for-granted discourse and correspondingly assume a disempowered, even hopeless attitude to the prospect of improvement (Busanich & McGannon, 2010). Simply put, if an athlete believes eating struggles are a result of their poor mental strength, they are unlikely to feel mentally strong enough for recovery. To illustrate, let's take the case of Jack, a varsity wrestler who has taken to extreme dieting and regular binge–purge episodes.

Concerned with how his behaviors have spiraled out of control, Jack begins to research what is happening to him. From his college dorm he browses the Internet late one night using the search term "eating disorder." A mass of information arrives in seconds. Most of the hits concern females. There are photos of models and talk of "vulnerable teenage girls" and "victimized models." He searches again. This time he types "eating disorders men" into Google. He learns that some men get eating disorders too but that it is mainly a "woman's disease." He reads about the men at risk. Perfectionist men, obsessive men, and sensitive men. Men who are "vulnerable." There was that word again. Vulnerable. He wondered if the other guys on the wrestling team struggled with eating. He doubted they did. Perhaps he was just weaker than they were. Less mentally tough. Perhaps, he wondered, he was just more vulnerable. He starts to feel depressed and useless. He starts to feel like it is all his fault. He starts to believe that he will never get better – it's just the way he is.

Given male athletes' limited involvement with professional eating disorder support (Hackler, Vogel, & Wade, 2010) and the absence of help-seeking behaviors in overtly masculinized athletes (Steinfeldt & Steinfeldt, 2010), such helplessness may fester without intervention.

Further, the focus on individual deficiencies may be uniquely damaging for male athlete eating disorders. The implied personal weaknesses are of course considered "female weaknesses," and are therefore in direct contrast to the masculine attributes exalted in sport – attributes such as self-confidence, bravery and physical and mental strength (see Clément-Guillotin & Fontayne, 2011). In addition, the incessant reproduction of disordered eating as a feminine phenomenon serves to position it as something normal for women to engage in and, by default, something "abnormal" for men to experience (Busanich & McGannon, 2010). The presence of an eating disorder is therefore an affront to both athletic identity and masculine identity. Eating problems threaten a male athlete's sense of self, the very essence of who they understand themselves to be. For example, men will invariably have their masculinity reinforced when immersed in sporting cultures. Consider the story of Brad, a college football player who struggles with bulimia nervosa.

As a young boy his father would emphasize the need to be tough if he was to succeed in sport. In high school he played injured through the entire state final and was celebrated by his coach and teammates for being a "brave warrior." From that point on he always had respect in the corridors. Others looked up to him. Brad bought into this macho identity and played his role well; he would risk injury on the field of play; he would never complain if he was hurt; he would train harder and longer than others. At college little changed. He was keen to show his new coach his aggression, strength and power; the very things that made him popular at school. It didn't take long for Brad to be known as one of the toughest players around. He quickly earned the respect he craved. Teammates, coaching staff and fans saw him as a role model. He was viewed as a "guy's guy" and the man who everyone turns to when the game isn't going to plan. Living up to his image was difficult. There was pressure to uphold this overtly masculine persona. Brad strived to achieve a muscularly defined physique but struggled. He looked powerful but not particularly muscular. He tried a variety of stringent diets but muscular definition eluded him. Eventually, he started engaging in self-induced vomiting as a means to purge the fat he believed was concealing his muscular body. He had a vague awareness that some women did this, models and actresses; he knew that the girlfriend of one of his teammates did it too. If people found out about his own purging they might compare him to these women. His reputation as the college tough guy would be finished, everything he thought himself to be would be lost. His identity would be gone. The very idea terrified him so he kept the truth quiet. He knew he was different to models and cheerleaders of course. He wasn't doing it to be thin; he was doing it to be muscular. He was doing it to be stronger, to be better at his sport. No pain no gain. This was the kind of sacrifice the very best had to make. Brad knew he was tough enough to make that sacrifice. It was all part of the game.

Much is made of men in sport being unwilling to admit their eating disorder to others, but the more significant issue might be whether or not men are willing to admit it to themselves. When one's sense of self and masculinity is at stake, there is much to lose in confronting an eating disorder.

Prevalence studies: hidden dangers

Prevalence studies are a means to identify the total number of disease cases in a given population (Hoek & Van Hoeken, 2003). Although essentially descriptive in nature, these studies are examples of reductionist positivism as they seek to pigeonhole high eating disorder risk into a specific known population. Typically, a self-report measure of disordered eating is administered to a specific group of interest; for example, "elite female athletes" (e.g. Torstveit, Rosenvinge, & Sundgot-Borgen, 2008) or perhaps athletes from a particular sport, such as "distance running" (e.g. Karlson, Becker, & Merkur, 2001). Men have often been included in this prevalence research, with many studies incorporating mixed sex samples (e.g. Martinsen, Bratland-Sanda, Eriksson, & Sundgot-Borgen, 2010; Martinsen & Sundgot-Borgen, 2013; Sundgot-Borgen & Torstveit, 2004). Unfortunately, involving men in prevalence work does not always constitute a positive step towards an increased understanding of male eating disorders in sport. The basis for this counterintuitive claim is that, as I have already emphasized, male athletes will consistently display significantly less disordered eating than female athletes (5 to 10 times less in some cases; Baum, 2006). As such, the major finding of interest in this work is invariably the inflated female prevalence, and it is this that investigators will go on to theorize about in their discussion pages. Rather than address reasons why some men *do* have eating disorders, explanations are offered as to why most men *don't* have eating disorders. Men are offered as the "gold standard," their relative absence of eating disorder symptoms used as means to judge the degree of "weakness" in their female counterparts. Men serve merely as a point of comparison and a means to illuminate the severity of the more significant issue: female athlete eating disorders. Men act as the blacked-out side of a looking mirror; hidden, unnoticed and used to help reflect something else – female eating behaviors. The practical implications of this abound; prevention efforts, coach education, athlete psychoeducation and inter-vention initiatives are almost exclusively geared towards female athletes, just as the research is. As well as marginalizing those men who could benefit from such support, the idea of an eating disorder as a female disease is further perpetuated, and men are silenced from discussing a "woman's problem" (Busanich & McGannon, 2010).

Petrie and colleagues produced a rare example of a study with a sole focus on male athlete eating disorder prevalence (Petrie, Greenleaf, Carter, & Reel, 2008). Eating disorders and other pathogenic weight control behaviors were measured in a sample of over 200 male collegiate athletes. Although almost 20% of athletes were classified as "symptomatic" (i.e. displaying disordered eating attitudes and behaviors), not a single participant was identified as possessing a clinical eating disorder. The authors, responsibly, are quick to exercise caution when interpreting what is a particularly low prevalence score. First, Petrie et al. acknowledged that the majority of the sample was drawn from a selection of sports where low body weight is relatively less of an issue. Specifically, less than a quarter of participants were involved in what may be described as "lean" or "aesthetic" based sports, such as distance running or diving. As such, male athletes most at risk have not been targeted. Second, Petrie et al. accepted the limits of a reliance on self-report given the great stigma associated with eating disorders, particularly male eating disorders. We can easily imagine that the archetypal American football player (over half the sample in this study) might feel somewhat reluctant to disclose struggles with an eating disorder. American football players, particularly those with a strong athletic identity, have been shown to conform to such masculine norms as winning, self-preservation, power over women and heterosexual self-preservation (Steinfeldt & Steinfeldt, 2012). Experiencing an eating disorder, a woman's disease, may well compromise these values, in particular the second two. Within the context of football culture and athlete ideals, can American football players fully preserve their heterosexuality if they suffer with a female illness? The answer is probably no, and, as such, these athletes are unlikely to have fully dis-closed to Petrie and colleagues. The dangers of social desirability are a well-worn caveat offered at the end of prevalence studies, yet the issue continues to plague such work. This is because, ultimately, whether via questionnaire or clinical inter-view with a therapist, identifying an eating disorder requires self-report in some guise. Rather than wrestle with this seemingly unfathomable conundrum, scholars might be better served by focusing their efforts on male athletes who are ready and willing to disclose. That is, by targeting specific cases of male athletes who have already self-identified as possessing an eating disorder or eating related problems, researchers can be sure they are able to address, or at least begin to address, the issue at hand. Recruitment will be tougher in such studies, but there is scope to achieve a depth of insight that far exceeds what is possible through prevalence work. Such an approach demands more interpretivist forms of research, which in turn demand that the shackles of a (post-)positivist psychology be shed, and that the reins of medical supremacy be abandoned. Only a few scholars have taken up this daunting challenge.

A different story: the role of interpretivism

Having problematized medical positivist approaches as decontextualized accounts that marginalize male athletes and overemphasize personal flaws ahead of cultural influences, I now turn to the alternative: interpretivism. Philosophically, interpretivism eschews reductionist science in favor of a science that accepts multiple, mind-dependent versions of reality. What we know is always a value-laden social construction, and, as such, interpretivists prioritize subjective meanings and how these meanings are formed within wider social auspices. Interpretivism fits well with the goals of a cultural sport psychology, and it provides a means to approach psychological questions in a way that differs from the medical approach that has frustrated so many (e.g. Bruner, 1990; Polkinghorne, 1988; Sarason, 1981).

Interpretive sport psychology research represents an ever-growing movement towards more meaning-centered understandings of psychological issues. Although interpretive methodological approaches are many – narrative inquiry, ethnography, autoethnography, interpretative phenomenological analysis, to name but a few – the common theme in all of these approaches is a focus on personal meanings as something socially and situationally constructed. Interpretive work seeks to explore the temporal, emotional and contextual nature of athletes' experiences (Smith, 2010). So how a male athlete understands self-induced vomiting is not a fixed phenomenon but rather a consequence of the broad cultural world they inhabit at any given moment. In certain circumstances the act of purging might bring relief, even happiness; in another environment, only guilt and depression. As such, an interpretive scholar's quest for knowledge must take into account the highly contextualized cultural environments in which meanings are formed (Busanich et al., 2012). The focus on meaning obviously dictates the types of research projects interpretive sport psychologists engage in and the sorts of questions they ask/are interested in. Within such projects, qualitative data is usually collected in the form of words or photographic images, as it is typically context- and meaning-rich in comparison to numerical data. For example, the interpretive researcher is concerned less with the *number* of eating disorder symptoms a male athlete engages in than with how the athlete *makes sense* of these symptoms – how do *they* explain their illness? How and where does it fit within their psychosocial world? Given the distinct difference in focus between (post-)positivist and interpretive approaches, the insights gleaned are very much different, and, as such, different and novel insights are gained. The subsequent section therefore outlines the unique progress made by interpretive research into male athlete eating disorders.

A few good men: speaking the unspeakable

Despite the fear of stigma and prejudice that disclosure might bring, a small number of male athletes have spoken of their struggles with an eating disorder. Often motivated by a need to help other male athletes, these men have dared to break a long-standing taboo for the benefit of scientific understanding. In one of the first studies to provide a detailed qualitative analysis of male athlete eating disorders, I conducted over 11 hours of in-depth life-history interviews with Mike, a former elite youth soccer player (Papathomas & Lavallee, 2006). In this study we were able to home in on what it was like for a male athlete to live with an eating disorder and explore *his* perceptions of why it occurred. We could be confident that Mike had experienced the issue under investigation as opposed to merely being at risk of it. Given that Mike's sport was soccer, an activity perceived as low risk, his atypical case may have been missed or considered insignificant and anomalous by the universal law-seeking positivist world. As such, the rich insights constructed in the analysis may never have come to pass without a move towards a more interpretivist sport psychology. The extended quotes included in the paper prioritized a voice that would typically have been silenced by the imperialistic governance of medical science. Theory, then, is built on, new understandings constructed, and a more inclusive, ethically conscious body of work prevails (Smith, 2010).

Atkinson (2011) claimed that the majority of the athlete eating disorder literature outright fails to attend to the complex sociocultural processes involved in the onset of self-starvation, and that this is particularly the case where male athletes are concerned. Dissatisfied with this oversight and frustrated by attempts to squeeze male athletes into existing theoretical models of female eating disorders, he sought to explore men's personal narratives of emaciation in sport through an ethnographic approach. Ethnography can be seen as an attempt to understand a given culture and is well suited to sport psychology research given the array of sub-cultures within sports settings (Krane & Baird, 2005). Atkinson immersed himself into the "culture of thinness" for a period of three years, competing in extreme endurance events and intentionally losing a third of his own body weight (over 30kg). Participants were recruited whilst in the field and later interviewed formally. In total, 102 competitive male athletes participated. Atkinson acknowledged that his own bodily changes may have alleviated the men's fear of stigma and judgment, encouraging them to disclose their behaviors to him.

Atkinson's (2011) analysis gave a range of fascinating insights into the cultural influences on male starvation in sport. For example, men justified their eating practices as the basic norm of an elite sporting environment. Dangerous eating habits were constructed as necessary for success, as part of an athletic identity and as something that characterizes only an exclusive group. Any challenges to this pervading attitude were "dismissed as incongruent with the norms of sport" (Atkisnon, 2011, p. 246). Given Atkinson's assertions, we might also speculate that by framing disordered eating practices as "sports-related," given the taken-for-granted meanings attached to sport (e.g. tough, competitive), males are able to minimize the accompanying female associations; eating disorders may be feminine, but competitive sport is culturally constructed as very much masculine (Messner, 2007). This framing of disordered eating practices as sports-related can thus help males legitimize emaciation as something "OK" for men to engage in. It may even help men construct their dangerous eating as something "different" from an eating disorder. Atkinson also discussed a process of *ethno-nutritionism*, whereby the eating practices of esteemed members of a sub-culture, for example high performing athletes, are uncritically adopted and reinforced by others within the group. Even when these eating practices are extreme and contrary to available scientific guidance, they are still considered valuable examples of "insider knowledge." I suggest this finding has intriguing implications for how male athlete eating disorder interventions are designed. Efforts at psycho-educational work may prove futile if targeted benefactors perceive that they or their fellow athletes "know better," and that the advice is out of touch with top level sport. It may be that well-intentioned but notoriously unsuccessful eating disorder intervention programs simply underestimate the power of cultural influences.

Engaging in a form of narrative inquiry, Busanich et al. (2012) elicited personal stories from five male and four female distance runners. Narrative is an interpretive tradition whereby its proponents see human experience and action as occurring through the stories that circulate within sociocultural realms (Smith, 2010). The majority of participants were interviewed on two separate occasions, allowing the authors to explore, in depth, their experiences of the body, food and exercise. The narrative analysis focused on the specific content of the stories, as well as the broader cultural contexts within which stories occurred. With regards to content, two opposing narratives were identified: the "*just do it*" narrative and the "*just do it better*" narrative. The former told of running for enjoyment and health, whereas the latter told of running for improvement and superiority. Consistent with the proposition that narratives *do things* on and for people (see Smith & Sparkes, 2009), each of the contrasting narratives impacted participants' eating and exercise behaviors in different ways. Specifically, those drawing from a "*just do it*" narrative had much more positive views of their bodies and emphasized the importance of fueling the body over self-starvation. On the other hand, runners whose experiences were shaped by the "*just do it better*" narrative were rarely satisfied with their bodies and described numerous unhealthy eating attitudes and behaviors. What is of particular interest is that of the study sample only two subscribed to the "*just do it better*" narrative, and both of these participants were male. The two males obsessed over their weight and engaged in extreme dieting and unhealthy exercising. These dangerous behaviors, which fit with many of the principal facets of an eating disorder, were constructed as a means of achieving athletic goals and sporting success, echoing the male voices depicted by Atkinson (2011). Busanich et al. (2012) suggested that such a downplaying of food- and body-related preoccupations was a way of protecting masculine identities. By conducting interpretivist research, we see that once again men separate disordered eating symptomatology from its feminine connotations by framing it as necessary for sporting achievement.

Concluding the chapter, not the story

This section may represent the conclusion of this chapter, but it should be read as a beginning. Nothing is concluded or finalized where an understanding of male athlete eating disorders is concerned. The unfortunate consequence of (sport) psychology's allegiance to a purely (post-)positivist science has been the overt marginalization of sporting men with eating problems. Prevalence studies, by their very nature, shine a light on the majority group and render the minority somehow less crucial, less pertinent, less worthy of our attention. Risk-factor researchers attempt to simplify complex biopsychosocial relationships in the hope of establishing the Holy Grail of *cause and effect*. This approach has not worked. For males, risk-factor studies may even intensify the stigma and shame experienced, the subtext being that this "female disease" is the result of their own personal weaknesses (Busanich & McGannon, 2010). Given the cultural discourses that construct eating disorders as female and view women as inferior (see Busanich et al., 2012), it can be no surprise when male athletes hide their illness from coaches, friends, family and even themselves (Papathomas & Lavallee, 2006).

As scholars we must be reflective and, in so doing, be willing to accept responsibility for our own role in reinforcing gender stereotypes with regards to eating disorders, and for creating a sporting culture in which having honest, open discussions on male eating issues is an enormously difficult task. Our studies and our insights contribute to the "truths" within the mass media, coach education programs and the running tracks and locker rooms where "common knowledge" is socially constructed. If we relentlessly rehash female prevalence studies and shy away from the complexities of male athlete eating disorder research, then we cement the female disease label and we force males with eating problems underground. Instead, we must seek the personal stories of the few good men who dare to speak to us. We must apply a diverse interpretive methodological repertoire to these stories to achieve a detailed understanding of what the lives of these men are like.

Portraying different stories in the literature via the use of a variety of methodological approaches may encourage a "counter-narrative" to enter cultural consciousness. Counter-narratives can be considered "the stories which people tell and live which offer resistance, either implicitly or explicitly, to dominant cultural narratives" (Andrews, 2002). In this respect, any story of a male athlete with an eating disorder can be seen as a counter-narrative as it resists the dominant notion that eating disorders are a female athlete phenomenon. It is the intricate details of each individual story that determine the degree of resistance offered. For example, the story of a bulimic male athlete from such an overtly masculine sport as soccer (e.g. Papathomas & Lavallee, 2006) is a powerful counter to the female figure skater stereotype. Similarly, Atkinson's (2011) persuasive account of culturally endorsed emaciation practices in vast numbers of male endurance athletes resists the notion that self-starvation is always an individual pathology that affects only the vulnerable. Other counter-narratives are needed. Stories that stand up to what we think we know and what we have taken for granted have the capacity and potential to challenge the accepted truth. Men may learn from these counter-narratives that, although a minority, they are most definitely not alone, and that their painful experiences are, unfortunately, not particularly exceptional. Comforted by the stories of others, more male athletes with eating disorders may gain the courage to speak openly to researchers, coaches or significant others; to admit their illness to health professionals or even just to themselves.

References

Andrews, M. (2002). Introduction: Counter-narratives and the power to oppose. *Narrative Inquiry, 12*, 1–6.

Atkinson, M. (2011). Male athletes and the cult(ure) of thinness in sport. *Deviant Behavior, 32*, 224–256.

Baum, A. (2006). Eating disorders in the male athlete. *Sports Medicine, 36*, 1–6.

Botha, D. (2009). Psychotherapeutic treatment for anorexia nervosa: Modernist, structural treatment approaches, and a post-structuralist perspective. *Counselling, Psychotherapy, and Health, 5*, 1–46.

Bruner, J. (1990). *Acts of meaning*. Cambridge, MA: Harvard University Press.

Busanich, R., & McGannon, K. R. (2010). Deconstructing disordered eating: A feminist psychological approach to the body, food and exercise relationship in female athletes. *Quest, 62*, 385–405.

Busanich, R., McGannon, K. R., & Schinke, R. J. (2012). Expanding understandings of the body, food and exercise relationship in distance runners: A narrative approach. *Psychology of Sport & Exercise, 13*, 582–590.

Clément-Guillotin, C., & Fontayne, P. (2011). Situational malleability of gender schema: The case of the competitive sport context. *Sex Roles, 64*, 426–439.

Goffman, E. (1990). *The presentation of self in everyday life*. London: Penguin.

Greenhalgh, T., & Hurwitz, B. (1999). Narrative based medicine: Why study narrative? *British Medical Journal, 318*(7175), 48–50.

Hackler, A., Vogel, D. L., & Wade, N. G. (2010). Attitudes toward seeking professional help for an eating disorder: The role of stigma and anticipated outcomes. *Journal of Counseling and Development, 88*, 424–431.

Hoek, H. W., & van Hoeken, D. (2003). Review of the prevalence and incidence of eating disorders. *International Journal of Eating Disorders, 34*, 383–396.

Hudson, J. I., Hiripi, E., Pope, H. G., Jr., & Kessler, R. C. (2007). The prevalence and correlates of eating disorders in the National Comorbidity Survey Replication. *Biological Psychiatry, 61*, 348–358.

Karlson, K. A., Becker, C. B., & Merkur, A. (2001). Prevalence of eating disordered behavior in collegiate lightweight women rowers and distance runners. *Clinical Journal of Sport Medicine, 11*, 32–37.

Krane, V., & Baird, S. M. (2005). Using ethnography in applied sport psychology. *Journal of Applied Sport Psychology, 17*, 87–107.

Krentz, E. M., & Warschburger, P. (2011). A longitudinal investigation of sports-related risk factors for disordered eating in aesthetic sports. *Scandinavian Journal of Medicine and Science in Sports, 23*, 303–310.

Lock, A., Epston, D., & Maisel, R. (2004). Countering that which is called anorexia. *Narrative Inquiry, 14*, 275–301.

Martinsen, M., & Sundgot-Borgen, J. (2013). Higher prevalence of eating disorders among adolescent elite athletes than controls. *Medicine and Science in Sport and Exercise, 45*, 1188–1197.

Martinsen, M., Bratland-Sanda, S., Eriksson, A. K., & Sundgot-Borgen, J. (2010). Dieting to win or to be thin? A study of dieting and disordered eating among adolescent elite athletes and non-athlete controls. *British Journal of Sports Medicine, 44*, 70–76.

Messner, M. A. (2007). *Out of play: Critical essays on gender and sport.* New York, NY: SUNY Press.

Murray, M., & Chamberlain, K. (1999). Health psychology and qualitative research. In M. Murray & K. Chamberlain (Eds.), *Qualitative health psychology: Theories and methods* (pp. 3–15). London: Sage.

Papathomas, A., & Lavallee, D. (2006). A life history analysis of a male athlete with an eating disorder. *Journal of Loss and Trauma, 11*, 143–179.

Papathomas, A., & Lavallee, D. (2012). Eating disorders in sport: A call for methodological diversity. *Revista de Psicología del Deporte, 21*, 387–392.

Petrie, T., Greenleaf, C., Carter, J., & Reel, J. (2008). Prevalence of eating disorders and disordered eating behaviors among male collegiate athletes. *Psychology of Men & Masculinities, 9*, 267–277.

Polivy, J., & Herman, C. P. (2002). Causes of eating disorders. *Annual Review of Psychology, 53*, 187–213.

Polkinghorne, D. E. (1988). *Narrative knowing and the human sciences.* Albany, NY: SUNY Press.

Ponterotto, J. G. (2005). Qualitative research in counseling psychology: A primer on research paradigms and philosophy of science. *Journal of Counseling Psychology, 52*, 126–136.

Ryba, T. V., Schinke, R. J., & Tenenbaum, G. (Eds.). (2010). *The cultural turn in sport psychology.* Morgantown, WV: Fitness Information Technology.

Sarason, S. B. (1981). An asocial psychology and a misdirected clinical psychology. *American Psychologist, 36*, 827–836.

Sarbin, T. (Ed.). (1986). *Narrative psychology: The storied nature of human conduct.* New York, NY: Praeger.

Schinke, R. J., & Hanrahan, S. J. (Eds.). (2009). *Cultural sport psychology.* Champaign, IL: Human Kinetics.

Smink, F. R. E., van Hoeken, D., & Hoek, H. (2012). Epidemiology of eating disorders: Incidence, prevalence and mortality rates. *Current Psychiatry Reports, 14*, 406–414.

Smith, B. (2010). Narrative inquiry: Ongoing conversations and questions for sport and exercise psychology research. *International Review of Sport and Exercise Psychology, 3*, 87–107.

Smith, B., & Sparkes, A. C. (2009). Narrative inquiry in sport and exercise psychology: What can it mean, why might we do it? *Psychology of Sport and Exercise, 10*, 1–11.

Steinfeldt, J. A., & Steinfeldt, M. C. (2010). Gender role conflict, athletic identity, and help-seeking attitudes among high school football players. *Journal of Applied Sport Psychology, 22*, 262–273.

Steinfeldt, M. C., & Steinfeldt, J. A. (2012). Athletic identity and conformity to masculine norms among college football players. *Journal of Applied Sport Psychology, 24*, 115–128.

Sundgot-Borgen, J., & Torstveit, M. K. (2004). Prevalence of eating disorders in elite athletes is higher than in the general population. *Clinical Journal of Sport Medicine, 14*(1), 25–32.

Torstveit, M. K., Rosenvinge, J. H., & Sundgot-Borgen, J. (2008). Prevalence of eating disorders and the predictive power of risk models in female elite athletes: A controlled study. *Scandinavian Journal of Medicine and Science in Sports, 18*, 108–118.

9 Sport-related concussion

Critical issues moving forward

Anthony P. Kontos and Erin Reynolds

Introduction

It is estimated that sport-related concussions affect between 1.6 and 3.8 million athletes each year in the United States alone (Langlois, Rutland-Brown, & Wald, 2006). These injuries are caused by direct or indirect forces to the head, and result in transient changes in mental status and function (McCrory et al., 2013). Concussions involve myriad symptoms, including cognitive (e.g., memory, concentration), somatic (e.g., headache, dizziness), emotional (e.g., anxiety, sadness), and sleep dysfunction, as well as cognitive (Aubry et al., 2002), vestibular (Johnson, Kegel, & Collins, 2011), and other impairments. Although most of these injuries can be resolved within days to a few weeks with proper management, approximately 20% of athletes experience a protracted recovery (Collins, Lovell, Iverson, Ide, & Maroon, 2006; Lau, Kontos, Collins, Mucha, & Lovell, 2011). The field of sport-related concussion has grown rapidly in the past decade with the advent of concussion specific clinics, numerous special issues in sports medicine and neuropsychology journals, and intense media coverage devoted to this issue. Sport-related concussions have even made their way into video games with the recent introduction of concussion as an injury that players might sustain while playing the Madden 2012 football game. As further evidence of the field's growth, a recent (June 2013) concussion-specific conference that we hosted at the University of Pittsburgh drew an audience of over 450 sports medicine professionals. However, this growth has often been outpaced by misinformation, media hype, and exaggerated claims of "concussion proof" equipment and silver bullet treatments that can "cure" concussion. Moreover, sport-related concussion researchers and clinicians are faced with several key challenges as the field continues to evolve. To that end, we have identified and will briefly discuss five critical issues facing the growing field of sport-related concussion. Specifically, we will examine the following issues: (1) lack of consensus in the field; (2) the need for evidence-based approaches to assessment and management; (3) a lack of awareness of the psychological issues that may accompany concussion; (4) health disparities in concussion management; and (5) a movement toward a more targeted approach to assessing and managing concussion.

Concussion consensus?

Prior to the development of concussion consensus statements, a series of at least 16 anecdotal-based guidelines predicated largely on the presence and duration of loss of consciousness (LOC) and/or post-traumatic amnesia (PTA) predominated the landscape of concussion management (Hayden, Jandial, Duenas, Mahajan, & Levy, 2007). However, during the past decade, concussion consensus and/or position statements have been developed and published by such groups as the American Academy of Clinical Neuropsychology (AACN), the American Academy of Neurology (AAN), the American Board of Professional Neuropsychology (ABPN), the American College of Sports Medicine (ACSM), the American Medical Society for Sports Medicine (AMSSM), Division 40 of the American Psychological Association (APA), the National Academy of Neuropsychology (NAN), the National Association of School Nurses (NASN), the National Collegiate Athletic Association (NCAA), and the National Athletic Trainers' Association (NATA). The most influential among the consensus statements was derived from the International Consensus Conference on Concussion in Sport group, which met in 2001 (Vienna), 2004 (Prague), 2008 (Zurich), and 2012 (Zurich), and published concussion consensus guidelines shortly after each meeting. The movement toward concussion consensus, which began in earnest in 2001, has dominated concussion policy, assessment, and management. Unfortunately, and in spite of a progressive start in Vienna, the recent consensus statements – which now number at least 10 – have lost traction and offer little in the way of change from previous incarnations. This trend is surprising, as concurrent research in sport concussion has exploded (see next section).

Much of the inertia in the development of consensus guidelines can be attributed to one of two causes: (1) practice boundaries and politics, or (2) a lack of quality empirical support (see next section). The former issue is evident in the number of published consensus statements from specific groups, wherein establishing practice parameters is often the primary focus. The evolution of these practice parameters has been mired in politics and a "stand your ground" mentality. Even the well-intentioned efforts to consolidate international consensus into one coherent statement exemplified by the 2012 Zurich Guidelines have been hampered by politics. As a result, there have been few changes to these guidelines since the 2008 meeting. Additionally, the politics of developing concussion consensus statements have been influenced by powerful sport and other organizations (e.g., FIFA for the Zurich Guidelines) and conflicts of interest (the COIs for the panel of experts on the Zurich Guidelines ran to an entire page). One might speculate that FIFA, which limits the number of substitutions in soccer and has traditionally been averse to rules changes, may oppose guidelines that advocate for the immediate withdrawal of potentially concussed players from games. Such a change could dramatically affect the outcomes of games. In contrast, if the substitution rules were changed such that soccer players who were removed from play with a suspected concussion could be replaced without the penalty to the team of a lost substitution, teams and players might exploit this rule by faking a concussion – which would be very difficult to disprove. As a result, such organizations as FIFA seem to support maintaining the status quo in concussion statements and guidelines, thereby stagnating the progression of change in how the injury is perceived and managed. What is needed is a research-driven consensus that includes a comprehensive review of the concussion literature and focuses on answering the question "What do we know about sport-related concussion?" instead of "What do we think about a limited sample of the research?"

Need for evidence-based concussion management and policies

The results of a recent search by these authors on PubMed for published research on "concussion" and "concussion and sport" demonstrate the rapid growth in published research on sport-related concussion since 1980 (see Figure 9.1). While publications on both concussion and sport-related concussion have grown exponentially since the 1980s, the focus on sport-related concussion has grown at a much more rapid pace. In fact, as evidenced in Figure 9.1, over half of all publications on concussion now involve sport-related concussion, whereas only 4% in the 1980s, 14.3% in the 1990s, and 44% in the 2000s involved sport-related concussion. Unfortunately, this growth in research quantity is not always accompanied by quality. As evidenced by the recent AAN consensus paper, few studies provide evidence beyond levels 1 and 2a (i.e., randomized and non-randomized control trials), leaving only research representing levels 2b (i.e., observational control) and 3 (i.e., case studies) from which to form evidence-based guidelines. Consequently, we must first produce more level 1 and 2a

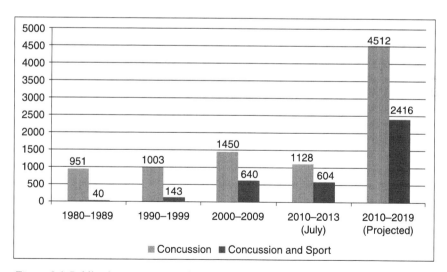

Figure 9.1 Publications on "concussion" and "concussion and sport" between 1980 and 2013 (July) and projected levels through 2019.

research on concussion to further refine current consensus statements, as well as clinical management and policies. This is especially true in regard to making safe return to activity decisions for athletes.

Current return to play criteria, as indicated by the 2012 Zurich Consensus statement, include a stepwise progression through six stages of exertion during recovery, with the first stage consisting of both cognitive and physical rest, and the sixth stage consisting of full contact game play (McCrory et al., 2013). This progression follows a return to baseline levels of symptoms, cognitive functioning, balance, and other parameters. This approach involves both cognitive and physical rest until athletes are asymptomatic for 24 hours and then outlines specific objectives for each exertion stage, along with examples of functional activities. Follow-up symptom evaluations are recommended before progression to the next stage. However, symptom evaluations alone may be insufficient to assess the readiness to return to activity. In one published study by McGrath and colleagues (2013), nearly 30% of athletes who reported no symptoms following approximately 20 minutes of aerobic exertion subsequently failed one or more cognitive tests. This finding suggests that we need to conduct post-exertion cognitive, balance, and other testing before returning athletes to activities where they might be reinjured. Additionally, athletes may intentionally minimize their symptoms so that they may return to play, or as a result of pressure from coaches and parents. Some athletes may simply not know what is and is not a relevant symptom. In contrast, some athletes may intentionally under-report symptoms due to their desire to return to play. This desire may relate to the temporary loss of their identity as an athlete, which has been caused by their time away from sport following their concussion. Regardless, relying on symptoms alone when making return to play decisions may needlessly place athletes at risk.

Given the individualized nature of concussion, and of the risk factors for each injured athlete, it is often difficult to implement these somewhat generic guidelines. For example, athletes with a history of migraine (Kontos et al., 2013b), with a history of the post-traumatic presence of anxiety, or with circumscribed symptoms with an identified source that do not affect one's ability to be physically active (such as oculo-motor impairments) may require different return to play criteria and exertion protocols. In these cases, a clinician may choose to progress the patient through initial stages of exertion prior to an asymptomatic status. Moreover, different types of physical exertion, such as static aerobic versus dynamic movement, stress different systems and may result in very different results based on an athlete's symptoms and impairment. For example, an athlete with a predominately vestibular (e.g., dizziness, balance) set of symptoms may report no symptoms and perform well on cognitive tests following aerobic exertion, but may fail post-exertion cognitive tests following a dynamic exertion protocol involving head turns and lateral movement. Surprisingly, no researchers to date that we are aware of have examined alternative approaches to return to activity decision-making and physical exertion, leaving many clinicians to rely on the "one size fits all" application of the consensus.

In addition to physical rest, it is important to consider the role of cognitive rest and the importance of introducing cognitive activity in a similar, stepwise progression. The focus by clinicians on physical exertion at times ignores the role of cognitive exertion in the recovery process. Researchers suggest that more than 80% of students aged 6 to 18 years old diagnosed with concussion show an increase in symptom severity while in school during the first two weeks of recovery (Gioia, 2012), and that one full week of cognitive rest results in decreased symptoms and improved neurocognitive performance (Moser & Schatz, 2012). Understanding the role of cognitive exertion may help inform treatment, particularly when considering a return to play progression. This becomes even more salient when one considers that not all providers see a large percentage of concussed patients in their practices. Recently, researchers reported that only 2 out of 89 pediatric primary care providers incorporated detailed recommendations regarding cognitive rest (Arbogast et al., 2013). The absense of a specific, evidence-based, "return to learn" plan is an area that warrants additional research to inform good clinical practice.

A recent example that highlights the need for evidence-based concussion policies involved the well-intentioned decision to limit contact practice time in youth football that was implemented by the Pop Warner youth football organization. This decision is another example of the "knee-jerk" approach to policy changes that pervades sport culture. Such changes have the effect of placating the public and media, but often fall short of their intended mark; in some instances, they may even have unintended consequences. Although the decision to reduce contact practice time was well intentioned and designed to reduce the number of concussions in youth football, the research does not support this change in regulations. Our authors (Kontos et al., 2013a) have recently demonstrated that the majority of concussions in youth football occur during games. Therefore, reducing practice time would likely have little effect on reducing concussion risk. Moreover, practice time is when proper hitting (tackling) technique is taught and reinforced in a much safer and controlled environment than in games. Limiting practices may not only have little effect on reducing concussions, but also actually increase the incidence of concussions in games via reduced time learning proper tackling in practice. A parallel analogy might be drawn with boxing, where limited "sparring" with headgear on might set the stage for increased concussions via less opportunity to practice avoiding being hit in the head. Ultimately, in order to reduce the likelihood of concussions in sport – especially among youth – future policy decisions need to be informed by empirical evidence to provide the most effective strategies to this end.

Psychological issues following concussion

To successfully understand and manage post-concussive symptoms, clinicians must be able to differentiate between true concussion symptoms and more pervasive symptoms that may be premorbid in nature. Symptoms of concussion during the first week can be conceptualized as a global cognitive-fatigue-migraine symptom cluster (Kontos et al., 2012), which may include affective, somatic, and sleep factors. It may be difficult to differentiate between post-concussive symptoms and generalized anxiety, depression, or more innocuous presentations, such as environmental or relationship stressors. Any pre-existing medical or mental health diagnosis, or underlying pathology, may become exacerbated during the recovery period, creating a complex web of symptoms for the clinician to begin disentangling.

From a clinical perspective, there are a number of concerns associated with treating a concussed patient with both diagnosed and undiagnosed pathology. This becomes particularly complicated when treating children who may have underlying learning difficulties or undiagnosed attention problems (Elbin et al., 2013), or unstable home environments (Ponsford et al., 1999). When broaching these sensitive subjects with the patient and family members, the clinician must be aware that there may be significant resistance in recognizing underlying pathology or familial discord. The skilled clinician will be cognizant of the delicate nature of these interactions in order to avoid disrupting the therapeutic alliance. Unlike psychotherapy, there is often less time available in treating a concussed patient to establish such an alliance and therefore the patient may not be as comfortable discussing the clinician's concerns. Likewise, it may be difficult for a parent to understand, or accept, that some of the child's presentation may be more pervasive in nature.

A strong clinical interview, as well as a comprehensive biopsychosocial history, is essential in providing insight into these complex clinical presentations. Utilizing more traditional psychology approaches, such as motivational interviewing or basic cognitive behavioral techniques, may allow for the clinician to establish an alliance of trust, while also navigating a somewhat ambiguous clinical presentation. Ultimately, the key to extricating these complex cases is an awareness of such ambiguity, and an ability to address difficult topics with the patient in a forthright, non-judgmental manner. Such an approach is often complicated by external pressures to return an athlete to play, which may come from coaches, sports medicine staff, parents, and others (Kontos, Russo, & Collins, 2004). In addition, and in contrast to the typical sport ethic of "no pain, no gain," some athletes may malinger and use their concussion to substantiate a withdrawal from sport, escape from the stress of competition, or some other tangible gain (Kontos et al., 2004). A concussion, with its individualized and disparate symptoms, offers athletes a good injury with which to malinger.

Health disparities in concussion management

Researchers have reported that groups that are traditionally underserved in regards to concussion management may be at a greater risk of neurocognitive impairment following concussion (Kontos, Elbin, Covassin, & Larson, 2010). Furthermore, researchers speculate that the greater risk may be due to a lack of access to appropriate care and follow-up treatment (e.g., Bazarian, Pope, McClung, Cheng, & Flesher, 2003). African American youth football players are noted as an example of an underserved group, and researchers have also found that African American children are more likely to have worse clinical outcomes following traumatic brain injury than other ethnic groups (Haider et al., 2007). Previously, researchers have speculated that a lack of resources to ensure the appropriate care and treatment of concussion, as well as a lack of knowledge of and awareness about concussion, may be leading to this disproportion (e.g., Bazarian et al., 2003; Kontos et al., 2010). Regardless of its source, the current health disparity in concussion management for underserved groups, particularly those in urban and rural areas, warrants attention and outreach efforts from both researchers and clinicians.

We recently completed a mixed-methods study of concussion-related health disparities in an at-risk group of youth football players, parents, administrators, and community leaders from seven predominately African American urban Pittsburgh communities. A total of 15 administrators participated in three focus groups to provide insight into concussion in their communities, to connect us with community resources for subsequent outreach efforts, and to assist us in the development of a written survey for parents and coaches. We focused our survey on concussion awareness, care, knowledge, attitudes, and injury rates. In addition, we included hypothetical situations related to concussion outcomes and decision-making. A total of 27 medically diagnosed concussions were reported across the sample. This represents a lifetime prevalence rate of approximately 25% in this population – which is much higher than rates reported in other populations. More importantly, 149 "bell ringers" (i.e., undiagnosed concussions) were reported, suggesting that up to 85% of youth with concussions received no care for their injuries. A total of 109 parents and coaches from across the seven communities completed the survey.

With regard to clinical care, the participants reported that most concussions were treated at the emergency room (65%), while only 16% of patients saw a specialist. Most parents of kids with diagnosed concussions reported using local emergency departments for initial care, but did not typically follow up with a specialist or their personal physician. The results of the study suggest that there is also a general lack of on-field management in these communities. Only one community utilized an appropriately trained sports medicine professional to provide medical coverage, but only during games. In addition, the participants reported that a lack of both insurance and an awareness of local clinics for concussion management and treatment were barriers to seeking appropriate care. The results of this preliminary study suggest that health disparities related to concussion do indeed exist in urban African American youth in the greater Pittsburgh area. As a result of this study, we were able to provide free baseline cognitive testing to between 500 and 1000 youth football players from these at-risk groups through the Heads Up Pittsburgh program sponsored by the Pittsburgh Penguins Foundation. This program provides baseline neurocognitive testing and concussion education to local Pittsburgh area non-scholastic youth sport athletes and their parents at reduced or no cost. However, the program had not specifically targeted under-served youth in the urban areas of the city, and the majority of participants were suburban youth. The combined effort of our research and outreach and the Heads Up program allowed us to target this underserved group and address the health disparity in concussion care and awareness. This effort represents an important first step in the right direction for these traditionally underrepresented groups, which have typically been excluded from concussion research and outreach efforts, as well as clinical care. It is our hope that this effort, which involved local youth and professional sport organizations, community groups, schools, coaches, parents, and athletes, can be extended to other urban and rural areas to address disparities in concussion awareness and care. To that end, additional research and outreach efforts focusing on other underrepresented, at-risk groups in both urban and rural locations is warranted. Empirical assessments of outreach efforts, such as the one described above, also need to be undertaken.

An individualized approach to concussion: clinical trajectories informing targeted treatment pathways

Although concussion is recognized as a heterogeneous injury, with multiple clinical phenotypes, current assessment and management approaches operate from a "one size fits all" framework. To target and treat concussions effectively, one must diagnose and characterize the specific problem(s) of individual patients. In so doing, one should also consider the unique context of each athlete, including socio-cultural (e.g., family, ethnic) and sport-specific (e.g., sport ethic, pain ethic) cultural factors that might influence an athlete's injury experience. Currently, there are no established empirically based subgroups and no concomitant proto-cols to enable targeted therapy for concussed athletes. As such, athletes are left with ambiguous diagnosis and prognosis and "shot-gun" approaches to treatment that involve trying multiple and often ineffective modalities in the hope that one approach will be effective. Effective treatment for sport-related concussion is likely to require an interdisciplinary set of assessment methods to characterize subtype or clinical trajectories, which can then be managed using targeted treatment pathways.

To date, there have been 28 clinical trials for pharmaceutical or neutraceutical treatments for traumatic brain injuries (TBI), including concussion (Maas, Roozenbeek, & Manley, 2010). Each of these trials has failed to result in a single Food and Drug Administration (FDA)-approved treatment for concussion (Xiong, Mahmood, & Chopp, 2009). The problem is not with the treatments per se, but rather the "one size fits all" approach taken by researchers and many clinicians in these studies and their work with concussed athletes. Concussions are highly individualized, or as one researcher put it, "They are like snowflakes, with no two being alike" (Guskiewicz, 2013). However, concussions are still mostly con-ceptualized as homogenous, which has led researchers and clinicians to adopt unidimensional approaches to assessing and managing the injury. This conceptual-ization stems from the stagnation of concussion statements and consensus, the search for a "silver bullet" assessment and treatment for concussion, and the adherence to traditional medical treatment paradigms. Consequently, and in spite of demonstrating statistical significance, most new assessments and treatments

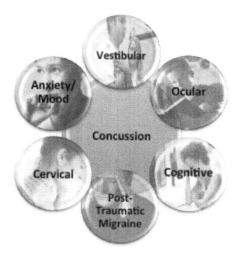

Figure 9.2 Clinical trajectories of concussion.

for concussion fail to demonstrate large clinical effects across a given sample. The heterogeneity of this injury obfuscates the efficacy of these new approaches to assessment and management. Hence, a new approach to conceptualizing sport-related concussion is warranted to better inform clinical care and direct research efforts.

Recently, we have developed such an approach at the University of Pittsburgh. Our approach is based on an evolving clinical trajectory model that partitions patients into six primary trajectories: vestibular, ocular, cognitive, post-traumatic migraine (PTM), cervical, and mood/anxiety (see Figure 9.2). Sleep dysregulation occurs across these primary trajectories and should be assessed and treated as well. Athletes may experience only one or a number of these impairments simultaneously, but will typically demonstrate a primary trajectory. Assessment should be matched to these trajectories and might involve the use of cognitive/ neuropsychological, vestibular, oculomotor, sleep, biomarker, imaging, and other analyses.

Based on the results of the interdisciplinary assessments discussed above and the insights of clinicians, each athlete is stratified into a clinical trajectory (e.g., primary vestibular with secondary post-traumatic migraine). An inter-disciplinary clinical consensus for targeted therapy to match each patient's clinical trajectory can then be implemented. This approach, which is currently being validated empirically, holds promise for accelerating the pace of the development of more individualized treatments for this injury.

Conclusion

The field of sport-related concussion has expanded rapidly during the past decade. Moving forward, researchers and clinicians are presented with both challenges and opportunities related to the critical issues discussed above. Concussion consensus statements that shape clinical care and policies need to be driven by empirical evidence rather than politics and protectionism. To that end, we need more and better quality empirical research on sport-related concussion to inform consensus, as well as safer return to activity decisions. Clinicians need to assess and differentiate between the psychological issues that often accompany concussion, and determine if they are premorbid or post-injury so that appropriate therapies can be implemented. Outreach efforts designed to enhance awareness and improve access to clinical care for underrepresented groups are warranted to mitigate the current disparity in concussion care. Most importantly, we need to re-conceptualize sport-related concussion to take into account the heterogeneity of the injury to better inform research and clinical care for injured athletes.

Acknowledgment

A portion of this chapter was made possible by Grant Number UL1 RR024153 from the National Center for Research Resources (NCRR), a component of the National Institutes of Health (NIH), and by NIH Roadmap for Medical Research. Its contents are solely the responsibility of the authors and do not necessarily represent the official view of either the NCRR or the NIH. Information on the NCRR is available at www.ncrr.nih.gov. Information on Re-engineering the Clinical Research Enterprise can be obtained from http://nihroadmap.nih.gov/clinicalresearch/overview-translational.asp.

References

Arbogast, K. B., McGinley, A. D., Master, C. L., Grady, M. F., Robinson, R. L., & Zonfrillo, M. R. (2013). Cognitive rest and school-based recommendations following pediatric concussion: The need for primary care support tools. *Journal of Clinical Pediatrics, 52,* 397–402.

Aubry, M., Cantu, R., Dvořák, J., Graf-Baumann, T., Johnston, K., Kelly J., Lovell, M., & Chamasch, P. (2002). Summary and agreement statement of the First International Conference on Concussion in Sport, Vienna 2001. *Physician and Sportsmedicine, 30*(2), 57–63.

Bazarian, J. J., Pope, C., McClung, J., Cheng, Y. T., & Flesher, W. (2003). Ethnic and racial disparities in emergency department care for mild traumatic brain injury. *Academic Emergency Medicine, 10,* 1209–1217.

Collins, M., Lovell, M. R., Iverson, G. L., Ide, T., & Maroon, J. (2006). Examining concussion rates and return to play in high school football players wearing newer helmet technology: A three-year prospective cohort study. *Journal of Neurosurgery, 58,* 275–286.

Elbin, R. J., Kontos, A. P., Kegel, N., Johnson, E., Burkhart, S., & Schatz, P. (2013). Individual and combined effects of LD and ADHD on computerized neurocognitive concussion test performance: Evidence for separate norms. *Archives of Clinical Neuropsychology, 28,* 476–484.

Gioia, G. A. (2012). Pediatric assessment and management of concussions. *Pediatric Annals, 41,* 198–203.

Guskiewicz, K. (2013). *The art and science of sport concussion: Translating data into concussion prevention.* Lecture presented at the annual meeting of the American College of Sports Medicine, Indianapolis, IN.

Haider, A. H., Efron, D. T., Haut, E. R., DiRusso, S. M., Sullivan, T., & Cornwell, E. E. (2007). Black children experience worse clinical and functional outcomes after traumatic brain injury: An analysis of the National Pediatric Trauma Registry. *Journal of Trauma, 62*, 1259–1262.

Hayden, M. G., Jandial, R., Duenas, H. A., Mahajan, R., & Levy, M. (2007). Pediatric concussions in sports: A simple and rapid assessment tool for concussive injury in children and adults. *Childs Nervous System, 23*, 431–435.

Johnson, E. W., Kegel, N. E., & Collins, M. W. (2011). Neuropsychological assessment of sport-related concussion. *Clinical Journal of Sports Medicine, 30*, 73–88.

Kontos, A. P., Russo, S., & Collins, M. W. (2004). An introduction to sports concussion for the sport psychology consultant. *Journal of Applied Sport Psychology, 16*, 220–235.

Kontos, A. P., Elbin, R. J., Covassin, T., & Larson, E. (2010). Exploring differences in computerized neurocognitive concussion testing between African American and White athletes. *Archives of Clinical Neuropsychology, 25*, 734–744.

Kontos, A. P., Elbin, R. J., Fazio-Sumrock, V. C., Burkhart, S., Swindell, H., Maroon, J., & Collins, M. W. (2013a). Incidence of sports-related concussion among youth football players aged 8–12 years. *Journal of Pediatrics, S0022-3476*(13), 00428–00429.

Kontos, A. P., Elbin, R. J., Lau, B., Simensky, S., Freund, B., French, J., & Collins, M. W. (2013b). Posttraumatic migraine as a predictor of recovery and cognitive impairment after sport-related concussion. *American Journal of Sports Medicine, 41*, 1497–1504.

Kontos, A. P., Elbin, R. J., Schatz, P., Covassin, T., Henry, L., Pardini, J., & Collins, M. W. (2012). A revised factor structure for the post-concussion symptom scale: Baseline and postconcussion factors. *American Journal of Sports Medicine, 40*, 2375–2384.

Langlois, J. A., Rutland-Brown, W., & Wald, M. M. (2006). The epidemiology and impact of traumatic brain injury: A brief overview. *Journal of Head Trauma Rehabilitation, 21*, 375–378.

Lau, B. C., Kontos, A. P., Collins, M. W., Mucha, A., & Lovell, M. R. (2011). Which on-field signs/symptoms predict protracted recovery from sport-related concussion among high school football players? *American Journal of Sports Medicine, 39*, 2311–2318.

Maas, A. I., Roozenbeek, B., & Manley, G. T. (2010). Clinical trials in traumatic brain injury: Past experience and current developments. *Neurotherapeutics, 7*, 115–126.

McCrory, P., Meeuwisse, W., Aubry, M., Cantu, B., Dvořák, J., Echemendia, R., & Turner, M. (2013). Consensus statement on concussion in sport: The 4th International Conference on Concussion in Sport held in Zurich, November 2012. *Physical Therapy in Sport, 14*(2), e1–e13.

McGrath, N., Dinn, W. M., Collins, M. W., Lovell, M. R., Elbin, R. J., & Kontos, A. P. (2013). Post-exertion neurocognitive test failure among student-athletes following concussion. *Brain Injury, 27*, 103–113.

Moser, R. S., & Schatz, P. (2012). A case for mental and physical rest in youth sports concussion: It's never too late. *Frontiers in Neurologym, 3*, 171.

Ponsford, J., Willmott, C., Rothwell, A., Cameron, P., Ayton, G., Nelms, R., Curran, C., & Ng, K. (1999). Cognitive and behavioral outcome following mild traumatic head injury in children. *Journal of Head Trauma Rehabilitation, 14*, 360–372.

Xiong, Y., Mahmood, A., & Chopp, A. (2009). Emerging treatments for traumatic brain injury. *Expert Opinion on Emerging Drugs, 14*, 67–84.

Part III

Self-reflection and reflexivity in sport psychology practice and research

10 BE, KNOW, DO model of consulting

An exploration of how experiences with soldiers affected me and how my notions of self affected soldiers' experiences

Shannon Baird

As the field of sport and performance psychology expands and advances, many researchers are devoted to examining variables that contribute to effective application (e.g., Anderson, 2000; Poczwardowski, Sherman, & Henschen, 1998). Though past research has focused on the actions and/or behaviors of effective practitioners, recent research has centered on the practitioner and what he or she brings to the consulting relationship (Lubker, Visek, Geer & Watson, 2008; Sharp & Hodge, 2011). Both reflective and reflexive practices have been advocated as means to explore the situated self of the practitioner (Cropley, Hanton, Miles, & Niven, 2010; Knowles, Gilbourne, & Niven, 2011; Knowles, Katz, & Gilbourne, 2012; Schinke, McGannon, Parham, & Lane, 2012; Smith & Sparkes, 2009a, 2009b; Sparkes, 2002) while adding another perspective to the existing corpus concerning effective mental skills training, a perspective that can be used to consider the messy art of application (Anderson, Knowles, & Gilbourne, 2004). In this chapter I use reflexivity to examine my applied work with soldiers in the United States Army in an effort to illustrate how one's own self-stories, narratives, and taken-for-granted notions can impact the effectiveness of applied interventions.

As an applied sport and performance practitioner working with the US Army, I have worked with soldiers in preparation for such daily performances as weapons qualification, Army Physical Fitness Test (APFT), combatives, interrogation training, board exams, and surgical residency. Also, I have assisted soldiers in their preparation to perform in more austere environments, such as a deployment to Afghanistan. Given the current inevitability of deployment for many of the soldiers I work with, I worry about my own effectiveness. The idea for this chapter came out of that worry and a desire to know more about Army culture.

In order to understand more about various Army performances, I have read a variety of Army Field Manuals (FM). As I was reading the Army Leadership Field Manual (FM 22-1), I began to notice elements that were empirically linked to effective consulting. In FM 22-1 Army leadership is explained through the BE, KNOW, DO model (Fig 1-1, p. 1-3). Simply put, there are certain things a leader must BE, KNOW, and DO to be effective. Each category describes different guidelines to help the soldier become an effective leader. FM 22-1 states that Army leadership begins with who a leader must BE. The BE category is described as the values and attributes that a soldier possesses and brings to situations. Leaders cannot expect to lead effectively if they do not have awareness of their values, beliefs, and attributes. The skills, knowledge, and competencies leaders possesses fall into the KNOW category. What a soldier KNOWs must go beyond technical knowledge or tactical skills to include such things as concept knowledge and communication skills. As soldiers advance to higher levels of leadership with greater levels of responsibility, so too must their knowledge advance. Though knowledge and character are vital to leadership effectiveness, they are not enough. According to FM 22-1, if a soldier cannot apply his or her character and knowledge, he or she is not an effective leader. Simply, a leader must act and DO what must be done.

Having been immersed in Army culture for nearly three years, it is not surprising that I began to draw parallels between effective consulting and the Army's BE, KNOW, DO model of leadership. Like an effective leader, there are certain things a practitioner must BE, KNOW, and DO to be effective. For example, practitioners must have a strong understanding of who they are and how they affect the world around them (BE) while drawing on vast knowledge and skills (KNOW) to implement useful mental skills training that evokes lasting positive change (DO). Unlike the leadership model, however, the BE, KNOW, DO elements of consulting are not prescriptive. That is to say, I am not using the BE, KNOW, DO categories to suggest that there is a single way to BE, a circumscribed set of theories one must KNOW, or a menu of actions one must DO to be an effective practitioner in an applied setting. I apply these categories as an interrogative tool. First, I use the BE, KNOW, DO model to consolidate recent research concerning effective practice. Then, the interrelationship between the BE, KNOW, DO elements of consulting are discussed. Specifically, the importance of understanding who one is as a practitioner (BE) is addressed. Lastly, I use my own experiences to illustrate the usefulness of reflexive practice to explore more thoroughly the BE elements of practice.

Fitting the BE, KNOW, DO leadership model to effective consulting

Over the last fifteen years a growing body of research has emerged focused on what makes the implementation of mental skills training effective beyond the scope of what skills are taught (Anderson, 2000; Lubker et al., 2008; Poczwardowski et al., 1998; Poczwardowski & Sherman, 2011; Sharp & Hodge, 2011). Three different areas of concern impacting consultant effectiveness are elucidated in this research, which can be addressed in terms of the BE, KNOW, DO model. First, the actions, or the things practitioners DO, or do not do, affect the quality of application (Poczwardowski et al., 1998; Poczwardowski & Sherman, 2011; Sharp & Hodge, 2011). However, effective practice is not determined solely by what practitioners DO because what practitioners do and how they do it are affected by both what they KNOW and who they are (Lubker et al., 2008; Schinke et al., 2012; Sharp & Hodge, 2011). In this way, the existing literature on consultant effectiveness indicates that effective consulting is a complex and somewhat muddy mixture of BE, KNOW, and DO.

DO

Prior to the year 2000, most research regarding consultant effectiveness focused on what skills practitioners teach (DO). Poczwardowski et al. (1998) codified and arranged research concerning effective practice in the Sport Psychology Service Delivery (SPSD) heuristic to help guide practitioners through-out stages of design, implementation, and intervention evaluation. Poczwardowski et al. (1998) identified the actions (DO) most often linked to effective consulting beyond the delivery of specific skills/tools (e.g., imagery, goal setting, thought stoppage). In their heuristic, the authors identified 11 factors related to effective practice, ranging from professional philosophy development, through imple-mentation, through to ending the consulting relationship. Simply, an effective practitioner must DO more than just teach mental skills. The practitioner must also evaluate needs, become immersed in the context, connect with the client, build rapport, ask meaningful questions, acknowledge weaknesses (both within themselves and/or within the client), and be willing to step away from the clients when ethical or personal boundaries are breeched (Poczwardowski & Sherman, 2011; Poczwardowski et al., 1998).

Though these actions (in addition to teaching mental skills) are related to effectiveness, current research indicates that the actions taken by practitioners to develop trust, rapport, and empathy may be the most important indicators of suc-cessful mental skills delivery (Anderson et al., 2004; Sharp & Hodge, 2011; Tod & Lavallee, 2011). In their interviews of 13 sport psychology practitioners, Sharp and Hodge (2011) found that effectiveness was less about what practition-ers taught and more about *how* they taught. Effective practitioners taught mental skills that met athletes' needs but did so by creating meaningful relationships with athletes. Lubker et al. (2008) found that for both athletes (n=124) and practitioners (n=80), the interpersonal techniques used by the practi-tioners were more crucial to effectiveness than the skills being taught. If the practitioner cannot connect with the client, the effectiveness of the training will suffer (Anderson, 2000).

In order to meet the needs of the client, develop rapport, and facilitate and maintain positive relationships, some researchers have suggested that practi-tioners use tools from fields outside traditional applied sport psychology. These researchers have suggested turning to consulting literature (Poczwardowski et al., 1998; Tod & Lavallee, 2011) or qualitative methodologies (Gilbourne & Priestley, 2011) to help fortify a practitioners' "DO" box. Gilbourne and Priestley (2011) suggested that actions based on qualitative methodologies can move applied sport and performance psychology forward by furnishing the practitioner with tools to help develop rapport and empathy while providing guidance on interview, observation, listening and analytical strategies. Moreover, a number of researchers (Anderson & Speed, 2011; Douglas & Carless, 2011; Smith & Sparkes, 2009a, 2009b; Strean & Williams, 2011) have advocated for the use of a narrative perspective in application. For example, Douglas and Carless (2011) discussed using a narrative perspective when working with athletes to better understand their lived experiences and behaviors. Paying attention to the stories clients tell and the metaphors they use can provide practitioners with insight into how clients construct and understand themselves in particular situations (Smith & Sparkes, 2009b), and can help practitioners develop rapport and interpersonal connection (Anderson & Speed, 2011). Using a narrative approach is advantageous because it is relationally focused, and can therefore enhance the tools practitioners employ to build and maintain relationships (Smith & Sparkes, 2009a).

KNOW

Tod and Lavallee (2011) observed that although the strength of the working relationship between practitioner and client accounts for most of the variance in application outcomes, far too often interventions are prioritized over the development of a strong working relationship. This means that a great deal of effectiveness depends on a practitioner's ability to engage in behaviors and actions (i.e., DO) that build rapport and trust. Thus, a practitioner must have knowledge beyond traditional psychological skills implementation. The practitioner must possess a diverse breadth of knowledge spanning multiple topics, such as communication (Anderson et al., 2004; Poczwardowski et al., 1998; Sharp & Hodge, 2011; Tod & Lavallee, 2011), observation (Anderson, 2000), listening (Anderson, 2000; Anderson & Speed, 2011), rapport building (Anderson, 2000; McCann, 2000; Sharp & Hodge, 2011; Tod & Lavallee, 2011), immersion (Anderson, 2000; Poczwardowski & Sherman, 2011), interpersonal skills (Poczwardowski & Sherman, 2011; Sharp & Hodge, 2011; Tod & Lavallee, 2011), sport culture (Poczwardowski & Sherman, 2011; Sharp & Hodge, 2011; Tod & Lavallee, 2011), and transference and counter-transference (Sharp & Hodge, 2011). This is not to say that one's knowledge concerning sport and performance psychology is irrelevant; quite the contrary, effective practitioners have extensive theoretical understandings of the psychological dimensions of performance, and can readily apply that knowledge to complex and ambiguous performance settings (Anderson, Miles, & Robinson, 2004; Gentner, Fisher, & Wrisberg, 2004; Gould, Tammen, Murphy, & May, 1991; Poczwardowski & Sherman, 2011; Poczwardowski et al., 1998; Sharp & Hodge, 2011). In other words, effective practitioners must possess a wide range of knowledge that includes and extends well beyond the traditional bounds of applied performance psychology. Despite its importance, knowledge without application does nothing for effectiveness. The importance of knowledge in action illustrates that the DO and KNOW categories are both equally important when understanding effective consulting.

Reflection has been suggested as a way to include "knowledge in action" in the sport and performance psychology literature (Anderson et al., 2004). Reflection is a cognitive process (Anderson et al., 2004; Cropley et al., 2010) that can take many forms (Knowles et al., 2011). On the one hand, technical and practical reflection can offer practitioners a framework for looking back at their application, evaluating implementation choices, and exploring personal meaning (Knowles et al., 2011). On the other hand, critical reflection or reflexivity pushes the practitioner to locate him- or herself within larger socio-cultural contexts to deconstruct taken-for-granted notions affecting application. Schinke et al. (2012) articulated clearly the distinction between reflection and reflexivity as a matter of magnitude. That is, reflexivity is a type of reflective practice (looking back), while reflexivity is a critical look at how the practitioner's location within the power structure affected the practitioner's behaviour, way of seeing, implementation strategy, and understanding of an applied context. All forms of reflection offer ways in which to facilitate personal growth and expand our professional knowledge (Anderson et al., 2004; Knowles et al., 2011). However, reflexive practices have specific benefits related to a better understanding of how situated-ness affects application by prioritizing notions of self and identity (McGannon & Johnson, 2009). Such a prioritization and exploration of self and identity allows practitioners to look at how their own notions of self and social position affect the behaviors they observe, the interpretations they make, the phenomena they remember, the questions they ask, and ultimately the interventions they choose.

BE

Reflexivity usually takes narrative form when shared (Knowles et al., 2011; Knowles, Gilbourne, Tomlinson, & Anderson, 2007; Smith & Sparkes, 2004). Not only do these narratives give voice to how practitioners put knowledge into action, but also the narratives provide a means to address the situated experiences of the practitioner. The exploration of who effective practitioners are and how they construct themselves (i.e., the BE category) is fairly new in the consulting effectiveness literature (Schinke et al., 2012). Yet who a practitioner is has been identified as vital to understanding the process of effective consulting (Anderson et al., 2004; Watson, Lubker, & VanRaalte, 2011). Researchers such as Anderson (2000) and Tod and Lavallee (2011) have indicated that the relationships practitioners enter into and sustain, as well as who the practitioners are within those relationships, are central factors related to the success of application. There is increased awareness within the literature that what a practitioner brings to the consulting relationship impacts consulting effectiveness; however, until recently, investigations concerning BE elements of effective consulting have focused on practitioner attributes and professional philosophy.

Athletes and practitioners have identified certain practitioner attributes that impact the effectiveness of the consulting relationship. Specifically, effective practitioners are able to be professional, confident, empathetic, authentic, willing to make mistakes, flexible, open-minded, honest, relaxed, respectful, and interested (Anderson, 2000; Lubker et al., 2008; Poczwardowski & Sherman,

2011; Poczwardowski, Sherman, & Ravizza, 2004; Sharp & Hodge, 2011). Though looking at practitioner attributes is important and begins to shift practitioners' attention inward, there are other aspects of who a practitioner understands him- or herself to be that deserve exploration. Such an exploration can help create a more holistic understanding of consulting effectiveness by exploring the relationship between how practitioners define themselves and how those definitions affect the questions they ask and the interventions they choose (McGannon & Johnson, 2009).

In the SPSD heuristic, Poczwardowski et al. (1998) addressed the importance of understanding oneself as a practitioner and identified professional philosophy as one of the factors necessary to effective delivery. In 2011, Poczwardowski and Sherman modified the SPSD heuristic, adding elements that reflect the interconnection between the practitioner and the client, elements that have been found to be fundamental to effective consulting (Lubker et al., 2008; Sharp & Hodge, 2011). Through their interviews with 10 accomplished practitioners, professional philosophy was identified not only as necessary, but also as crucial to a practitioner's success because one's philosophy influences all other aspects of service delivery.

Poczwardowski and colleagues (2004) stated that one's professional philosophy, partially made up of values, beliefs, and theoretical perspectives, is foundational to effective practice because it guides the questions asked and the manner in which practitioners conceive of and conduct their practice. However, how individuals listen, what they hear, and the way in which they interpret are not influenced by philosophy and theoretical perspective alone. A practitioner's understanding of the world is also couched in his or her experiences, attitudes, and histories, and the various aspects of intersecting self-identities. In other words, the BE element of consulting effectiveness cannot be defined exclusively through professional philosophy or personal attributes. The BE category is multiple, contextual, and negotiated because the identities of practitioners are multiple, contextual, and negotiated, and because the lines between self, other, and culture are mutable (McGannon & Johnson, 2009; Smith, 2010; Smith & Sparkes, 2007; Sparkes, 2002). That is to say, practitioners' identities are not isolated from other concepts of self, other people, or the environments within which they live and work. In order to understand more fully how notions of self affect consulting, sport and performance psychology practitioners must prioritize self-awareness and begin to move away from looking at the tools they use (DO) toward looking inward at who they are as situated players within the consulting context (BE) (Anderson et al., 2004; Petitpas, Giges, & Danish, 1999; Poczwardowski et al., 2004; Werthner & Coleman, 2008).

Reflective and reflexive practice address the importance of BE elements of consulting

Recently, researchers have suggested borrowing from qualitative methodologies and critical theory to explore more thoroughly the practitioner's role as a situated and socially constructed individual (i.e., the BE elements) in effective practice (Gilbourne & Anderson, 2011; Gilbourne & Priestley, 2011; Schinke et al., 2012). Specifically, self-reflection and reflexivity have been suggested as means to improve practice, gain more knowledge of self, situate one's self as a practitioner in an environment, and share tacit knowledge (Anderson et al., 2004; Douglas & Carless, 2011; Schinke et al., 2012; Watson et al., 2011).

More specifically, Schinke et al. (2012) have suggested that the process of reflexivity allows the practitioner to develop self-knowledge and address the reciprocal relationships between environment, culture, practitioner, and client. Reflexive practice involves both reflecting on one's own interventions, choices, and interpretations and the critical scrutiny of how one's notions of self, taken-for-granted assumptions, and positions of power influenced one's intervention, choices, and interpretations. In this way reflexive practice allows practitioners to generate knowledge concerning how their beliefs, biography, history, experiences, and storied lives can affect their practices (Douglas & Carless, 2011; Knowles et al., 2011). Furthermore, by engaging in reflexive practice practitioners share how they negotiate their own self-stories to provide quality service. Reflexive accounts of applied work contribute to the applied genre by demonstrating how practitioners' notions of self and location within a given power structure (i.e., the BE) can affect what they know and do. Additionally, reflexive writing can provide examples of how practitioners negotiate self, society, and culture to achieve successful outcomes in practice.

The product of reflexivity, reflexive writing, typically takes on a narrative form (Knowles et al., 2007, 2011; Smith & Sparkes, 2004). The representation of this narrative can come in various styles, but at its heart lies situated meanings experienced by the practitioner. Narratives are stories told over time that help individuals make meaning of experiences (Carless & Douglas, 2008; Douglas & Carless, 2010; Smith, 2010; Smith & Sparkes, 2009a, 2009b). The stories one tells are simultaneously individual and culturally situated. Individuals have the autonomy to construct a narrative of their choosing; however, the narrative threads used to create meaning are borrowed from the larger fabric of culture (Carless & Douglas, 2008; Smith, 2010; Smith & Sparkes, 2009b). Moreover, there is not a culture, singular. There are many cultures and sub-cultures each with their own dominant and accepted discourses. This means that in order to create and apply interventions with diverse poulations effectively, practitioners must be willing to contextualize the experiences of others within specific cultural frameworks (Schinke et al., 2012) while avoiding labeling, which can limit the experiences of others and perpetuate taken-for-granted notions of "normal" or "right" (Strean & Williams, 2011).

The narratives individuals construct help them make sense of the world, consolidate the chaos of experience, guide behavior, know others, and know themselves (Smith, 2010). Though these dominant narratives provide a framework for making sense of experiences, dominant narratives also concurrently blind us to other ways of seeing (Douglas & Carless, 2011; Smith & Sparkes, 2004). If we accept our initial understanding of behaviors or situations without question, we are not allowing for other possible experiences to exist, such as those experiences that reside outside of our own frame of reference (Douglas & Carless, 2011; Schinke et al., 2012). Strean and Williams (2011) warned that ascription to particular narratives can limit what others experience, which can, according to Schinke and colleagues (2012), severely limit our ability to deliver meaningful interventions. Therefore, it is imperative for practitioners to know how they construct reality, understand experience, and know themselves in relation to others. Specifically, practitioners must be willing to excavate their own self-stories and experience to question the ways in which the narratives they choose to create limit their understanding of the contexts or the individuals they work with.

Much can be learned from the narratives practitioners share concerning their practice. Specifically, according to Smith and Sparkes (2009a, 2009b), narratives can rationalize the messiness and complexity of human experience. Ultimately, with continued exploration of effectiveness in applied sport psychology, practitioners are learning that the relationship between client and practitioner determines, most strongly, the effectiveness of the intervention. In this way, reflexive practices allow practitioners to investigate the complexity of the relationships between practitioner and client and to mine their own and others' experiences in an effort to understand more completely what it means to BE an effective practitioner. Furthermore, reflexive practices allow practitioners to explore how the BE (i.e., who they are) can affect what they know about the people they work with and how they deliver mental skills training. Also, the publication and sharing of reflexive practice creates space for individuals to share how they have negotiated the BE, KNOW, and DO of consulting.

Sport and performance psychologist in the field with (her)os

In this section I engage in what Sparkes (2002) has referred to as a confessional tale. I share my own journal entries concerning the first day I met the Female Engagement Team (FET) soldiers. After sharing the story of that day, I look specifically at how my own FET narrative and self-story occluded my understanding of the FET environment and impacted my consulting.

Contextualizing the FET

A FET is a team of two or three women. FETs are tasked with engaging the female population of Afghanistan. Specifically, FETs develop and maintain positive relationships with Afghan women to foster Afghan solutions to such issues as the long-term sustainment of justice, security, healthcare, and economic opportunities (Center for Army Lessons Learned, 2011). Their objectives are imperative given the pending withdrawal of US troops from Afghanistan.

Though they are not acting as infantry soldiers or military intelligence, their position on the front line, embedded with maneuver elements, requires them to be proficient at infantry tasks and attentive to potential intelligence concerning hostile forces while remaining focused on their mission to advance relations amongst Afghan civilians. The job is described in Army doctrine as rigorous and challenging, a job that requires high levels of motivation and extensive training.

Until recently, FET training took place as a part of Special Operations. However, due to the recent success of FETs, NATO mandated that all Stryker Brigade Combat Teams (SBCT) carry at least one FET for every Company (CO) in a maneuver battalion (BN) in the brigade (BDE).

The mandate has meant that infantry brigades across the Army are now responsible for training FET soldiers to meet the NATO standard. A local brigade developed a taskforce to meet the needs of the NATO mandate. During the intake meeting, the Officer in Charge (OIC) of the taskforce, First Lieutenant Ash (1LT), explained that the brigade would hold FET Selections. She explained that she wanted to enlist my help in the development of challenges for Selections that would require mental agility, self-regulation, and teamwork. The purpose of Selections was to pare down a list of 71 volunteers to 45 candidates who could handle the mental and physical demands of the FET mission while still operating as a successful member of a small team. The brigade would eventually need a total of 62 females to be trained. 1LT Ash believed that she could build up a more formidable platoon of FET-trained soldiers if she started from a pool of 45 exceptional performers and recruited the remaining 17 over the course of the year. Once Selections were complete, I was to remain an integrated part of FET training leading up to the platoon's deployment to Afghanistan. The following is a vignette of my initial meeting and psychological skills training with the FETs. In this vignette I share the subtle ways in which dominant narratives and my own notions of self influenced my understanding of FETs and shaped my interactions with the soldiers. At the end of this vignette I explore my own shortcomings to illustrate the importance of BE elements to effective sport and performance psychology interventions.

"Voluntold" to volunteer

> Candidates for FET should arrive mentally prepared, physically fit, and highly motivated.
>
> > (Center for Army Lessons Learned, 2011, p. 26)

> All FET members should be volunteers, not voluntolds (nonvolunteers directed to participate).
>
> > (Center for Army Lessons Learned, 2011, p. 19)

I reach out and hold on to the back of LT's seat as the Humvee rebounds sideways over a series of deep holes. The weight of my helmet pulls at one side of my head and wobbles loosely with each bounce. My gloved hands pull uselessly at the straps in a vain attempt to secure the helmet on my head. Eventually I surrender, wipe at my nose with the back of my glove, and sniff against the cold. My helmet and I are not the only things jumping around inside the cab. Gear and personnel alike shift, lurch, and jingle as the Humvee cuts through the forest. The canvas doors shutter as we bound along the gravel road. I double-check that the door is still closed and, to my surprise, the rusted latch has maintained its reluctant grip. My thoughts return to our departure from BDE headquarters (HQ) this morning, and I wonder if anyone saw me fighting with the mechanism in the parking lot before we rolled out. I shake my head at the memory and look out the plastic window to my right. Even if the windows were not clogged with grime, there would be nothing to see. 05:30 is inky darkness and the dense forest blocks out all hope of light. Occasionally the light from the Blue Force Tracker (BFT) bounces off the plastic just right and I can see my distorted smile winking back at me from the surface of the crinkled window. I am consumed in the experience of riding in a Humvee, wearing body armor, and listening to convoy chatter on the radio. I'm about to be a part of history.

I can see Selections in my mind. Though the women are in digital camouflage and standing at parade rest, the scene I create is familiar. It feels like regional team tryouts for rugby. Physically fit women awaiting judgment and the opportunity to shine. Unlike regional team hopefuls, the FET candidates stand ready to make a difference in the world and in the US Army, serve their country, and walk toward grave peril. Yet, their features are set and stoic. They know only a few will be selected to become FET soldiers, to be trained and honed as tactical athletes.

The Humvee lurches and I'm jolted askew in my seat and the drip-pan skitters on to my lap. We tip forward abruptly. The horizon is swallowed by mud and earth and we descend into a deep embankment. Again, I brace against LT's seat and she calls out over her shoulder, "We're almost there, Doc!" I grunt in acknowledgment and think, "So fucking cool."

It's raining . . . or maybe it's snowing. We've been delayed and I can't feel my toes. 1LT Ash ordered Second Lieutenant (2LT) Mars to bring required equipment to the training sight. However, she has been lost for an hour. Understandably, 1LT Ash is angry and disconcerted by the bad example set by 2LT Mars. I am a little befuddled by the behavior relative to this population. It will be difficult for these elite level soldiers to take an officer seriously who cannot find her own way to the training site on time. I note how this may affect trust, cohesion, and motivation. Captain (CPT) Shore, 1LT Ash's commanding officer (CO), walks over to us. 1LT Ash and CPT Shore discuss 2LT Mars. I note their differing perspective. 1LT Ash is more angry than the CPT. It's almost as if CPT Shore cannot see the importance of Mars's behaviour. I scratch another note to myself, and as I write a snowflake plops on to my field notes, "So it's definitely snowing."

We're waiting in a forest clearing without shelter. The tree line is 100 yards away and does little more than block the big gusts of wind. Every one of the candidates is sitting on a mound of dirt and rock. They are not really engaged in conversation; mostly they just sit hunched against the cold. I can overhear the occasional "this sucks," "what are we waiting for," and "this is dumb." I try to jot down a note concerning motivation but have to pause to breathe on my pen. As I coax the frozen ink, I realize that I don't think this sucks. I love that the conditions are miserable. Perhaps the anticipation of working with the most elite forces of female soldiers obscures all discomfort.

"So . . . things are different than we thought," 1LT Ash remarks from just behind me.

"Wha'?"

"Scare ya?"

"Na, just thinkin'."

"I just came over to tell ya, of the 71 we had, only 37 showed up this morning."

"Oh, whoa! What's that mean?"

"Well, we can't cut anyone. We don't have the minimum number of soldiers we need. So . . . you mind teaching them some stuff to help them get through Selections? We need to keep as many as we can."

"How much time can I get?" I ask.

"As much as you need. No tellin' when Mars will show, better to have 'em be productive than just sittin' around."

I hesitate only long enough to consider needs, wants, outcomes, and come up with a workable solution that can be executed in a reasonable amount of time. As we walk over to where the 37 volunteers sit, I decide to teach a specific tool (i.e., thought stoppage) after having a discussion about their reasons for becoming a FET soldier. After 1LT Ash introduces me, I scan their obscured faces and ask a simple question: "Why are you here?"

Based on the FET narrative I constructed long before I asked that question, I expected to hear responses centered on volunteering. For example, having the opportunity to serve, giving Afghan women a voice, being in combat, and being elite were all motives that fitted the FET narrative I had constructed and were, therefore, responses I expected. Consequently, when the soldiers indicated that they "were ordered to attend" and that they "have no idea what this is all about," they voiced experiences outside my FET narrative. In that moment, however, their experiences did not change my understanding of FET soldiers. I was reflective enough to realize that my initial strategy to leverage their intrinsic motivation to help them refocus would not work, and so I adjusted that plan to match their needs. In this regard, I provided space for the soldiers to speak and worked with the soldiers to help improve their motivation. Though I observed the soldiers and their behaviors, asked questions concerning meaning, listened to how they constructed their experience, and looked for ways to interact and provide support, I was still missing information. Though I was reflective, I was not reflexive enough to see that my own romanticized FET narrative was affecting my perception and therefore affecting my intervention strategies. I was DOing the right stuff, backed by KNOWledge I possessed; however, I was not considering myself (BE). For the remainder of this chapter, I will use the above vignette to illustrate how reflexivity is an important component of effective consulting. In particular, I will examine how the BE affected my ability to provide effective consulting. First, I address how my own self-stories, experiences, and values led to the construction of a romanticized FET narrative. Then, I discuss how that narrative affected what I observed and "knew to be true" of the FET soldiers. Lastly, I address how my own taken-for-granted notions affected my approach to the soldiers.

Romanticizing the soldier

It was easy for me to construct a romanticized FET narrative because I grew up around the military. My mom was a "lifer" and served her country through two wars before retiring. As a result, I have very specific ideas of what it means to be in the military. As a child, I was inundated with positive images of patriotism, valor, and service. America's war-fighters, across all armed forces, were my first heroes. In fact, I can remember playing war with a replica M-16, mucking about in a drainage ditch, and reciting parts of the US Military Code of Conduct (e.g., "I will never surrender of my own free will. If captured I will continue to resist by all means available"). These early experiences shaped who I am and how I see others. In the months before I met the soldiers I worked with, even as I read Army regulations, I was constructing a narrative of FET that was consistent with my own beliefs and experiences. I admit it was a narrative that looked like a strange amalgam of *Red Dawn* (1987), *GI Jane* (1997), *Rambo* (1982), and *Glory* (1989).

We know, as practitioners, that one of the first things we have to do when working with a new client or team is learn about the people we are going to work with (Poczwardowski et al., 1998). It is important that the practitioner possesses an understanding (or at least a working knowledge) of the sport, sport culture, or team in order to contextualize mental skills (Lubker et al., 2008; Poczwardowski & Sherman, 2011; Sharp & Hodge, 2011). As such, the first question I asked myself after I met with 1LT Ash was, "Who are these women?" I looked for answers in Army doctrine, talked to other FET soldiers, and read media coverage concerning FETs. Prior to entering the field, I delved into any materials that would help me better understand FET soldiers, but I neglected to ask a vital question; I entered the field without first asking, "Who am I?" This self-examination is necessary because how one defines one's self in any moment affects what and how the world is perceived (Schinke et al., 2012; Smith & Sparkes, 2007). As a result of my own lived experiences, history, and self-stories, coupled with existing cultural narratives concerning military service, I constructed a limited FET narrative with constrained notions of expected behaviors and acceptable self-stories. As a result, I perceived certain taken-for-granted truths that may or may not have been related to the soldiers' experiences. The ease with which I constructed the FET narrative and the inflexibility of that narrative had to do with who I am, or the BE. In this regard it is apparent that we cannot, nor should we try to, remove ourselves from our practice. As a result, reflexivity and reflective practice serve as ways to locate ourselves within our practice and better address how we affect our own practice.

Anderson (2000) has suggested that we know very little about what it looks like when practitioners stand in the way of their own effectiveness. The above vignette, its content and structure, illustrates what it looked and felt like when I got in my own way. Specifically, it felt comfortable, right, and effortless. It was effortless to measure the candidates I worked with against my FET narrative because the narrative was aligned with my own beliefs and views concerning military service.

In other words, when I stood in my own way it was comfortable, because I was locating myself in a well-rehearsed way of seeing and knowing. Moreover, as suggested by Smith (2010), my embodied experience of joy, excitement, and elation gave credence and weight to the narrative I constructed. In this way dominant narratives of selves and others are seductive.

The FET narrative I constructed prescribed identities and proscribed experience (Smith & Sparkes, 2009b). Without intending to, I defined FET soldiers as strong women who were intrinsically motivated to make the ultimate sacrifice for their country. In other words, either they were intrinsically motivated to be FET members or they were not FET soldiers. I listened to their stories, but did not question how my FET narrative was shaping what I heard. The narratives a practitioner creates obscure the senses and limit clients' lived experiences (Strean & Williams, 2011), thereby limiting what practitioners can see as viable applications.

Poczwardowski and Sherman (2011) indicated that being immersed and observing are important, as observations can provide the practitioner with valuable information about the environment and can help build rapport. My observations serve as one of my sources of information concerning what, how, and when to teach. However, the observations were filtered through the lenses of my own experiences, history, knowledge, and self-identities, and were consolidated into a particular FET narrative. The truly unpleasant part of looking back and asking critical questions of my own behavior has made me all too aware of my own sexism and privilege. I was unable to see that my FET narrative was shaped by heteronormative ideals concerning bravery, strength, and heroism. Furthermore, this experience has allowed me to see my own pitfalls. Understanding how self and identity affect behavior choices relative to performance outcomes is important to me. Despite this I never once stopped to find out who these women were. I applied the FET narrative I constructed from field manuals and personal experience. Specifically, I tended to see lack of motivation as the primary issue affecting their various performances because they were not acting in a way that was consistent with my romanticized FET narrative. Perhaps what I was seeing was not lack of motivation but more of a struggle to reconcile the dominant FET discourse with who they saw themselves to be. I may have served them better by listening to their stories and helping them craft their own FET narratives that would have fitted with their own self-stories. Alas, that was not the path I took.

I interpreted behavior through the filter of my FET narrative. For example, as time passed and I became a fixture in the platoon, I interpreted missed meetings and eye-rolls as confirmation of lack of motivation. What I failed to account for was the possibility that my position and education may have affected how the soldiers behaved around me (Schinke et al., 2012). Introduced as a trainer and supported by their commanding officer, I may have been perceived by the candidates as a gatekeeper to Selections. That is, they may have perceived me as someone evaluating their performance and thus avoided expressing performance concerns with me for fear of negative evaluation. In this way, soldiers may have made decisions to avoid contact with me for fear of negative reprisals, such as negative counseling statements that could lead to not getting promoted or getting dismissed from the team (which would also negatively affect their career).

Additionally, I may have inadvertently distanced myself from the soldiers in the way I approached the environment. In the above vignette, my desire to "help" the soldiers toward deployment could be understood as an othering mechanism. Despite my desire to work with the soldiers toward achievement, there was still a clear distinction in my thinking between myself and *them* that was articulated in such thoughts as, "I want to help them." In this thought alone I reveal a bit about my beliefs and my privilege. I am essentially claiming that I possess the knowledge to fix them. The assumption here is that they need fixing and that I am an authority and can bring knowledge to them, rather than working with them to create mutual growth. Moreover, in the vignette there is a theme to my thoughts that I have already figured out the women I was going to work with. That is to say, I knew who FET soldiers were, and if the women I met did not fit into that discourse, they were something less or other than FET soldiers.

Furthermore, as indicated in my vignette, I stood physically separate from them, distancing myself from them which could also have sent a clear message that I was different from them. In addition, they may have felt distanced from me as a result of my level of education and position as a contractor. The US Army is a hierarchical culture. As a result, it is often difficult for individuals to know how to interact with civilian contractors. As such, I have found that using my title places me within the hierarchy and eases most soldier populations. As one soldier explained, "Doctor is your rank, so I know how to treat you." However, by using my title, I may have simultaneously garnered credibility and distanced myself from these soldiers.

Though I built rapport (Poczwardowski & Sherman, 2011; Sharp & Hodge, 2011), made myself available (McCann, 2000), listened to their stories (Anderson, 2000), and focused on matching their needs (Poczwardowski & Sherman, 2011; Poczwardowski et al., 1998; Sharp & Hodge, 2011), I may still have created a perceivable distance between myself and the soldiers. This distance may have resulted, in part, from my own perceptions of self and others. I distanced myself from them in my own narrative (Smith & Sparkes, 2009b). My behaviors and what I taught told these women exactly who I thought they were. This may have sent the very clear message that I was there only to help individuals who fitted my FET mold. Anyone not defining themselves in the same manner may have felt that I was not a resource for them. Moreover, I used the metaphor of sport to facilitate my understanding of the FET environment. Due to my experiences, the sport metaphor was readily available and helped me make sense of a new performance environment. Though this metaphor provided insight, it also constrained my understanding. By comparing FET soldiers to athletes, I adhered to a myopic view of performance that privileged deployment. The focus on the October deployment blinded me to other issues.

I was focused on the reality of war and preparing them for combat; consequently, I overlooked the daily battles they fought, such as gender stereotypes. Resistance to FET soldiers was relayed by both covert and overt means. Covert resistance was more systemic. For example, the FET platoon was not given resources or information concerning daily operations. Moreover, the employing battalions were unfamiliar with the FET mission, and OICs would employ the FET soldiers for non-relevant tasks (e.g., working in the motor pool). This affected the soldiers' willingness to commit completely to their roles as FET soldiers. Instead of providing a space for these soldiers to explore their own notions of self and give voice to their gendered experiences, I focused on preparation for deployment (i.e., how to accept uncontrollable situations).

Additionally, these women had to cope with more overt discrimination. For example, many of the women had to cope with continual sexual innuendos, scorn, and vilification. At times, this disparagement came from family members. One soldier indicated that her husband, who had been deployed for nine months during the previous year, was refusing to let her deploy because he could not be expected to "do everything" (i.e., care for the kids, maintain the house, go to work) while she was gone. Upon hearing this comment I began to realize that my romanticized FET narrative was significantly gendered and singular. In my romanticized narrative, the soldiers just needed to focus on performance; I did not allow for the complex experiences of gender negotiation and, in this way, silenced these women. My desire to help, deployment centered training, and romanticized FET narrative all obscured experience and impacted consulting effectiveness.

Concluding remarks

Originally, when I came to judge the effectiveness of my intervention with the FETs, I looked at performance outcomes and survey responses. According to these measures, my involvement was a success; however, the reflexive process allowed me to reflect on what might have been different had I considered my own self-stories and romanticized FET narrative. I shared the above vignette to illustrate that knowledge, skills, and action are not enough when questions of effectiveness are posed. Practitioners must also be willing to acknowledge who they are. To be effective, practitioners must both understand who the client is and understand who they are in relation to the client.

Reflexive practice gives practitioners the chance to explore their situated selves within the applied domain and acknowledge how the BE elements can affect application. Through reflection, practitioners can situate themselves and make more informed decisions concerning the clients they work with. In its many forms, reflection allows practitioners to explore decisions and experiences to better understand and manage the self in the consulting environment while simultaneously moving the field of applied sport psychology forward (Anderson et al., 2004; Cropley et al., 2010; Knowles et al., 2011, 2012). In the sharing of our lived experiences, we are passing on our tacit knowledge and helping to achieve growth in the applied domain (Anderson et al., 2004; Martens, 1987).

Effectiveness in consulting is a negotiation of who we are, what we know, and what we choose to do. Reflexive practice not only contributes to current research on effective consulting by critically looking at how practitioners affect their own practice, but also provides new and experienced practitioners with a frame of reference for how BE, KNOW, and DO are negotiated. By sharing more stories that illustrate the messy mistakes of application, we generate numerous practitioner narratives.

However, the negotiation of self and others as practitioners is largely absent from the literature. Practitioners who have experienced success or failure, objectively or subjectively, have stories to share. These stories can elucidate the various ways in which practitioners are navigating the waters of social interaction. The more we share, explore, and reveal in an authentic, honest way, the more we will know, which can be used to enrich personal practice, develop the professional corpus, and aid mentorship.

References

Anderson, A. G., Knowles, Z., & Gilbourne, D. (2004). Reflective practice for sport psychologists: Concepts, models, practical implications and thoughts on dissemination. *The Sport Psychologist, 18*, 188–203.

Anderson, A., Miles, A., & Robinson, P. (2004). Evaluating the athlete's perception of the sport psychologist's effectiveness: What should we be assessing? *Psychology of Sport and Exercise, 5*, 255–277.

Anderson, M. B. (Ed.) (2000). *Doing sport psychology*. Champaign, IL: Human Kinetics.

Anderson, M. B., & Speed, H. D. (2011). The practitioner and client as storytellers: Metaphors and folktales in applied sport psychology practice. In D. Gilbourne & M. B. Anderson (Eds.), *Critical essays in applied sport psychology* (pp. 84–104). Champaign, IL: Human Kinetics.

Carless, D., & Douglas, K. (2008). Narrative identity and mental health: How men with serious mental illness re-story their lives through sport and exercise. *Psychology of Sport and Exercise, 9*, 559–720.

Center for Army Lessons Learned. (2011). Commander's guide to female engagement teams, version 1. (CALL No. 11-38). Fort Leavenworth, KS: US Army Combined Arms Center.

Cropley, B., Hanton, S., Miles, A., & Niven, A. (2010). Exploring the relationship between effective and reflective practice in applied sport psychology. *The Sport Psychologist, 24*, 521–541.

Douglas, K., & Carless, D. (2010). Restoring connections in physical activity and mental health research and practice: A confessional tale. *Qualitative Research in Sport and Exercise, 2*, 336–353.

Douglas, K., & Carless, D. (2011). A narrative perspective: Identity, wellbeing and trauma in professional sport. In D. Gilbourne & M. B. Anderson (Eds.), *Critical essays in applied sport psychology* (pp. 3–22). Champaign, IL: Human Kinetics.

Gentner, N. B., Fisher, L. A., & Wrisberg, G. A. (2004). Athletes' and coaches' perceptions of sport psychology services offered by graduate students at one NCAA division I university. *Psychological Reports, 94*, 213–216.

Gilbourne, D., & Anderson, M. B. (Eds.). (2011). *Critical essays in applied sport psychology*. Champaign, IL: Human Kinetics.

Gilbourne, D., & Priestley, D. (2011). Epiphanies and learning: A rejection of the performance-based myopia. In D. Gilbourne & M. B. Anderson (Eds.), *Critical essays in applied sport psychology* (pp. 217–230). Champaign, IL: Human Kinetics.

Gould, D., Tammen, V., Murphy, S., & May, J. (1991). An evaluation of U.S. Olympic sport psychology consultant effectiveness. *The Sport Psychologist, 5*, 111–127.

Knowles, Z., Gilbourne, D., & Niven, A. (2011). Critical reflections on doing reflective practice and writing reflective texts. In D. Gilbourne & M. B. Anderson (Eds.), *Critical essays in applied sport psychology* (pp. 59–72). Champaign, IL: Human Kinetics.

Knowles, Z., Katz, J., & Gilbourne, D. (2012). Reflective practice within elite consultancy: Diary extracts and further discussion on a personal and elusive process. *The Sport Psychologist, 26*, 454–469.

Knowles, Z., Gilbourne, D., Tomlinson, V., & Anderson, A. G. (2007). Reflections on the application of reflextive practice for supervision in applied sport psychology. *The Sport Psychologist, 21*, 109–122.

Lubker, J. R., Visek, A. J., Geer, J. R., & Watson, J. C. (2008). Characteristics of an effective sport psychology consultant: Perspectives from athletes and consultants. *Journal of Sport Behaviour, 31*, 147–165.

Martens, R. (1987). Science, knowledge, and sport psychology. *The Sport Psychologist, 1*, 29–55.

McCann, S. C. (2000). Doing sport psychology at the really big show. In M. B. Anderson (Ed.), *Doing sport psychology* (pp. 209–222). Champaign, IL: Human Kinetics.

McGannon, K. R., & Johnson, C. (2009). Strategies for reflexive cultural sport psychology research. In R. J. Schinke & S. J. Hanrahan (Eds.), *Cultural sport psychology* (pp. 57–75). Champaign, IL: Human Kinetics.

Petitpas, A. J., Giges, B., & Danish, S. J. (1999). The sport-athlete relationship: Implications for training. *The Sport Psychologist, 13*, 344–357.

Poczwardowski, A., & Sherman, C. P. (2011). Revision to the sport psychology service delivery (SPSD) heuristic: Explorations with experienced consultants. *The Sport Psychologist, 25*, 511–531.

Poczwardowski, A., Sherman, C. P., & Henschen, K. P. (1998). A sport psychology service delivery heuristic: Building on theory and practice. *The Sport Psychologist, 12*, 191–207.

Poczwardowski, A., Sherman, C. P., & Ravizza, K. (2004). Professional philosophy in the SPSD: Build on theory to practice. *The Sport Psychologist, 18*, 445–463.

Schinke, R. J., McGannon, K. R., Parham, W. D., & Lane, A. M. (2012). Toward cultural praxis and cultural sensitivity: Strategies for self-reflexive sport psychology practice. *Quest, 64*, 34–46.

Sharp, L. A., & Hodge, K. (2011). Sport psychology consulting effectiveness: The sport psychology consultant's perspective. *Journal of Applied Sport Psychology, 23*, 360–375.

Smith, B. (2010). Narrative inquiry: Ongoing conversations and questions for sport and exercise psychology research. *International Review of Sport and Exercise Psychology, 3*, 87–107.

Smith, B., & Sparkes, A. (2004). Men, sport, and spinal cord injury: An analysis of metaphors and narrative types. *Disability & Society, 19*, 613–626.

Smith, B., & Sparkes, A. (2007). Sport, spinal cord injury, and body narratives: A qualitative project. *Health Psychology Update, 16*, 26–33.

Smith, B., & Sparkes, A. C. (2009a). Narrative inquiry in sport and exercise psychology: What can it mean and why might we do it? *Psychology of Sport and Exercise, 10*, 1–11.

Smith, B., & Sparkes, A. C. (2009b). Narrative analysis and sport and exercise psychology: Understanding lives in diverse ways. *Psychology of Sport and Exercise, 10*, 279–288.

Sparkes, A. C. (2002). *Telling tales in sport and physical activity: A qualitative journey.* Champaign, IL: Human Kinetics.

Strean, W. B., & Williams, D. J. (2011). Playful deviance. In D. Gilbourne & M. B. Anderson (Eds.), *Critical essays in applied sport psychology* (pp. 129–144). Champaign, IL: Human Kinetics.

Tod, D., & Lavallee, D. (2011). Taming the wild west: Training and supervision in applied sport psychology. In D. Gilbourne & M. B. Anderson (Eds.), *Critical essays in applied sport psychology* (pp. 193–216). Champaign, IL: Human Kinetics.

Watson, J. C., Lubker, J. R., & VanRaalte, J. (2011). Problems in reflective practice: Self-bootstrapping versus therapeutic supervision. In D. Gilbourne & M. B. Anderson (Eds.), *Critical essays in applied sport psychology* (pp. 157–172). Champaign, IL: Human Kinetics.

Werthner, P., & Coleman, J. (2008). Sport psychology consulting with Canadian athletes and coaches: Values and ethical considerations. *Athletic Insight: The Online Sport Psychology Journal, 10*(4). Retrieved from http://www.athleticinsight.com/Vol10Iss4/Canadian.htm.

11 "Standing in the question"

Teaching a critical perspective to developing sport psychology consultants

Leslee A. Fisher and Alicia J. Johnson

Over the last 10 years or so, I (Leslee, Associate Professor of Sport Psychology) have taught *Women, Sport, and Culture*, an elective sport psychology graduate seminar that meets twice a week at a university in the Southeastern United States. The stated course description from the syllabus is:

> The purpose of this course is to critically examine the experiences of girls and women in America from a psycho-socio-cultural perspective with a particular emphasis on the constructs of gender, race, class, and sexuality and how these constructs both independently and collectively mediate the female sport experience. This course will explore theories and interpretive frameworks from sport studies, feminist studies, race studies, psychology, and cultural studies.
>
> (Fisher, 2013, p. 1)

The stated course objectives from the syllabus are:

> To seriously take up the critical study of sport as one of America's most pervasive cultural forms; to trace the development of women's involvement in American sport; to gain an understanding of the parallels between women in society and women in sport and physical activity; to understand the importance of sport and physical activity as an empowering force in the lives of girls and women; to gain an understanding of the psycho-socio-cultural and ideological issues of oppression with which the female sport participant is confronted; to gain an understanding of feminist theoretical frameworks and women's ways of knowing.
>
> (Fisher, 2013, p. 1)

The semester is broken up into three major sections (similar to the structure of the textbook that some of the readings come out of; see Heldke & O'Connor, 2004). The first section (one-third of the class) focuses on readings by theorists who write about *oppression*, the second third on *privilege*, and the last third on *resistance* strategies. I also use theoretical underpinnings and readings from sport psychology, sport sociology, and queer studies. Some course reserve readings are directly related to sport and some are not. However, all are written by scholars who have lived experiences of being oppressed, privileged, or both simultaneously. In addition, most of the scholars are women who are marginalized in some way in the United States.

From 2000 to 2006, I co-taught this class with a fellow faculty member in a unique (in America) cultural studies of sport program. In this program, we had two sport psychology professors, one motor behavior professor, one sport sociology professor, one sport history professor, one sport philosophy professor, a cultural studies of education professor, a philosophy of education professor, and a history of education professor. The sport sociology professor developed the original course, and she and I co-taught the course upon my arrival. It was common in the program to co-teach courses together, to attend a weekly seminar with our students together, and to write together.

The sport sociology professor and I have since been separated from each other due to departmental reconfiguration. The cultural studies program was moved out of our department entirely to educational psychology and counseling. My two sport psychology and motor behavior colleagues and I were moved to kinesiology, while the sport sociology professor and another colleague were moved to recreation and sport management but within the same department.

Until the program reconfiguration – when I began to teach the course by myself – we had not included the last section of this class about theorizing resistance strategies in sport. Looking back, I am not sure why I did not implement resistance sooner. Implicit in the previous sentence is the notion that I could have resisted if I had wanted to; perhaps resistance is also made easier when one's position is secure. However, perhaps I did not resist immediately because my position was not secure – I was co-teaching a course that had already been designed by my co-instructor, and I had not yet received tenure. Perhaps it was because since the day I had joined the class, we had upset parents calling us about why we were teaching their "children" about the "f" (feminism, feminist, and "femi-nazi") word. Perhaps it was because we are in the "Bible belt" of America, where there are many students who are Caucasian, middle-class fundamentalist Christians and it was hard enough to help them understand that there was oppression in the world, including religious oppression (almost all of the students in the various departmental programs were Caucasian and in a master's degree program). And, the real kicker was that many of the students in the course had graduate assistantships related to NCAA Division I Athletics and hoped to work in that environment one day, either as sport psychology consultants, athletic trainers, sport managers, or coaches.

To be sure, there was already much resistance in these students to the fact that NCAA Division I Athletics is a big business that privileges some (e.g., themselves as those on assistantships) while marginalizing and in some cases damaging others (e.g., athletes). However, one of my commitments in my work (Fisher & Anders, 2010) is to make sure that those who want to be future sport psychology professionals explore their own privilege and power, as well as how to become change agents for the betterment of athlete welfare in this system. Many students are resistant to these ideas, perhaps because they have been the very beneficiaries of privilege via Division I Athletics as a big business.

I decided that I needed to incorporate strategies for social change into the last third of the course. What has been heartening is that there are always a few students in the class who have an "aha" moment and are interested in examining their own privilege and seeing systematic change within both the psychology of sport and Division I Athletics. However, it is usually depressing for them at first. As Heldke and O'Connor (2004) stated, "the actions of one individual, no matter how noble her intentions, cannot make these [oppressive] systems 'go away' – not even in the life of an individual. Such a realization cannot fail to be disheartening" (p. 561). Further, as Peggy McIntosh (2004) so eloquently put it, as is often the case, once one sees that there is oppression and privilege, one becomes newly accountable for changing it. However, most people, like our students, do not know how to do it because they have been in positions of power their entire lives via their demographic status (e.g., able-bodied, Caucasian, middle to upper-middle class, heterosexual, Christian in the Southeastern United States).

As part of this chapter, I (Leslee Fisher) address how I have attempted to engage graduate students in one Southeastern US university in/with sociocultural difference and the development of a critical perspective about sport and sport psychology practice. It is also important to remember that what stimulated discussion and deep reflection among the students in the Southeastern region of the United States in 2013 may not work for anyone else, at this time or at any other; this is because all knowledge is local and historically specific, not set in stone. An important first step toward understanding the complexity of oppression and privilege is to wrestle with their definitions; the definitions from the course readings are cited here. In addition, as my comrades in the cultural sport psychology movement have suggested (see McGannon & Johnson, 2009; McGannon & Schinke, 2013; Ryba, Schinke, & Tenenbaum, 2010; Schinke & Hanrahan, 2009), becoming more critically reflective is also important. To this end, some critical reflection questions and activities that have been useful in this particular class are highlighted. After one of the activities is described, Alicia (the second author, a PhD student who completed the course in May of 2013) writes about her own experience of bringing and presenting this activity to her classmates.

What has been particularly useful for me is an adapted version of Richard Rohr's (2009) process of learning. This includes lessons from monks as well as how "wondering" can lead us out of the academic "rabbit hole" of answering questions to asking the "right" questions instead of seeking the "right" answers. In my experience, there is also great mystery and individuality in terms of what will spark a desire in students to examine social justice issues. As previously mentioned, there is also often great resistance to these ideas, which instructors must prepare for.

Definitions: what are oppression, privilege, and resistance, and how do they relate to sport?

According to Heldke and O'Connor (2004), the very nature of *oppression* and *privilege* and the models used in the United States to define these constructs are extremely complex and thorny. To be sure, sexism, racism, heterosexism, and homophobia (not an exhaustive list by any means) are "enormous, multifaceted systems of oppression" (p. 561), which function together in complicated ways. First of all, *oppression* is not one thing; what Heldke and O'Connor have defined as the systematic and unfair marginalization of an entire group of people (see p. vii), Young (2004) described as "the disadvantage and injustice some people suffer . . . because of the everyday practices of a well-intentioned liberal society" (p. 39). Further, Young asserted that to be oppressed, people have to have experienced one or more of the following five faces of oppression: (1) *exploitation* ("a steady process of the transfer of the results of . . . labour of one social group to benefit another") (p. 46); (2) *marginalization* ("a whole category of people is expelled from useful participation in social life and thus potentially subjected to severe material deprivation and even extermination") (p. 50); (3) *powerlessness* ("the labor of most people in the society augments the power of relatively few") (p. 52); (4) *cultural imperialism* ("the universalization of a dominant group's experience and culture, and its establishment as the norm") (p. 54); and (5) *violence* ("members of some groups live with the knowledge that they must fear random, unprovoked attacks on their persons or property, which have no motive but to damage, humiliate, or destroy the person") (p. 56).

As you can see in this brief review of selected US theorists, some theoretical models and definitions of oppression have an individual focus while others focus on collective oppression. Many models are even in tension with one another. However, this should not stop us from engaging in and with the material.

In terms of *privilege*, Peggy McIntosh (2004) used her own experience as a US Caucasian female professor and the metaphor of an "invisible knapsack" to investigate her own white privilege. This knapsack is filled with special maps and provisions that only white people can use to navigate the world; further, it is an invisible knapsack that people of color do not have access to. Heldke and O'Connor (2004) asserted that while oppression is the systematic and unfair *marginalization* of an entire group of people, privilege is its opposite – the systematic and unfair *granting of advantage* to an entire group of people (see p. vii). And Bailey (2004) posited that privilege is "unearned assets conferred systematically" (p. 305). In addition, Bailey suggested that while "all privilege is advantageous . . . not all advantages count as privilege" (p. 305). We also each can experience both oppression and privilege simultaneously.

Scholars are taking up these ideas and writing about them within sport psychology. The areas of critical reflection and the examination of privilege are growing (e.g., Blodgett et al., 2010; Butryn, 2010). In addition, because oppression is not just one "thing" but a systematic process, there are multiple ways to resist it

(Heldke & O'Connor, 2004). Heldke and O'Connor defined *resistance* as taking collective action to work against existing systems to create social change (see p. vii). Since there are missing threads, holes, gaps, and inconsistencies in oppressive and privileged ideologies, such gaps can provide ideal locations for resistance.

Heldke and O'Connor have described six resistance strategies: (1) *education*; (2) *treason/traitorousness/disloyalty*; (3) *separatism and identity politics*; (4) *revolution*; (5) *coalition-building*; and (6) *neither/nor thinking*. In other words, they suggested that in order to disrupt the status quo, individuals can commit to becoming educated about these systems, reject or disrupt the privilege that they are given, stymie or disrupt the expectations that others have of them based on these systems, identify with a particular group and split off entirely from the mainstream, revolt, build coalitions to fight social injustice, and/or refuse to engage in neither/nor thinking. However, as they rightly pointed out, unfortunately we are often not even aware of the systems of oppression and privilege that we live in because they are constituted in such a way that many of us have a stake in "things remaining the way they are" (p. 562).

In my (Leslee's) experience, this critical idea – about the "hiddenness" of privilege – is at the heart of why it is necessary to educate future sport psychology professionals about these complex social justice constructs. Upon entry, many graduate students report believing that sport (and the field of sport psychology) is a "meritocracy" that "anyone" can benefit from, if they just put in the necessary time and effort. Therefore, many of these students appear completely unaware of how US NCAA Division I sport (and the field of sport psychology) is constituted in such a way as to make sure that we help it *stay the way it is*. If students are not exposed to the resistance strategy of education about their own privilege and positions of power (both within and outside of sport and sport psychology), as well as about such ideologies as "sport is a meritocracy" and "anyone can practice sport psychology," then they may never work through their own privilege with reflective practice – defined as "challenging, focused, and critical assessment of one's own behaviour as a means toward developing one's own craft" (Osterman, 1990, p. 134) – and may be doomed to (unconsciously) oppress others with whom they work.

In the remainder of this chapter, educational activities as the primary *resistance* strategy used in the class are explored. These activities serve as a first step toward exploring the question of how to engage students in critically reflecting about themselves as future sport psychology professionals, as well as in learning to question the world around them in order to create social change.

Process: can developing sport psychology practitioners learn to see as the mystics see?

> Elitism, classism, torture, homophobia, poverty, and the degradation of the earth are still largely unaddressed . . . I list all these not to be negative, but to let us see the very real limitations of the over-defining and over-asserting of

the individual self and its private salvation … the individual became "individuated" in the West, without any keen awareness of the common good or the harmonizing of body, mind, heart, and community.

(Rohr, 2009, p. 42)

Richard Rohr – critical scholar, ordained Catholic priest, and the founder of the Center for Action and Contemplation (www.cac.org, 2013) – asked the world's religions to critically reflect on the goal of religion and what it does and should "equip us to learn, see, or become" (p. 39). In a similar vein, to begin the process of critical self-reflection, students in the *Women, Sport, and Culture* class are asked: what do you think the end goal of sport studies is, and what does and should it equip you to learn, see, or become? How is your training affected by being in a relationship (e.g., assistantship, swag, etc.) with US NCAA Division I Athletics? In what ways does US NCAA Division I Athletics embody elitism, sexism, homophobia, racism, classism, ablebodiedness, etc.? To what extent is US NCAA Division I Athletics over-defined and over-asserted by a focus on the "individual self" versus a focus on "the common good" or "harmonizing the body, mind, heart, and community"? What *kind* of sport practice do you think you should have (i.e., what are the principles that will ground your practice) when you are finished?

What we want students to end up with is a different (i.e., critical, self-reflective) way of seeing and knowing. Rohr (2009) posited that one can gather all the knowledge in the world, or what Buddhists call "the ten thousand things" (p. 59). He wrote, however, that:

all the information in the world does not of itself accumulate into wisdom … wisdom is not the gathering of more facts and information, as if that would coalesce into truth. Wisdom is precisely a different way of seeing and knowing those ten thousand facts.

(p. 59)

Rohr (2009) has invited us to reflect on how wisdom is not gained through finding the "perfect answers" to questions, but by refining the questions themselves, by systematically asking more and more questions, by opening up to "wonder," and by becoming more curious. Rohr's definition of the three components of wonder is very helpful: "Standing in disbelief … Standing in the question itself … [and] Standing in awe before something" (p. 46). In his book *The Naked Now: Learning to See as the Mystics See* (Rohr, 2009), he illustrated this type of learning via a story about young monks in training at a Tibetan monastery:

during the young novice's training, he or she is presented over a period of three years with each and every one of the Buddha's teachings. During that time, she has to name all of the difficult and problematic consequences that would follow from observing this teaching. After each answer, the older monks clap their hands in approval, and smile at one another. When all of the possible negative consequences are exhausted, they move onto the good consequences. The same procedure is followed until all of the good consequences have been unpacked, no matter how many hours or days it takes. And, again, after each answer, the masters clap their hands, and they smile at one another.

(p. 43)

As Rohr believed, this type of training fosters discipline in "nonpolarity thinking" and in "broader reflection and discrimination" (Rohr, 2009, p. 44). What's more, there is no one "perfect" answer or any "wrong" answer. In fact, the goal is to teach trainees to understand both good and bad consequences of a system and how to weigh the pros and cons of each. This is an entirely different learning structure from the one used in most US universities, where classrooms are filled with a Socratic type of debate style in which there is usually one winner and one loser.

Other critical reflection questions that students are asked to engage with have developed out of the experiences and writings of former PhD students on the program. These include but are not limited to: what should our role be (as educators, practitioners, etc.) in resisting or challenging oppression in sport? Should sport psychology graduates be "social change agents" in the systems they are about to work and interact in or not? If so, when (Fisher, Butryn, & Roper, 2003, 2005; Fisher, Roper, & Butryn, 2009)? In addition, critical reflection questions come directly from the readings: what if universities were "conceived as institutions in the business of *challenging* racism, sexism, and heterosexism?" (Heldke & O'Connor, 2004, p. 561). By extension, what if sport psychology training programs were in the business of challenging racism, sexism, and homophobic thinking in athletic departments, teaching what Rohr calls "broader reflection and discrimination" and "nonpolarity thinking" about social justice issues in addition to mental training issues?

As referenced by McGannon and Johnson (2009), reflective cultural sport psychology (CSP) practice should include critical reflection based on such definitions as Hatton and Smith's (1994). These authors suggested that "making judgments about whether professional activity is equitable, just, and respectful of persons or not . . . critical reflection locates any analysis of personal action within wider socio-historical and politico-cultural contexts" (Hatton & Smith, 1994, p. 35, as cited in McGannon & Johnson, 2009, p. 58). What follows in the last part of this chapter is a series of six educational, critical reflection activities that have been undertaken in one Southeastern US university elective *Women, Sport, and Culture* graduate class. Each activity is both an individual and a group activity done by every member of the class. In addition, the classroom itself is structured so that the desks are arranged in a circle; this is an attempt to diminish the power that I (Leslee) have "over" the students.

Activity #1: creating a critical consciousness – discussion of definitions. The purpose of this activity is to create an environment in which University of

Tennessee (UT) students can examine their own critical consciousness and personal politics, their role in UT sport, the effect their participation has had on their personal development and on society, and the relationship between UT intercollegiate athletics and higher education (see Fisher et al., 2003). In order to create a *critical consciousness* in students (Friere, 2000) and to help students talk about the ways in which they are both privileged and oppressed (Collins, 2000; hooks, 2006), I begin with definitions of critical consciousness, personal politics, a brief summary of US second-wave feminism, consciousness-raising, and potential consciousness-raising discussion topics. I discuss US second-wave feminism because that is where the birth of critical consciousness occurred around issues of social justice, particularly as they related to gender roles and identity. *Critical consciousness* has been defined as "the ability to perceive social, political, and economic oppression and to take action against the oppressive elements of society" (www.hermes-press.com, 2006). *Consciousness-raising* has been described as "when people get together and put a name to their experience," as well as "increasing one's awareness and memory of certain experiences" (Lox, Martin-Ginis, & Petruzzello, 2006, p. 421). A brief *summary of second-wave feminism* during the 1960s begins with 1963 and the publication of Betty Friedan's *The Feminine Mystique*. In addition, there were major theoretical debates framed around Marxism. In 1970, Shulamith Firestone's *The Dialectic of Sex* was published, followed shortly thereafter by marches, demonstrations, "bra burnings," "consciousness-raising," and the development of *Ms.* magazine and N.O.W. by Gloria Steinem. Hornacek (2004) defined *10 Essential Men's (and Women's) Consciousness-Raising Topics* as (1) childhood training for sex roles; (2) marriage, monogamy, jealousy; (3) work and housework; (4) fathers and sons (mothers and daughters; com-binations); (5) rape; (6) sexual orientations, e.g., LGBTQQIAA, homosexuality, heterosexuality, bisexuality; (7) the nuclear family as a bastion of sexism; (8) maleness and masculinity (femaleness and femininity); (9) sensuality and sexuality; and (10) intimacy with women, intimacy with men (Hornacek, 2004). In the *Women, Sport, and Culture* class, each of these is discussed in relation to sport.

Personal politics, on the other hand, are "the sum total of skills necessary to navigate a situation in which my values, standards or boundaries are in conflict with another's or others'" (Bornstein, 2004, p. 767). The concepts of "social group," "group identity," and what "identity politics" mean are also important. According to Young (2004), the concept of a social group is "a specific kind of collectivity [with] ... specific consequences for how people understand one another and themselves" (p. 40); group meanings also *partially* constitute peoples' identities. Students are asked to wrestle with: how do you think these definitions relate to the group "athletes"? How do these definitions mirror or not mirror your own understanding/experience of these concepts, of being an athlete, of working with athletes? In most cases, students describe that they have never thought about nor been exposed to these issues before.

Activity #2: examining your own privilege. The purpose of this activity is to encourage students to self-reflect critically on the individual privileges that they have been afforded based on their connections with UT Athletics. Students are asked: what privileges do you get via your assistantship/job/being a student at university? What would it be like to give it up? What would you do with the "goods," "swag," status, assistantship, etc.? This activity proves challenging for students, especially if they have been connected to athletics at various levels their entire lives.

Activity #3: examining your social group privilege. The purpose of this activity is to encourage students to examine critically the group privilege that they have been afforded based on a variety of group identities. In this activity, a legal pad-sized piece of paper with the phrase "An athlete is . . ." written at the top is given to each person in the group. Everyone is then asked to complete the sentence with whatever descriptor comes to mind. S/he then passes the paper to the person seated on his/her left, who completes the sentence with a descriptor such as "strong." After each person has written something different, the group leader reads the descriptors out loud. Group discussion then occurs using the following four questions: (1) how do these descriptions reflect a "stereotypical" view of "athletes"? (2) How do they challenge it? (3) Is there anything in your experience that supports these descriptions? If so, what? (4) Is there anything in your experience that challenges these descriptions? If so, what? The instructor can also do this with additional descriptors, e.g., "male," "female," "Caucasian," "Christian," "African-American female," "sport psychology consultant," "sport psychology graduate student," etc. (modified from www.teachingtolerance.org, 2006). Students invariably are challenged when they see how many of the descriptors for "athlete" are related to "male" athletes and traditional notions of masculinity.

Activity #4: examining your own personal politics. The purpose of this activity is to encourage students to reflect critically on their own personal politics. The following questions are discussed: (1) do you choose your friends solely on the basis of their identities [yes/no/somewhat]? (2) Which is more important to you [your identity/your principles]? (3) Exactly how have you determined the principles of those around you? (4) What criteria do you use? (5) What qualities or values do you look for in a friend? (6) Now measure your political affiliations by the same standards by which you choose your friends. Note the similarities and differences (adapted from Bornstein, 2004). Students report that they have never thought about the ways in which they select their friends or their friends' identities.

Activity #5: broader social issues – "coming out" star activity. One of the broader social issues tackled in the class is homophobia and how to combat it. There are two class periods related to homophobia, as I have found that there are a considerable number of students in the class who have not been exposed to this issue. Alicia brought this activity to class and led her classmates through it during her required class presentation.

Materials needed: colored paper (four different colors) cut into the shape of a star, writing utensils, and the story script given below. Preparation: this activity should take between 20 and 30 minutes, depending on the debriefing at the end and the group size. The facilitator should prepare one paper star for each person in the class or education session.

Directions: the facilitator should explain to the participants that a story will be read aloud by the facilitator, and that there should be no other talking while the story is read out. Everyone should receive either a blue, pink, red, or yellow paper star. The participants should be in a circle so they can see one another. Jeff Pierce (n.d.) of the University of Southern California LGBT Resource Center created the following story script that should be read by the facilitator.

Imagine that this star represents your world, with you in the center and those things or people most important to you at each point of the star. So we'll begin by writing your name in the center of the star, making it your very own! [Pause to allow the participants to write their name.] You are now all someone who identifies as lesbian, gay, bisexual, or transgender and is about to go through the coming out process. Select a side of the star to begin with. Choose a friend who is very close to you. Someone that you care about very much. A best friend or a close friend, it doesn't matter. Write his/ her name on a point of the star. [Pause to allow the participants to write their friend's name.] Next, think of a community that you belong to. It could be a sport team, religious community, organization, student group or just a group of friends. Take the name of that group that you are a part of and write it on the next point of the star, going clockwise. [Pause to allow the participants to write the community name.] Now, think of a specific family member. Someone that you have always turned to for advice or maybe who knows how to cheer you up when you're sad. A mother, father, aunt or grandparent . . . any family member who has made a large impact in your life. Please write his/her name on the next point of the star. [Pause to allow the participants to write their family member's name.] What job would you most like to have? It could be anything from president to professor to sport psychology consultant. Whatever your career aspiration is, please write it on the next point. [Pause to allow the participants to write their career aspiration.] Lastly, what are some of your hopes and dreams? Maybe you want to do sport psychology consulting with elite athletes, start a family, travel the world, and give time to charitable causes. Think of a few hopes and dreams and write them on the last point of the star. [Pause to allow the participants to write their hopes and dreams.]

   You decide that it will be easiest for you to come out to your friends first, since they have always been there for you in the past and you feel that they need to know. If you have a BLUE star, your friend has no problem with it. They have suspected it for some time now and thank you for being honest with them. Luckily, they act no different toward you and accept you for who you are. If you have a PINK or a YELLOW star, your friends are kind of hesitant. They are a little irritated that you have waited so long to tell them, but you are confident that soon they will understand that being LGBTQ is just a part of who you are . . . you just need to give them some time. Please fold back this point of the star. If you have a RED star, you are met with anger and disgust. This friend who has been by your side in the past tells you that being LGBTQ is wrong and they can't associate with anyone like that. If you have a red star, please tear off this point and drop it on the ground. This friend is no longer a part of your life. [Pause.]

With most of you having such good luck with your friends, you decide that your family probably deserves to know. So, you turn to your closest family member first so that it will be a little easier. If you have a YELLOW star, the conversation doesn't go exactly how you planned. Several questions are asked as to how this could have happened, but after some lengthy discussion, this person who is close to you seems a little more at ease with it. Fold this point of your star back, as they will be an ally, but only with time. If you have a BLUE star, you are embraced by this family member. They are proud that you have decided to come out and let you know that they will always be there to support you. If you have a PINK or RED star, your family member rejects the thought of being related to a person who is LGBTQ. Much like some of your friends, they are disgusted and some of you are thrown out of your house or even disowned. You are now part of the 20% of the homeless youth who identify as LGBTQ [National Alliance to End Homelessness, 2013]. If you have a PINK or RED star, please tear off this point and drop it on the ground. [Pause.]

Having told your friends and family, the wheels have started to turn and soon members of your community begin to become aware of your sexual orientation. If you have a YELLOW or BLUE star, your sexual orientation is accepted by your community. They continue to embrace you like anyone else and together you celebrate the growing diversity in your community. If you have a PINK star, you are met with a mixed response. Some accept you and some don't know what to think. You remain a part of the community, and with time, will fit in as you once did. If you have a PINK star, please fold back this point. If you have a RED star, your community reacts with hatred. They tell you that someone like you does not belong in their community. Those who had supported you in your times of need no longer speak to you or acknowledge you. If you have a RED star, tear this point off and drop it on the ground. [Pause.]

You have heard that rumors have started circulating at work regarding your sexual orientation. In the past, you have made it a point to confront these rumors as soon as they began, but now you're not sure if that will do more harm than good. But, unfortunately, you don't have the chance. If you have a BLUE star, your co-workers begin to approach you and let you know that they have heard the rumors and that they don't care, they will support you. Your bosses react the same way, letting you know that you do good work and that is all that matters. If you have a YELLOW star, your workplace has become quite interesting. Everyone seems to think that you are LGBTQ, even though you haven't mentioned it to anyone or confirmed any of the rumors. Some people speak to you less, but the environment has not seemed to change too drastically. If you have a YELLOW star, please fold back this point. If you have a RED or a PINK star, you continue to work as though nothing is happening, ignoring the rumors that have spread throughout your workplace. One day, you come in and find that your office has been packed up. You are called into your boss's office and they explain to you that you are being fired. When you ask why, they tell you that lately your work has been less than satisfactory and that they had to make some cutbacks in your area. If you have a RED or PINK star, please tear off this point and let it drop to the ground. [Pause.]

Now, your future lies ahead of you as a person who identifies as LGBTQ. Your hopes and dreams, your wishes for the perfect life . . . for some of you these are all that remain. If you have a YELLOW, BLUE, or PINK star, these hopes and dreams are what keep you going. Most of you have been met with some sort of rejection since beginning your coming out process, but you have managed to continue to live a happy and healthy life. Your personal hopes and dreams become a reality. If you have a RED star, you fall into despair. You have been met with rejection after rejection and you find it impossible to accomplish your lifelong goals without the support and love of your friends and family. You become depressed and with nowhere else to turn, many of you begin to abuse drugs or alcohol. You have thoughts where you feel that your life is no longer worth living. If you have a red star, please tear it up and drop the pieces to the ground. You are now aware that 40% of all suicide victims identify as lesbian, gay, bisexual, queer or trans [source not identified in script].

(Pierce, n.d.)

Debriefing points: (1) validate that the participants may be feeling a variety of emotions right now and thank them for participating in the activity; (2) ask the participants to write about what they are feeling, while remaining silent, for 1–2 minutes; (3) ask if anyone would like to share what he or she is feeling now and/ or what was felt throughout the activity (if there is time, allow everyone who would like to speak share his or her experiences. Many people might need to process the activity verbally); (4) ask the participants how this activity might help them to be a more culturally competent sport psychology consultant; and (5) once again, validate and thank the participants. The facilitator should also be available for further processing, and should also be able to provide referrals to local counseling centres. Alicia now describes what it was like to lead the *"Coming Out" Star Activity* with her classmates.

Alicia's experience of presenting this activity. Prior to starting my doctoral studies at the University of Tennessee, Knoxville, I had already begun to awaken my self-awareness as to how my identities positioned me in this world, especially within the world of sport psychology. For most of my life I have been made aware of the identities that put me at a disadvantage – being female and being of a low socioeconomic status. However, it was not until I took a multicultural counseling course during my master's program that I started to examine my privileges –

being Caucasian, heterosexual, able-bodied, Christian, well educated, and a US citizen. From that course onward, I was continuously looking to process the ways that I have been disadvantaged and advantaged throughout my life. During this time of seeking, I engaged in reflexivity through journaling and processing verbally with a counselor and trusted peers. When I got to my PhD program and registered for the *Women, Sport, and Culture* course, I knew this would be a safe space for me to continue that processing because of Dr. Fisher's experiences and background. I had full confidence in her ability to create a safe and welcoming environment.

My experience in the class was likely very different from that of the master's students. Many of these students had not been exposed to active critical thinking regarding how their identities have positioned them in this world. I say this because I lost count of the number of times I heard "I've never thought about it like that before" from my peers over the course of the semester. Since I had already begun processing such topics, I felt as though I was at an advantage because I was able to process beyond how such topics relate to myself and excavate deeper to connect with how the material and course experience relate to my future career.

As part of the course all students have to give a presentation and lead the discussion on one of the course topics. The topic I chose was scheduled for the second day of the homophobia/lesbians in sport discussion. I was both excited and nervous about presenting this topic. I identify as a strong ally to the LGBT community, but I knew there were several people in the class who did not share my beliefs, mainly because of religious reasoning. Because I could not predict what the tone of the conversation would be, I was nervous about leading the discussion.

My opening activity was the *"Coming Out" Star Activity* described above. This is an activity that I had facilitated before, but I always remind myself that every group is different and I can never predict where the discussion will go. I pondered: *Am I prepared to facilitate this for my peers?* I found myself preparing by separating my identities into "my classmates' peer" and "the discussion leader." This separation of identities led me to conclude that I needed to lead the activity and discussion as if I were instructing my own (future) class. I felt this way because I was facilitating the activity in a state that has banned same-sex marriage by law. This was challenging for me as I had recently moved from Massachusetts, a state that legally recognized same-sex marriage almost a decade ago. The "acceptable" discourse varies greatly between the two geographic regions. However, this did not mean that I didn't want to challenge the students to think beyond political or religious stances. I saw the responsibilities of my role as facilitator of the class to include challenging the students' current thinking, helping them see how the topic connects with their role as a future professional, and leaving them intrigued so they are eager to continue processing and to seek understanding beyond the classroom.

I allocated several minutes to self-reflection after the activity prior to beginning the discussion. Several people really seemed to be processing while some people were clearly not willing to connect with the activity. When opening the floor to discussion, I could feel the nervousness rising in my throat. The students began discussing how the activity really allowed them to walk in the shoes of someone who is going through the process of coming out as LGBT. There was also some discussion surrounding how every star's experiences were different, and how, when the students saw the person sitting next to them tear off a point of their star but theirs remained, they could feel their hearts sink. And then a very important voice in the discussion came forward.

A student who had previously disclosed to the class that she identifies as a lesbian spoke about how, during the activity, she had felt as though she was reliving her actual experiences of coming out to her family, friends, and other networks. I had wondered if she would take part in the discussion of the activity, but knew I didn't want to single her out, as she was the only student to disclose identifying as LGBT. If she was going to speak, it had to be on her terms. While she was speaking, I tried to balance good eye contact with her, in an effort to show her support, with looking around the room at the facial expressions of other students. It was clear to me when looking at the facial expressions of the other students that the activity became even more real in that moment of disclosure.

After the opening activity's discussion I moved through the rest of my presentation material, which included LGBT equality in sport advocacy groups and organizations. At the end of each presentation, the students give anonymous feedback to the presenter. Much of the feedback I received was positive, but one note stood out. The comment on the note was that this person would now consider being an ally to lesbians but could not ever imagine being an ally to gay men. When I read that note, I wondered if I had missed something in my presentation. On the one hand, it was great that this person was considering becoming an ally to a particular group. But why was this person willing to be an ally only to lesbians but not to gay men? I wish I knew who had written the note so I could understand their reasoning for making that comment. If I could better understand the comment, then perhaps I could help this person process further. *Is that even my place?*

What this presentation ended up being for me was a practice run for my future career. It helped me realize that I will not convince everyone to be an advocate for social justice issues. However, watching other students begin the familiar path to self-awareness during my presentation and over the course of the entire semester was an important piece of my professional development. This self-awareness and continued critical reflection on everyone's part will help us better understand ourselves and, therefore, become better practitioners. Overall, the course represented a chance for me to help future sport practitioners think deeply and critically about issues related to the interconnectedness of women, sport, and culture while continuing on my own path of self-awareness.

Activity #6: taking action. It is one thing to articulate one's identities and social categories and how they are experienced. It is quite another to think about taking action to change oppressive systems or people, especially when one may be living in an oppressive state or is getting benefit from that particular system. The final activity presented in this chapter focuses on moving from critical self-reflection to action.

Students are asked to complete, reflect on, and discuss the following exercise: on a scale of 1 (never) to 5 (always), how often do you: Interrupt someone telling a racist or ethnic joke? Read about the achievements of people with physical disabilities? Challenge friends expressing a gender stereotype? Send emails to TV or radio stations who broadcast news stories with cultural or racial biases? Examine your own language for unconscious bias or stereotypes? Ask foreign student-athletes about their countries of origin? Think about the definition of "rape"? Protest against unfair or exclusionary practices in an organization? Think about ways in which you belong to oppressor or oppressed groups? Examine your own level of comfort around issues of sexual orientation? Celebrate your uniqueness? Examine your responses for patterns. Did you surprise yourself in any way? Are there behaviors you would like to engage in less frequently? More frequently? How will you implement those changes? (Modified from www. teachingtolerance.org, 2006.)

Concluding remarks

In this chapter, we have presented strategies for engagement with future sport professionals at one Southeastern US university at one particular point in time related to sociocultural difference in sport and the development of a critical perspective. It is evident from the selectively reviewed course material taken from one *Women, Sport, and Culture* class and our experiences that racism, sexism, homophobia, etc. exist within sport contexts, and that these are often ignored or unexplored due to "taken for granted" dominant norms and understandings within sport. As the editors of this book pointed out in a review of this chapter, by drawing attention to what is "taken for granted," future sport professionals can begin to become more open and understanding – through critical self-reflection – about multiple, intersecting identities and oppression within the sport context. In this way, students can potentially move from trying to answer questions about social difference the "right way" (or what some have called being "politically correct") to seeking wisdom by trying to refine the questions themselves, by systematically asking more and more questions about their role in maintaining such oppressive and privileged systems as those found within some parts of athletics, by becoming more curious about others who are "different" from them, and by opening up to "wonder." As Rohr (2009) suggested, this entails "Standing in disbelief . . . Standing in the question itself . . . [and] Standing in awe before something" (p. 46). Standing in the question itself can serve as the *beginning* of the development of a critical consciousness related to these issues. However, it is by no means the end of our exploration.

References

Bailey, A. (2004). Privilege. In L. Heldke and P. O'Connor (Eds.), *Oppression, privilege, and resistance: Theoretical perspectives on racism, sexism, and heterosexism* (pp. 301–316). Boston: McGraw-Hill.

Blodgett, A. T., Schinke, R. J., Fisher, L. A., Yungblut, H. E., Recollet-Saikkonen, D., Peltier, D., … Packard, P. (2010). Praxis and community-level sport programming strategies in a Canadian Aboriginal reserve. *International Journal of Sport and Exercise Psychology, 8*, 262–283.

Bornstein, K. (2004). This quiet revolution. In L. Heldke & P. O'Connor (Eds.), *Oppression, privilege, and resistance: Theoretical perspectives on racism, sexism, and heterosexism* (pp. 767–786). Boston: McGraw-Hill.

Butryn, T. M. (2010). Interrogating whiteness in sport psychology. In T. V. Ryba, R. J. Schinke, & G. Tenenbaum (Eds.), *The cultural turn in sport psychology* (pp. 127–152). Morgantown, WV: Fitness Information Technology.

Collins, P. H. (2000). *Black feminist thought: Knowledge, consciousness and politics of empowerment.* New York, NY: Routledge.

Fisher, L. A. (2013). KNS 543: *Women, sport, and culture.* Course taught at the University of Tennessee, Knoxville, Spring, 2013.

Fisher, L. A. & Anders, A. D. (2010). Critically engaging with sport psychology ethics through cultural studies: Four commitments. In T. V. Ryba, R. J. Schinke, & G. Tenenbaum (Eds.), *The cultural turn in sport psychology* (pp. 101–126). Morgantown, WV: Fitness Information Technology.

Fisher, L. A., Butryn, T. M., & Roper, E. A. (2003). Diversifying (and politicizing) sport psychology through cultural studies: A promising perspective. *The Sport Psychologist, 71*, 391–406.

Fisher, L. A., Butryn, T. M., & Roper, E. A. (2005). Diversifying (and politicizing) sport psychology through cultural studies: A promising perspective revisited. *Athletic Insight, 7*(3). Retrieved from www.athleticinsight.com.

Fisher, L. A., Roper, E. A., & Butryn, T. M. (2009). Revisiting diversity and politics in sport psychology through cultural studies: Where are we five years later? In R. J. Schinke (Ed.), *Contemporary sport psychology* (pp. 105–120). Hauppauge, NY: Nova Science Publishers.

Friere, P. (2000). *Pedagogy of the oppressed* (30th anniversary ed.). New York, NY: Continuum International Publishing Group.

Hatton, N. & Smith, D. (1994). Facilitating reflection: Issues and research. Paper presented at the *Conference of the Australian Teacher Education Association* (24th, Brisbane, Queensland, Australia, July 3–6, 1994).

Heldke, L., & O'Connor, P. (2004). *Oppression, privilege, and resistance: Theoretical perspectives on racism, sexism, and heterosexism.* Boston: McGraw-Hill.

hooks, b. (2006). *Outlaw culture: Resisting representations.* New York, NY: Routledge Classics.

Hornacek, P. C. (2004). Anti-sexist consciousness-raising groups for men. In L. Heldke & P. O'Connor (Eds.), *Oppression, privilege, and resistance: Theoretical perspectives on racism, sexism, and heterosexism* (pp. 594–599). Boston: McGraw-Hill.

Lox, C., Martin-Ginis, K., & Petruzzello, S. J. (2006). *The psychology of exercise: Integrating theory and practice.* New York, NY: Holcomb Hathaway.

McGannon, K. R., & Johnson, C. R. (2009). Strategies for reflective cultural sport psychology research. In R. J. Schinke & S. J. Hanrahan (Eds.), *Cultural sport psychology* (pp. 57–78). Champaign, IL: Human Kinetics.

McGannon, K. R., & Schinke, R. J. (2013). *The psychology of sub-culture in sport and physical activity: A critical approach.* Florence, KY: Psychology Press (Taylor & Francis).

McIntosh, P. (2004). White privilege and male privilege: A personal account of coming to see correspondences through work in women's studies. In L. Heldke & P. O'Connor

(Eds.), *Oppression, privilege, and resistance: Theoretical perspectives on racism, sexism, and heterosexism* (pp. 317–327). Boston: McGraw-Hill.

National Alliance to End Homelessness. (2013). LGBTQ Youth. Retrieved from http://www.endhomelessness.org/pages/lgbtq-youth.

Osterman, K. F. (1990). A new agenda for education. *Education and Urban Society, 22*, 133–152.

Pierce, J. (n.d.). Coming out stars. *University of Southern California LGBT Resource Center*. Retrieved from http://sait.usc.edu/lgbt/files/ComingOutStars.pdf.

Rohr, R. (2009). *The naked now: Learning to see as the mystics see*. New York, NY: The Crossroad Publishing Company.

Ryba, T. V., Schinke, R. J., & Tenenbaum, G. (2010). *The cultural turn in sport psychology*. Morgantown, WV: Fitness Information Technology.

Schinke, R. J., & Hanrahan, S. J. (2009). *Cultural sport psychology*. Champaign, IL: Human Kinetics.

www.cac.org (2013). The Center for Action and Contemplation.

www.hermes-press.com (2006). Social justice definitions.

www.teachingtolerance.org (2006). Social justice activities for teachers.

Young, I. (2004). Five faces of oppression. In L. Heldke & P. O'Connor (Eds.), *Oppression, privilege, and resistance: Theoretical perspectives on racism, sexism, and heterosexism* (pp. 37–63). Boston: McGraw-Hill.

12 Caged quandaries

Mixed martial arts and the politics of research

Matthew A. Masucci and Ted M. Butryn

Introduction

While the modern-day phenomenon of professional mixed martial arts (MMA) and its most prominent organization, the Ultimate Fighting Championship (UFC), began in earnest (in the United States at least) in 1993, it has been less than a decade since MMA earned more mainstream acceptance within established sporting cultures. Not surprisingly, with the increase in popularity of this aggressive combat sport, which most often takes place in a caged ring, scholars from several academic fields, including sport sociology and critical media studies, have started to devote their efforts to understanding the growing sport and to grappling with the implications of its newfound status as a pay-per-view juggernaut and major television network-aired spectacle (Abramson & Modzelewski, 2011; Andrew, Kim, O'Neil, Greenwell, & James, 2009; Garcia & Malcom, 2010; Hirose & Pih, 2010; Lim, Martin, & Kwak, 2010; Milton, 2004; Spencer, 2009, 2012; van Bottenburg & Heilbron, 2006). In this chapter, we attempt to add to this body of scholarly work not by addressing MMA or the UFC in general, but through a nuanced critical interrogation of the *process of investigating the sport* and the tensions that can, and arguably should, arise when those invested in any sort of cultural sport psychology (CSP) project are faced with a research topic that is always and already imbued with social and political issues. Further, we will suggest that such tensions should indeed be highlighted, problematized, contested, and then contextually negotiated. One aim for this chapter, therefore, is to offer up a real-world examination, self-reflection, and critique of the often contradictory goals of our academic pursuits in the ongoing project of our research on mixed martial arts. To this end, we draw on sport studies and CSP research that, in general terms, has cultural praxis at its core, and, more particularly, utilize a narrative autoethnographic approach (Markula & Denison, 2005) that makes use of reflection and storied representation to help contextualize the ongoing examination of the meaning and value of sport psychology-based research on MMA.[1]

Situating the authors

While Ted and I have sport philosophy and sport psychology backgrounds, respectively, we both went through the doctoral program in Cultural Studies and

Sport at the University of Tennessee, one of the places where, at the time, some of the ideas central to cultural sport psychology were beginning to take root. Now colleagues at San José State University, in the past few years we have conducted five studies (both solo and in collaboration) on the growing sport of mixed martial arts. The work took two fairly distinct research trajectories: one prong focused on how professional MMA fighters coped with stressors before, during, and after fights, while the other was based, more broadly, on sociological issues related to MMA, including the media's role in its legitimatization (Masucci & Butryn, 2013), as well as ethnographic and autoethnographic work on MMA training and gym culture, which was conducted solely by Matt.

Over the past eight years, we have presented versions of these MMA-related research projects at sport psychology (Association of Applied Sport Psychology: AASP), sport sociology (North American Society for the Sociology of Sport: NASSS), and sport history (North American Society for Sport History: NASSH) conferences. It was during the NASSH conference that a few of our female colleagues asked how were we able to reconcile doing critical cultural studies and pro-feminist-informed work with the seemingly a-critical sport psychology work that has as one of its aims to instruct athletes and coaches in how to perform better at their violent combat sport? In the years since, we have talked sporadically about how we make sense of the apparent tensions our colleagues pointed out. While Matt's autoethnographic work on MMA training clearly exposed some of these tensions (we discuss this in greater length later in the chapter), it remains unclear from both an ethical and/or a methodological perspective how our research, and the expanding body of work on the psychology of MMA in general, can ever be completely reconciled with the culture of violence, perpetuation of heteronormative masculinity, and gender politics, as well as class exploitation, often revealed in combat sport research. As Schinke, McGannon, Parham, and Lane (2012) stated, cultural praxis aims to "blend theory, lived culture, and social action with a 'self-reflexive sensibility' to raise awareness as to how one's own values, biases, social position, and self-identity categories impact participants within the research and/or consulting realms" (p. 35). More specifically, we draw on the work of several authors (e.g., Holt & Strean, 2001; McGannon & Metz, 2010; Schinke et al., 2012; Smith, 1999; Sparkes, 2002; Sparkes & Smith, 2003) on self-reflexivity in an attempt to consider how our previous work on MMA has concealed, or at least de-emphasized, some of the issues and practices CSP often seeks to place at the forefront of any research agenda, including issues of violence, gender identities, and self-reflexivity. In examining our work on MMA, and specifically the first author's research on an MMA gym and his subsequent autoethnographic work, we, perhaps unwittingly, are directly in line with this vital process of self-reflexivity, because as Schinke and colleagues (2012) noted, such work involves researchers situating themselves in the research, with the "self of the researcher becoming the site of analysis and the subject of critique" (p. 35).

While we are both consumers of MMA and the UFC in particular, having watched many pay-per-view events and attended the first legally sanctioned MMA event in California, as well as the first ever UFC event in San José, we arrived at this moment, both personally and academically, via different routes. Ted's background is in mainstream sport psychology, with an emphasis on performance enhancement. While later trained in a sport psychology program within a critical cultural studies unit, he continues to provide mental training services for university athletes. In addition, his initial interest in researching MMA was due to the perceived lack of sport psychology work being done with MMA athletes. In one study, for example, 20 professional, male MMA fighters were interviewed using an interview guide developed in part from the previous mainstream sport psychology work on stress and coping. In an additional study, two UFC fighters were interviewed following each MMA competition over a 13-month period.

The focus of this chapter, however, will be on methodological and paradigmatic issues related to two studies that I (i.e., Matt) conducted at an MMA gym, and on my own experiences training there. With an athletic background in wrestling – one of the core disciplines of MMA training – and an academic background in philosophy and cultural studies of sport, I was interested in exploring the meaning and value that amateur practitioners of MMA linked to their participation in the activity. Moreover, and perhaps as a legacy of my historical participation in wrestling (as well as the traditional masculine sport of American football and, later, rugby), and, perhaps, because I considered myself a fan of boxing growing up, I was intrigued by the combative and individualistic nature of the sport. The raw physicality of the sport, coupled with my own personal sporting history, had piqued my curiosity, while at the same time – as I shall explain below – also providing the foundation for a conflicted relationship with the subject. Drawing on my background in critical sport studies, I conducted an ethnographic research project at an MMA training facility in San José, California – one of the hotbeds of this increasingly popular sporting discipline. During both the course of the investigation and the subsequent analysis of the data that emerged, I began to struggle with a palpable tension that arose from my simultaneous participation in and critique of the sport of MMA. While not conceived of as "sport psychology research," Ted and I look to this ethnographic and autoethnographic work as an exercise in self-reflection that stands in contrast to our other MMA-related sport psychology research in order to explore the ways in which multiple robust lines of inquiry, from a variety of sport-related disciplines, may ultimately bolster CSP-informed research on MMA. In short, in a parallel autoethnographic project, I attempted to articulate the tensions between, for example, participating in the hyper-masculine culture of MMA and the critical political and theoretical underpinnings of my academic training through a series of reflexive *self-bracketing vignettes* (Masucci, 2006).

Brief history of MMA and subsequent increase in research

MMA is a combat sport that combines several traditional martial art practices, including kick-boxing, Brazilian jiu-jitsu, wrestling, and judo. While the sport is generally thought to have originated in ancient Greece in the form of the Pankration, the modern, and most commercially viable, version of MMA – the

Ultimate Fighting Championship – began in the United States in the early 1990s as a way to demonstrate the superiority of one "fighting system" over another. Ostensibly, the introduction of the original "no-holds-barred" pay-per-view spectacle helped to promote so-called Gracie jiu-jitsu, a particular style of Brazilian jiu-jitsu (BJJ) imported into California by the Gracie family of Rio de Janeiro, Brazil (Masucci, 2013).

In the mid-1990s there was a concerted effort, led in part by Arizona senator John McCain, to ban cable operators from broadcasting the lucrative UFC events on pay-per-view, although the sport still maintained its cult-like fan base through gate receipts at live shows and a brisk video cassette sale and rental market. With a change of ownership and several shrewd business and marketing moves, the effort to bring the UFC (and thus MMA) out of the shadows and into the mainstream had begun. By highlighting new rules and seeking sanctioning from state athletic commissions, the company was well on its way to rebranding itself as a legitimate sporting practice. This effort culminated in the state of California legalizing the sport in 2005, opening the floodgates for other states, with the notable exception of New York, to follow suit.

As MMA became more popular, in part due to the introduction of the Spike TV reality show *The Ultimate Fighter*, as well as the increasingly uncritical stance of many mainstream media sources, who willingly bought both fact and fiction from charismatic UFC president Dana White (Masucci & Butryn, 2013), scholars in media and communication studies, sport sociology (Abramson & Modzelewski, 2011; Garcia & Malcom, 2010; Hirose & Pih, 2010; Spencer, 2009, 2012; van Bottenburg & Heilbron, 2006), sport management (Andrew et al., 2009; Lim, Martin, & Kwak, 2010), and sport psychology (Jensen, Roman, Shaft, & Wrisberg, 2013; Massey, Meyer, & Naylor, 2013; Milton, 2004) began, somewhat sporadically, to develop research agendas around MMA in general, and the UFC in particular.

The diversity of the academic foci, methodological approaches, and, importantly for this chapter, politicized or apoliticized stances of the growing body of work on MMA illustrates how scholars from different academic areas who study other violent sports (e.g., American football) often have very contradictory notions of what "important" research topics are when it comes to the now-mainstream space and practice of MMA. In addition, these studies necessarily used a range of methodological approaches. Abramson and Modzelewski (2011), Milton (2004), and Spencer (2009, 2012) used ethnographic methods and phenomenology, and, following the work of Wacquant on boxing, sought to understand the subculture of MMA fighting by training themselves.

Perhaps the major focus of attention in the sport studies research on MMA has to do with issues concerning the reproduction of problematic masculinities, the moral acceptability of violent sport, and the process by which MMA eventually gained mainstream acceptance in the mid-2000s (Masucci & Butryn, 2013; Santos, Tainsky, Schmidt, & Shim, 2013; van Bottenburg & Heilbron, 2006). While other research on gender and sexuality will undoubtedly emerge following the inclusion of female fighters in the UFC in 2013, the research conducted on

MMA thus far has been primarily male-centered; indeed, in the case of the first author's ethnographic study of MMA gym culture, men dominated the space of the MMA gym. In this regard, we now turn to a (re)interpretation of the first author's (i.e., Matt's) research studies as an example of what the process of critical self-reflexivity might offer to future work on the psychology of MMA.

Entering the space of MMA: notes on politics, identity, and (auto)ethnographic work

While this chapter addresses the work conducted by both authors, the first author's work on an MMA gym is highlighted here; thus, all references to the first person that follow are the first author's. As suggested above, a possible tactic for the reconciliation (or perhaps rationalization) of the seemingly disparate trajectories of our work on MMA is that a multi-perspectival approach to understanding the sport may yet yield a more critically informed sport psychology. For example, only through such a comprehensive interrogation of the sport from historical, sociological, psychological, and philosophical vantage points have we begun to understand some of the nuances of the sport that may have been easy to overlook by working only within narrow interpretations of the CSP framework. Taking seriously the call to move beyond "uncritical dichotomizations" in the examination of sporting practices (Giardina & McCarthy, 2005, pp. 165–166), the MMA projects we have conducted, when taken as a whole, can provide subtle and nuanced contours of MMA that we may not have had otherwise, and thus (at least) create an opening for new ways to think about a CSP-infused (or at least CSP-aware) union of theory and practice.

One of the early projects in my work on MMA involved an ethnography of an MMA training academy. I signed up for classes at a local gym and participated in classes over a 13-month period. While the main goal of the research project was to understand the motivations and meanings that gym members associated with their participation in MMA training, ongoing reflection of the research process and topic yielded an unexpected yet correlated exposition. In particular, I was interested in understanding, not the elite experience that is so often the focus of sport studies and sport psychology research, but the experiences of those "regular folks" who spent their hard-earned money and time on this physical activity. Much of the data, gleaned from observation and both formal and informal interviews, confirmed the conclusions articulated above – namely, that the MMA gym constituted a "safe space" for the reproduction of particular kinds of heteronormative masculinities. Many of the casual conversations during and after class, and some of the language used by the instructors, tended to calcify the ridged gender and sexual orientation roles that are readily available as a consistent critique of contemporary sport in the sport studies literature. For example, the uncritical use of the feminine as a pejorative, the overtly homophobic and sexist banter before and after class, and the unspoken yet obvious (at least initially) masculinity-affirming posturing when new male members entered the gym space were all clearly observable in the gym. Indeed, it was a challenge to assess how women perceived the space, since, as indicated above, there were only a handful of occasions during the course of the study where women practiced with men – though there was no overt prohibition to do so.

Over the course of the ethnographic study it became clear that when women were present in the training space of the gym, there was a profound segregation of men and women in all but a handful of instances. Interestingly, in the year that I was taking classes at the MMA gym, women were seen participating in the main striking and grappling session on only one occasion. While the sessions were not ostensibly closed to the participation of women, it was interesting to note their marginalization within the gym space. In one of the sessions (a striking session) where one woman was present, it was clear, by observation and from comments made by the instructor, that she was a high-level kick boxer. As such, her abilities eclipsed the skill level of all the male participants in the room. Interestingly, with her obvious skill, and the novice status of those men training that night, the woman at this particular training session was accorded a level of status equal to her obvious skill. She was seen helping other students and was used as a demonstration partner for the main (male) instructor. On the other hand, in all other instances, when women were seen participating in the gym, it was either in a male-led "self-defense" class or in a cardio boxing type of class. In both cases, my perception was that the gym space was highly segregated and (save for the female kick boxer mentioned above) women in the gym were relegated to the periphery, either working in the membership office or taking classes specifically designed "for women" and, thus, not as complex or intense as the regular "submission fighting" that the men were engaged in.

Other sociological scholars of combat sport and contact sports, however, have found that violence is far from a one-dimensional construct. DeGaris (2000) found that as opposed to seeing their jobs as mindless violence, some boxers were often supportive of one another, and shared intimate stories of family, aging, and notably vulnerability. Lane (2009) also found that, in his consulting experiences, there was very little evidence that fighters had any intent to injure their opponents, and that "aspects of skill, emotional control and physical fitness" (p. 255) were the major factors related to performance. This finding was true in the noticeable majority of the MMA participants the first author encountered, few of whom expressed a desire to impose their violent wills on their opponents. On the other hand, one interesting observation from the ethnography was the policing of unrestrained aggression by those members who become regulars at the gym. In one instance, a prospective member was participating in a class for the first time and was very vocal about his desire to learn MMA skills in order to be able to fight and "handle his business" out on the street. As the session progressed, the person was becoming increasingly fatigued, due to the intense and regimented conditioning that was common in the class, and frustrated, due to the lack of "contact" that we were engaging in. When he began to participate in skill drills, it was evident that he was attempting to participate very aggressively when, as a matter of course, the rest of the class always knew to work at half-speed in order to practice skill development but also to reduce potential injury. At several points in the practice, as the prospective member's frustrations seemed to be mounting, due to a lack of real fighting, various members of the practice session admonished him for going too hard. Interestingly, the would-be member never returned to the gym during the course of the ethnographic study. While seemingly minor, this unspoken etiquette of policing overly aggressive practice behavior was prevalent in the gym setting.

On the other hand, some of the interactions and relationships between men at the gym fostered in the practice setting corroborated findings related to supportive, inclusive, and non-judgmental environments (DeGaris, 2000; Waquant, 2006). Indeed, once insider status was established, both for myself as the researcher and for the members of the class as they continued to become more familiar with one another, a spirit of cooperative learning and mutual encouragement began to emerge. Despite these findings, an interesting side project began as I embedded myself further into the MMA ethnography.

As part of my ongoing work, I began to make a habit of recording field-notes immediately upon completion of each MMA class. As I began to reflect on my notes, and during a short recuperation from injury sustained in one of my MMA classes, I noticed that many of the entries were filled as much with self-reflections, inner doubts, and personal ambiguities *about the nature and value of the project* as they were with observations of the participants at the gym – the supposed aim of the study in the first place. In an attempt to reconcile this emerging conflict, I turned to the work of those sport studies scholars who have been advocating for re-casting the representation of research "findings," up to and including the *enmeshment* that the researcher has with the research project. In particular, the work of Markula and Denison (2005), Sparkes (2002), and Smith (1999; Smith & Sparkes, 2010) has informed the attempt to situate myself within (and beyond) the MMA ethnography project by offering a clear articulation of the value and purpose of the research through alternative forms of narrative representation. While this project was originally designed as a sport studies undertaking, it is important to note the growing body of reflexive work in CSP that could be drawn on that would undoubtedly strengthen this type of view. Nonetheless, as the researcher's privileged position is interrupted, the (often uncomfortable) space of self-reflection (and simultaneous reflection by others) demands that one positions oneself with respect to particular privileges, not only as a researcher but also, importantly, as a co-creator and interpreter of meanings and contexts within and beyond the research milieu. As Markula and Denison (2005) stated:

> In addition to considering more carefully how to represent their research subjects' experiences, and considering the possibility of story writing, qualitative researchers today are also concerned with how their own experiences influence the research process. For this reason, many qualitative researchers insert their own selves into their research texts. They do this not only by writing in the first person, but by also discussing how their own biases and values intersect with their subjects' values.
>
> (p. 165)

Struggling to make sense of my conflicted location relative both to the MMA study and to the co-related tensions beyond the dojo walls that had emerged since I had started my work as a "student" – including negotiating injury, disentangling notions of objectivity, questioning my intellectual commitment, and navigating increasingly strained personal relationships – I turned to Denison and Markula's work on storied research as an opportunity to excavate, reflect, and reframe my narrative as it relates to the work of ethnography.

Therefore, as a reflexive experiment in contemplating my dual position as both a researcher and a participant at the MMA gym, and considering the escalating reservations about the nature and purpose of the MMA research study in general, I created a brief version of what I called *autoethnographic self-bracketing vignettes*. This work was intended to share (however thinly) a kinship with the process of a "bracketing interview," which has often been deployed in qualitative inquiry in order to, among other things, safeguard against biases (Dale, 2000). Despite the personal nature of this work, and charges of self-indulgence, I share with sport psychology and sport sociology scholars (e.g., Dzikus, Fisher, & Hays, 2012; Rinehart, 1998; Rowley, Earle, & Gilbourne, 2012; Smith, 1999, 2010; Sparkes, 2002) the notion that no story, however personal, makes sense outside of contextualization and the relation-ality to others (Smith, 2010).

While the idea of autoethnographic representation is not uniform across academic disciplines, my autoethnography of the MMA gym research project leaned extensively on the iteration suggested by Sparkes (2002). In one of his essays, Sparkes (2002) included a section entitled "No conclusion." While his purpose was to convey the unsettled and ambiguous relationship between the process of research and the creation and interpretation of the textual and self-reflexive account of that work, I found his summation of the process to be a clear articulation of how this kind of work can foster ongoing inquiry and con-templation. Despite the (often exceedingly) uncomfortable process of self-reflection and expression, I believe – as Sparkes has articulated – that the value of autoethnography in particular, and of self-reflection on the process of research in general, holds great promise, since "even if 'narratives of the self' do nothing else but stimulate us to think about issues in the sociology of sport, then they will have made a significant contribution to the field" (Sparkes, 2002, p. 38).

Moreover, and notwithstanding the various and often competing versions of autoethnography across academic disciplines, I leaned on the iteration suggested by Ellis, Adams, and Bochner (2011) in order to provide a framework for my autoethnography:

> As a method, autoethnography combines characteristics of autobiography and ethnography. When writing an autobiography, an author retroactively and selectively writes about past experiences. Usually, the author does not live through these experiences solely to make them part of a published document; rather, these experiences are assembled using hindsight.
>
> (2011, para. 4)

Finally, I took liberties with the following representations by creating fragments of narrative histories, by reconsidering and reinterpreting personal artefacts, and by the re-signification of traditional data sources. The larger function of this type of reflexive engagement, as it relates to the purpose of this chapter, is to illustrate how working in this simultaneous way – from both a non-traditional and an introspective standpoint, as well as from a more conventional qualitative perspective – can yield important insights about the meaning and purpose of the work, which ultimately can help to inform the more critical practice suggested by CSP.

In this way, my aim was to use the form of the auto-narrative as a way to perhaps re-position myself within the MMA ethnography project. As a result of this intense self-reflexive interrogation, the more I considered undertaking an ethnographic examination of the MMA academy, the less sure I felt about my rationale and/or intent. Finally, following the work of McGannon and Johnson (2009), Schinke et al. (2012), Smith (2010), and others, I hoped that this experiential excavation, the reflexive and reflective work, and the (collaborative) reframing of my history(s) would contribute to my conceptualizations of both MMA in the space of the study (the local) and MMA's place in society as a whole. In the small segment that follows, I attempt to present two such self-bracketing vignettes: one that suggested an academic and personal conflict in the MMA ethnography, and one that revealed itself during a series of conversations over the course of a camping trip in the Eastern Sierra Mountains with my partner:

Bridgeport, CA

The swirl of beer and flexeril are scarcely taking the edge off the pulsing pain in my neck. "At least I'm on god-damned vacation" I mutter to myself in fleeting contentment; yet with every dull "thump-thump" pushing fresh blood to my neck, the unmistakable smell of the gym mats skulk in my consciousness. I struggle to focus on Sarah's voice. "Yep . . . mmm, huh . . ." I've vanished; my thoughts are drifting now . . . Jesus Christ!, what if the nerve damage is permanent? Two more Rolling Rocks arrive and temporarily buoy my optimism for the remainder of our Sierra exploit. We are disjointed. The local tavern is drenched in clichés – bulletin board photographs of the Locals' wish-you-were-here 4th of July party – a weathered rack of antlers, taken I'm told, 15 years ago up near Antelope Valley – *Achey Breaky Heart* on the Jukebox . . .

When I signed up for the evening classes, I didn't think about coming home glassy eyed, dead-tired, famished and angry – at 9:30 each night of the week. Sarah's clipped and frosty "hello" manages to communicate – in five short letters – her utter indifference to my "hard work."

"How was class?" she offers from the back room, not even bothering to inflect one ounce of "I give a crap." I lie and say it was fine, *not wanting to get into it*, as I paw frosted mini-wheats from the box for supper.

This *IS* important work for Christ's sake, I think to myself!

As we sit in Rhino's I am holding my neck unnaturally. The muscles in my back strain to ballast my body and I feel awkwardly vulnerable despite visualizing combinations – right cross, uppercut, outside kick . . .

"Well . . . *this* is a blast" Sarah finally says, breaking 15 minutes of silence.

I'm simmering now; my face is flush with beer, pain, and the unmistakable knowledge that *EVERTHING* is my fault. "You know" I say much more angrily than I intend, "my arm could really be permanently fucked-up . . ."

"I just don't get it Matt, I mean why are you doing this . . . why are you doing this to yourself . . . As a feminist . . . you know . . . it is hard to watch. *Do you really like this stuff*?? Because it's a side of you I don't know . . ."

In my best pompous professor-who-knows-you-couldn't-possibly-understand-the-value-of-my-work voice, I respond by babbling something about "tropes of masculinity" and "interrogations" and "hetero-normative dialectics of . . ."

"But why *THIS*? Why are *YOU* doing *THIS*??" her voice trailing off . . .

And so there it was . . . my hull is breeched. I'm foundering.
I stare blankly at the foamy residue clinging to the side of my glass.
The question, in its elegant simplicity, was demanding to be answered . . .

Interpretation and implications

In the above short vignette, I attempt to articulate the academic, social, and interpersonal tensions I (and perhaps others in a different research context) experienced when taking on a project that was counter to my stated professional and political standpoint. Hopefully, it becomes clear for the reader that these conflicts are always and already messy. Where, for instance, does our personal life and our professional life begin and end? In what ways do our own personal historical contingencies impact and shade the work that we do? How do the subjectivities of others force us as researchers to provide an accounting of the projects that we decide to take up, and in what way do those choices impact the trajectory of those investigations? In the end, this moment – as told in the above story – compelled me to face a host of questions about my motives, my ideological position, and the larger intent of the project. While recounting the story alone will not carry the weight of the reflexive process, in my case, struggling to craft and revise the tale and the subsequent hours of reflection that this process necessitated certainly helped keep these issues to the fore as Ted and I moved forward with subsequent MMA research projects.

Hypocrisy or reconciliation: final thoughts on applied work with MMA athletes

In her afterword to the edited text *The Cultural Turn in Sport Psychology* (Ryba, Schinke, & Tenenbaum, 2010), Cole noted that a CSP project "proposes a more responsible, accountable, and reflexive psychology: a situated scholarship that is at its best when it intervenes in normalizing functions" (p. 401). Clearly, none of our work has directly intervened to problematize the normalization of male violence within the context of gender identities, consumption, self-damage, and fighter exploitation. On the other hand, when the data and methodological decisions are re-evaluated through a more nuanced lens that is focused by a CSP-oriented interrogation of these MMA research projects, flickers of possibility begin to reveal themselves. One of the broader challenges, therefore, is to deftly stitch together work from an imaginative coalition of research perspectives and paradigms. As Fisher, Roper, and Butryn (2009) wrote, "our research theories and methodologies could be based on this critical intellectual sensitivity toward athlete oppression, privilege and resistance" (p. 108), within the context of athlete identities and power structures. Ryba and Wright (2010) added that sport psychology should "not be glossing over the profound implications of practicing the performance discourse for identity, subjectivity, and well-being of sport and exercise participants" (p. 22). The hard work, of course, resides in the meaning-making dialog among and between the co-constructors of the knowledge and, further, in the assessment of the best way to "activate" the results in the applied domain of sport psychology. From our experience, no one epistemological vantage point or research result should hold *potential* interpretations captive. In the end, perhaps conducting these multiple lines of research can provide a subtle and nuanced understanding of the contours of MMA that we may not have had otherwise, and thus create an opening for new ways to think about a CSP-infused (or at least CSP-aware) fusion of theory and practice.

The idea that there are obviously problematic aspects to the sport and culture of MMA does not necessitate that it *has* to be problematic in certain types of practice. However, sport psychology scholars should understand the multiple meanings of participant motivation, meaning, and fulfillment in order to help facilitate the potentially less problematic aspects of the activity (Lane, 2009). Maybe the reconciliation of doing CSP work while simultaneously engaging in performance-enhancing projects related to MMA is future work informed by deep critical understanding of the psychological and phenomenological accounting of MMA.

In conclusion, our work to date on the sport of MMA has revealed a number of encouraging and potentially problematic methodological choices when viewed through the critical lens of CSP. We suggest that sport psychology researchers should attempt to address issues of athlete agency and empowerment, identity politics, and economic issues in their future work, if possible integrating these issues into studies aimed at developing successful mental training techniques and other performance-enhancing protocols. Certainly, as this chapter and several other works on self-reflexivity (e.g., Butryn, 2009; Knowles & Gilbourne, 2010;

McGannon & Johnson, 2009; McGannon & Metz, 2010; Ryba & Wright, 2005; Schinke et al., 2012) have illustrated, it is possible simply to continue to expand the research base on a given phenomenon in sport psychology without addressing, paradigmatically or methodologically, any of the CSP work and its accompanying politics. Yet we hope that it is also readily apparent why this should not be the trajectory of future studies. The degree to which these two notions can be teased out still presents a challenge; however, it is clear through our combined understanding of MMA in this case that there are valuable (and less problematic) outcomes that a CSP-informed practice could serve to illuminate.

Note

1 As a matter of clarification, in the remainder of the chapter, when "I" is used, it will refer to Matt, since the voice is solely that of the first author commenting on an ethnography he conducted in an MMA gym. The use of "we" will refer to Ted and Matt.

References

Abramson, C. M., & Modzelewski, D. (2011). Caged morality: Moral worlds, subculture, and stratification among middle-class cage-fighters. *Qualitative Sociology, 34*, 143–175.

Andrew, D. P. S., Kim, S., O'Neil, N., Greenwell, C., & James, J. D. (2009). The relationship between spectator motivations and media and merchandise consumption at a professional mixed martial arts event. *Sport Marketing Quarterly, 18*, 199–209.

Butryn, T. M. (2009). (Re)examining whiteness in sport psychology through autonarrative excavation. *International Journal of Sport & Exercise Psychology, 7*, 323–341.

Dale, G. A. (2000). Distractions and coping techniques of elite decathletes during their most memorable performances. *The Sport Psychologist, 14*, 17–41.

DeGaris, L. (2000). Be a buddy to your buddy: Male identity, aggression, and intimacy in a boxing gym. In J. McKay, M. A. Messner, & D. Sabo (Eds.), *Masculinities, gender relations, and sport* (pp. 88–108). Thousand Oaks, CA: Sage.

Dzikus, L., Fisher, L. A., & Hays, K. F. (2012). Shared responsibility: A case of and for "real life" ethical decision-making in sport psychology. *The Sport Psychologist, 26*, 519–539.

Ellis, C., Adams, T. E., & Bochner, A. P. (2011). Autoethnography: An overview [40 paragraphs]. *Forum: Social Research/Sozialforschung, 12*(1), Art. 10, http://nbn-resolving.de/urn:nbn:de:0114-fqs1101108.

Fisher, L. A., Roper, E. A., & Butryn, T. M. (2009). Engaging cultural studies and traditional sport psychology. In R. J. Schinke & S. J. Hanrahan (Eds.), *Cultural sport psychology* (pp. 23–34). Champaign, IL: Human Kinetics.

Garcia, R. S., & Malcolm, D. (2010). Decivilizing, civilizing or informalizing? The international development of mixed martial arts. *International Review for the Sociology of Sport, 45*, 39–58.

Giardina, M. D., & McCarthy, C. R. (2005). The popular racial order of urban America: Sport, cinema, and the politics of culture. *Cultural Studies/Critical Methodologies, 5*, 145–173.

Hirose, A., & Pih, K. K. (2010). Men who strike and men who submit: Hegemonic and marginalized masculinities in mixed martial arts. *Men and Masculinities, 13*, 190–209.

Holt, N. L., & Strean, W. B. (2001). Reflecting on initiating sport psychology consultation: A self-narrative of neophyte practice. *The Sport Psychologist, 15*, 188–204.

Jensen, P., Roman, J., Shaft, B., & Wrisberg, C. (2013). In the cage: MMA fighters' experiences of competition. *The Sport Psychologist, 27*, 1–12.

Knowles, Z., & Gilbourne, D. (2010). Aspiration, inspiration and illustration: Initiating debate on reflective practice writing. *The Sport Psychologist, 24*, 504–520.

Lane, A. M. (2009). A profession of violence or a high contact sport? Ethical issues working in professional boxing. In R. J. Schinke (Ed.), *Contemporary sport psychology* (pp. 253–261). New York, NY: Nova Science Publishers.

Lim, C. H., Martin, T. G., & Kwak, D. H. (2010). Examining television consumers of mixed martial arts: The relationship among risk taking, emotion, attitude, and actual sport-media-consumption behavior. *International Journal of Sport Communication, 3*, 49–63.

Markula, P., & Denison, J. (2005). Sport and the personal narrative. In D. Andrews, D. Mason, & M. Silk (Eds.), *Qualitative methods in sport studies* (pp. 165–185). New York, NY: Berg.

Massey, W. V., Meyer, B. B., & Naylor, A. H. (2013). Towards a grounded theory of self-regulation in mixed martial arts. *Psychology of Sport & Exercise, 14*, 12–20.

Masucci, M. A. (2006, November). *As real as it gets? An autoethnographic examination of a mixed martial arts academy.* Paper presented at the annual meeting of the North American Society for the Sociology of Sport (NASSS), Vancouver, BC, Canada.

Masucci, M. A. (2013). Mixed Martial Arts/Ultimate Fighting Championship. In M. R. Nelson (Ed.), *American sports: A history of icons, idols and ideas*. Santa Barbara, CA: ABC-CLIO Publishing.

Masucci, M. A., & Butryn, T. M. (2013). Writing about fighting: A critical content analysis of newspaper coverage of the Ultimate Fighting Championship from 1993–2006. *Journal of Sport Media, 8*(1), 19–44.

McGannon, K. R., & Johnson, C. R. (2009). Strategies for reflective cultural sport psychology research. In R. J. Schinke & S. J. Hanrahan (Eds.), *Cultural sport psychology* (pp. 57–75). Champaign, IL: Human Kinetics.

McGannon, K. R., & Metz, J. L. (2010). Through the funhouse mirror: Understanding access and (un)expected selves through confessional tales. In R. J. Schinke (Ed.), *Contemporary sport psychology* (pp. 153–170). Hauppauge, NY: Nova Science Publishers.

Milton, M. (2004). Being a fighter II: "It's a positive thing around my male friends." *Existential Analysis, 15*, 285–297.

Rinehart, R. (1998). *Players all: Performances in contemporary sport*. Bloomington, IN: Indiana University Press.

Rowley, C., Earle, K., & Gilbourne, D. (2012). Practice and the process of critical learning: Reflections of an early stage practitioner working in elite youth level rugby league. *Sport & Exercise Psychology Review, 8*, 35–50.

Ryba, T., & Wright, H. (2005). From mental game to cultural praxis: A cultural studies model's implications for the future of sport psychology. *Quest, 57*, 192–212.

Ryba, T., & Wright, H. (2010). Sport psychology and the cultural turn: Notes toward a cultural praxis. In T. V. Ryba, R. J. Schinke, & G. Tenenbaum (Eds.), *The cultural turn in sport psychology* (pp. 3–28). Morgantown, WV: Fitness Information Technology.

Ryba, T. V., Schinke, R. J., & Tenenbaum, G. (Eds.). (2010). *The cultural turn in sport psychology*. Morgantown, WV: Fitness Information Technology.

Santos, C. A., Tainsky, S., Schmidt, K., & Shim, C. (2013). Framing the octagon: An analysis of news-media coverage of mixed martial arts. *International Journal of Sport Communication, 6*, 66–86.

Schinke, R. J., McGannon, K. R., Parham, W. D., & Lane, A. (2012). Toward cultural praxis: Strategies for self-reflexive sport psychology practice. *Quest, 64*, 34–46.

Smith, B. (1999). The abyss: Exploring depression through a narrative of the self. *Qualitative Inquiry, 5*, 264–279.

Smith, B. (2010). Narrative inquiry: Ongoing conversations and questions for sport and exercise psychology research. *International Review of Sport and Exercise Psychology, 3*, 87–107.

Smith, B., & Sparkes, A. (2010). The narrative turn in sport and exercise psychology. In T. V. Ryba, R. J. Schinke, & G. Tenenbaum (Eds.), *The cultural turn in sport psychology* (pp. 75–100). Morgantown, WV: Fitness Information Technology.

Sparkes A. C. (2002). *Telling tales in sport & physical activity: A qualitative journey*. Champaign, IL: Human Kinetics.

Sparkes, A. C., & Smith, B. (2003). Men, sport, spinal cord injury and narrative time. *Qualitative Research, 3*, 295–320.

Spencer, D. C. (2009). Habit(us), body techniques and body callusing: An ethnography of mixed martial arts. *Body & Society, 15*, 119–143.

Spencer, D. C. (2012). *Ultimate fighting and embodiment: Violence, gender, and mixed martial arts*. New York, NY: Routledge.

van Bottenburg, M., & Heilbron, J. (2006) De-sportization of fighting contests: The origins and dynamics of no-holds-barred events and the theory of sportization. *International Review for the Sociology of Sport, 41*, 259–282.

Wacquant, L. (2006). *Body & soul: Notebooks of an apprentice boxer*. New York, NY: Oxford University Press.

13 Confessions of the disc

A Foucauldian analysis of ethics within Ultimate Frisbee

Hamish Crocket

Ultimate Frisbee (Ultimate) is an invasion-style team sport played with a flying disc. Its emergence within the context of the 1960s counter-culture movement can still be seen through the notion of *Spirit of the Game*—a code of fair play that constitutes the first clauses of the rules—and, relatedly, the game being self-officiated (Crocket, 2012; Thornton, 2004).[1] Yet, Leonardo and Zagoria (2005) have documented ongoing debates about interpretations of Spirit of the Game throughout Ultimate's history. Moreover, interpretations of Spirit of the Game vary between and within levels of competition (Crocket, in press a). Spirit of the Game, then, should not be regarded as having an essential meaning; rather, it is produced and re-produced in a range of forms through on- and off-field performances.

As I have suggested elsewhere (Crocket, in press a), Spirit of the Game might be thought of, in rather loose terms, as a willingness to accept limits in the pursuit of victory. Examples of such limits include honesty, respect, adhering to rules, and avoidance of contact. Spirit of the Game is ethically significant insofar as it offers a code that involves various forms of concern for self and others. In this chapter, I will offer an account of ethics that is contextualized within Ultimate's subculture.

As with many other lifestyle sports (see Wheaton, 2004), Ultimate players vary in the extent of their involvement. Fringe players might participate in local leagues or pick-up games, while committed or 'core' players travel significant distances for weekend tournaments and devote hours to training and preparation (Crocket, 2013). Committed players regularly spend thousands of dollars each season (e.g., Greenough, 2013). Players socialize extensively with their teammates and players from other teams both at tournaments and outside their commitments to Ultimate. Unsurprisingly, in the context of this major commitment, 'core' Ultimate players develop a distinctive subculture, sharing a common argot, "a 'sense' of irony" (Hutcheon, 1994, p. 92; see also Crocket, 2012), and wearing Ultimate-related clothing—a mélange of whimsical, ironic, and athletic styles (Crocket, 2012; see also Leonardo, 2007).

Moreover, Ultimate remains relatively unrecognized by those not involved in the sport. It has little media coverage beyond a few Ultimate-specific websites and efanzines, and to many outsiders its credibility as a sport is weak (e.g., Bombjay, 2010; Gentile, 2009). In contrast to participants in mediatized sports, Ultimate players find that their stories of participation are unintelligible to non-players (e.g., Bara, 2012). In this way, Ultimate's lack of recognition by outsiders reinforces the distinctiveness of its subculture.

Nevertheless, as Wheaton (2007) and others (e.g., Maffesoli, 1996; Muggleton, 2000; Wilson, 2008; Young & Atkinson, 2008) argued, the notion of subculture is challenged by the internal diversity and fluidity of 'subcultural' groups. In this context, it is important to note that while aspects of Ultimate, such as Spirit of the Game, might be seen as distinct or even oppositional to dominant sporting culture, Ultimate's subculture is better characterized in more fluid terms as formed from a range of debates (cf. Rinehart, 2000). Aspects of Ultimate that appear oppositional to dominant sporting culture should be balanced with the recognition that many Ultimate players aspire to have Ultimate recognized as a mainstream sport (e.g., Korber, 2012). I do not suggest, then, that Ultimate might be regarded as an ethical alternative to mainstream sports. Rather, I offer this brief background of Ultimate's subculture as part of a localized, contextual psychology of ethics.

My involvement with Ultimate

I started playing Ultimate in 2003 as a deliberate attempt to move away from institutionalized sports, in which I was finding it increasingly difficult to tolerate others'—and contain my own—'win-at-all-costs' behaviors. Yet, after five years immersed within Ultimate's subculture I realized that my binary positioning of Ultimate as ethical and more mainstream sports as unethical was at best a naïve simplification of both ethics and these differing sports. Subsequently, I decided to undertake postgraduate study focusing on the possibilities and limitations of ethical athletic subjectivities within Ultimate using ethnographic methods (e.g., Crocket, 2012, 2013, in press a and b; Pringle & Crocket, 2013).

My critical, qualitative research has consisted of fieldwork as a player at numerous social and competitive tournaments in Australasia and Europe, in-depth semi-structured interviews with players from New Zealand, Europe, and North America, and textual analysis of documentaries, books, DVDs, and websites. For more information on ethnographic methods in sport psychology research, I refer readers to Krane and Baird (2005) and Thorpe (2009, 2010).

Since beginning my research in 2008, I have seen Ultimate players making increasing use of the Internet and social media, including such efanzines as *Skyd Magazine* and *Ultiworld*, such forums as rec.sport.disc/nospam and reddit.com/r/ultimate, and such open-access email list servers as Britdisc and Eurodisc, to discuss myriad issues. Increasingly, elite games are offered in live stream or download formats, and reviews of games and tournaments have been posted online (e.g., *Skyd Magazine*, 2013). Focusing on a case study of a controversial play from a game that was posted online (see Shardlow, 2008), I show how players' on-field and online performances both take on ethical dimensions within Ultimate's subculture.

A critical psychology of ethics

In this section I offer a critical perspective on the psychology of ethics in two related parts. First, I critically review reductionist approaches to ethics developed within mainstream sport psychology. Second, I outline a Foucauldian interpretation of ethics and subjectivity, which offers a nuanced and localized way to undertake a critical psychology of ethics within sporting subcultures.

Sport psychologists have devoted significant attention to the prevalence of, and factors correlated with, what might be considered ethically problematic sporting behaviors, such as aggression, violence, and cheating (e.g., Coulomb-Cabagno & Rascle, 2006; Kavussanu, 2008; Keeler, 2007; Kirker, Tenenbaum, & Mattson, 2000; Shields & Bredemeier, 1995).[2] As examples, ego-orientated athletes and those athletes who are in a perceived ego-involved motivational climate are more likely to cheat or aggress than task-orientated athletes, or those athletes who are in a perceived mastery-involved motivational climate (Kavussanu, 2008). Moreover, acceptance of aggressive behavior is more likely from older rather than younger athletes, male rather than female athletes, elite rather than social athletes, and contact sport rather than non-contact sport athletes (Coulomb-Cabagno & Rascle, 2006).

While these studies have offered important insights into ethical behavior in sport, there are limitations to the approaches these studies have taken. These studies have typically relied on surveys of athletes, observation of video footage, and quantification of predefined types of behaviors. In this regard, the psychology of sports ethics has been conceptualized as the examination of "identifiable meas-urable behavior resulting from existent mental structures" (Baird & McGannon, 2009, p. 380). Such an approach assumes an unproblematic distinction between an internal psychological self and external social influences (McGannon & Mauws, 2000). Consequently, these studies have avoided "genuine psycho-logical topics such as *subjectivity* – subjective personal experiences and the meanings that human beings attribute to these experiences" (Theo, 2009, p. 37, emphasis in original). One aim of critical psychology is to bring questions of subjectivity to the fore, rather than reduce subjectivity to a series of dependent and independent variables.

A growing number of sport psychology researchers (e.g., Fisher, Butryn, & Roper, 2003; McGannon & Mauws, 2000; Smith and Sparkes, 2009; Ryba & Wright, 2005) have contributed to a broad critique of reductionist tendencies within sport psychology. As Gilbourne and Richardson (2006) argued, much of sport psychology assumes:

> a clean, linear world that seeks to control variables in order to find a specific answer to a specific question. Yet the soccer world (and the world in general) is unpredictable, sometimes irrational, often emotional. A three way ANOVA is none of these things.
>
> (p. 332)

In simple terms, these authors question whether the reduction of complex and contradictory lived realities to predefined, measureable variables offers an adequate representation of the complex, inconsistent social environments in which sport is performed. Subsequently, psychologists working from a range of alternative approaches have adopted different modes of analysis and presentation, ones that allow a greater focus on subjectivity (e.g., Gilbourne & Andersen, 2011; Krane & Baird, 2005; Ryba, Schinke, & Tenenbaum, 2010). These approaches have given voice to previously silenced issues, such as culture, language, and power relations.

An equally problematic assumption within these psychological studies of sports ethics is the reduction of ethics to specific sets of rules and duties from which correct behavior may be defined regardless of context (cf. Baird & McGannon, 2009). In contrast, Foucault (1984) argued "given a code of actions . . . there are different ways to 'conduct oneself' morally, different ways for the acting individual to operate, not just as an agent, but as an ethical subject of this action" (p. 26). Subsequently, it is important to realize that ethical actions cannot simply be 'read' from a code; instead, codes require interpretation, opening up possibilities for divergent actions. For example, in Ultimate, some players insist on following the rules to the letter, whereas others prefer to follow the rules more loosely. This can lead to differences in what is interpreted to be acceptable behavior, yet these behaviors arise from the same moral code.

Moreover, as Bauman (1993) observed, "the choice is not between following the rules and breaking them, as there is no one set of rules to be obeyed or breached" (p. 20). Subsequently, we cannot with any authority define a moral code in advance of understanding the context. A critical psychology of ethics, then, should focus on subjective understandings and experiences of ethics within a specific context, rather than seek to describe correlations between behaviors and predefined ethical norms. In order to develop an understanding of ethical subjectivities in such sporting subcultures as Ultimate, a more localized, flexible, and interpretive approach is required. In this context, an interpretive approach seeks to understand individuals' perspectives in subcultural terms. Postmodern ethical theories, such as Foucault's (1984, 1988), offer one way in which an examination of ethical subjectivities might be pursued.

Foucault's ethics: subjectivity and truth

Numerous scholars in sport and exercise have sought to examine subjectivities in sport and exercise through Foucauldian theorizing (e.g., Crocket, 2012, in press b; Denison, 2010; Markula & Pringle, 2006; McGannon, 2012; McGannon & Busanich, 2010; McGannon & Spence, 2012; Pringle & Crocket, 2013; Pringle & Hickey, 2010; Shogan, 2007). Moreover, Foucault's genealogies were central to critical psychology's revision of the individual subject (Henriques, Hollway, Urwin, Venn, & Walkerdine, 1984). In this section, then, I describe how Foucauldian theory can further inform a critical psychological understanding of ethics in the subculture of Ultimate.

Foucault (1984) envisioned ethics as an ongoing process through which subjects negotiate a sense of self in relation to particular truths. His historicist revisions of freedom, power relations, truth, and the subject are central to understanding this process. Foucault (2000a, 2000b; see also Markula & Pringle, 2006) did not see power as something possessed by institutions or individuals. Rather, he primarily saw power as something exercised relationally. Simply put, a power relation is the strategic attempt to influence another person's behavior. Although Foucault rejected the idea that one could ever be free from power relations, he believed that rather than power relations deterministically controlling individuals' behavior, "there are always possibilities of changing the situation" (Foucault, 2000b, p. 167). As examples, Markula and Pringle (2006) and McGannon (2012) both used autoethnography to examine how they negotiated new possibilities in relation to their engagement with exercise and the dominant discourses of Western femininity.

Foucault (2000a) came to emphasize freedom within power relations as central to any consideration of ethics. More specifically, he suggested that "freedom is the ontological condition of ethics. But ethics is the considered form that freedom takes when it is informed by reflection" (Foucault, 2000a, pp. 283–284). For Foucault, then, we all have some socio-historically produced freedoms available to us. To act ethically requires consideration of the specific possibilities for acting, which are available within a particular setting. In the context of Ultimate, we might consider freedoms related to the game being self-refereed. Players are free to call rule violations as they see them occur. Yet, concomitantly, because there are no harsh penalties within the game for deliberate fouls, players might also be seen as free to violate rules to their advantage. An ethical question for Ultimate players, then, is to consider how they might limit or shape their self in relation to these contextual freedoms.

Foucault's understanding of truth was also strongly anti-essentialist. He rejected notions of pure, unchanging, or ahistorical truths. Instead, he suggested that truth is spoken, or constructed, by "free individuals who establish a certain consensus, and who find themselves with a certain network of practices of power and constraining institutions" (Foucault, 2000a, p. 297). His understanding of truth, then, was contextual and historical, rather than ontological. For Foucault, the ontological status of truth was of far less interest than effects of truth on the formation of particular subjectivities. From a Foucauldian point of view, then, an investigation of ethical subjectivities within Ultimate's subculture might focus on players' relationships to subcultural 'truths,' such as Spirit of the Game. For example, a player is 'free' to make a call they know to be false, such as calling themselves in-bounds when they know they are out of bounds. However, in deciding whether or not to exercise this freedom, they develop a relationship to Spirit of the Game, as this subcultural truth suggests players should be honest in such situations (see Crocket, in press a).

Foucault suggested one way in which the self was produced in relationship to truth was through the confession. Foucault (1978) noted, "Western societies have established the confession as one of the main rituals we rely on for the production of truth" (p. 58). Although the confession was initially a religious practice, "in the 18th century confession developed as a complex technology of secular discourses proliferating in pedagogy, medicine, psychiatry, and literature" (Besley & Peters, 2007, p. 16). The confession was a central means by which modern individuals were expected to produce truth about their selves, which would otherwise remain hidden. For example, through confessing to a psychologist or psychiatrist, a person might come to recognize their madness, or through confessing in a court of law, a person might admit their criminal status.

Most importantly, in his initial interpretation of the confession, Foucault (1978) argued:

> It is also a ritual that unfolds within a power relationship, for one does not confess without the presence (or virtual presence) of a partner who is not simply the interlocutor but the authority who requires the confession, prescribes and appreciates it, and intervenes in order to judge, punish, forgive, console, and reconcile.
>
> (p. 61)

Confessions, then, involved a strongly asymmetric power relationship between the confessor and the expert judge who received the confession. Markula and Pringle (2006) referred to such situations as relations of domination, as the possibilities for changing the situation within these power relations are highly constrained, particularly on the part of the confessor. In a sporting context, an asymmetric confession might occur between an athlete accused of doping and those sporting bodies who judge such cases.

However, in his later writing, Foucault considered the potential for confession to be "*an ascetic practice of self-formation*" (Besley & Peters, 2007, p. 22, emphasis in original). In this context, Foucault saw potential for a confession to be a process of critically accounting for how one had exercised or limited specific freedoms available to them. This shifted the emphasis of confession from the revelation of hidden secrets to accounting for one's acts in relation to "a collection of rules of conduct that he [*sic*] had learned" (Foucault, 1993, p. 207). Put very simply, because there are few harsh penalties for rule infractions in Ultimate, players have the freedom to cheat in order to win. Yet, the subcultural truths of Spirit of the Game ask players to give up that freedom and limit their actions to those that show respect for others and for the rules. In this way, we might expect a confession within Ultimate to occur when a player accounts for their actions in relation to the truths of Spirit of the Game. I now present and then analyze a specific example of confession within Ultimate.

Ultimate confessions: an example of the subcultural construction of ethics, subjectivity, and truth

In order to demonstrate the Foucauldian approach I outlined above, I provide the following mediated example. I examine an online response to the publication of a 'clip of the day' by a niche Ultimate media company, Pushpass Productions. This UK-based company featured a clip on their website from a semi-final of a major tournament (see Shardlow, 2008). The clip showed a spectacular diving catch by Pete 'Rodders' Wright in the end zone. Although his team celebrated, and the 40-odd spectators on the sidelines cheered the play, he was immediately involved in a discussion with his defender. The clip showed the discussion, and while the audio did not pick up the conversation, heckles could be heard from the crowd, and numerous players from both teams attempted to intervene. Most people assumed that a legitimate point had been scored, and that Rodders's marker was mistakenly disputing the play. Following this discussion a turnover was called, much to the surprise of the other players and the crowd.

After a link to the ambiguous, low-resolution clip was posted on the open-access UK Ultimate mailing list, BritDisc, Rodders clarified his behavior by emailing a confession to BritDisc:

> Just to clear it up. I caught it clean. I was in. But, as is clear on the video replay, it pops out of my hand during the hilarious combat role after the catch, and I kind of sweep it up off the ground with the cone. I knew it had popped out (and seemingly I was the only person that knew this) so I took [my defender] to one side, and told him this, and asked if he had fouled me, and he said no. I believed him. No score!

> (Wright, 2008)

In confessing through BritDisc, Rodders "was authenticated by the discourse of truth he was able or obliged to pronounce concerning himself" (Foucault, 1978, p. 58). It is significant, however, that Rodders's confession was not forced, and that the receiver of the confession was not an interpreter who became "the master of truth" (Foucault, 1978, p. 67). It is important to recognize that Rodders's confession was still embued with relations of power; however, in contrast to the asymmetric confessions Foucault analyzed within modern "pedagogy, psychiatry, medicine and literature" (Besley & Peters, 2007, p. 16), we might envisage a more symmetrical power relationship between Rodders and his peers on Britdisc who received his confession. This is because the roles of confessor and receiver of confession in Ultimate are temporary and fluid: while in this example Rodders was the confessor, in a subsequent situation he could receive another player's confession. Relatedly, Rodders's confession did not seek to reveal a hidden aspect of himself, or to renounce an aspect of himself. Instead, his confession sought to relate his actions "to rules of conduct he had learned" (Foucault, 1993, p. 207).

Through his confession—and his on-field actions—Rodders produced his self as a spirited player as his behavior was guided by the subcultural truths contained within Spirit of the Game. This was the point Foucault made when he argued that an ethical self could "not be conceived without a relation to truth" (Foucault, 1984, p. 86). Rodders's confession, then, might be thought of as an example of self-mastery involving self-knowledge and care of the self.

Although Foucault's ethics focused on the creation of an ethical self through coming to know the self and care for the self, his ethics was not solipsistic. Instead, he argued that care of the self "is also a way of caring for others" (Foucault, 2000a, p. 287). We can see this through Rodders's on-field acknowledgment of his turnover. Moreover, in confessing his actions to BritDisc, Rodders demonstrated care for his defender, who, because of the ambiguity of the clip, might otherwise have been assumed to have made a poorly judged, or 'unspirited,' call.

Moreover, it is notable that both the clip and Rodders's confession sparked further discussion on BritDisc not only about the ethical merits of Rodders's on-field actions, but also about those of the spectators who heckled, and, more broadly, whether the honesty shown by Rodders was expected or exceptional. It is through discussions such as these, whether confessional or otherwise, as well as through on-field actions, that Ultimate players produce their selves as ethical subjects while simultaneously reproducing, recreating, or modifying truth within Ultimate.

Although space does not allow exploration of further examples of the confession, I note that apologies, delivered both in person and online, are a noticeable, albeit non-compulsory and non-uniform, practice within Ultimate's subculture. I suggest such apologies might also be productively analyzed as confessions in relation to Ultimate's truths. I that argue the role of the confession within Ultimate has significant consequences for sport psychology. First, because confessions are a non-compulsory practice, this offers an example of the complexity and diversity of ethics within sporting subcultures. Just as Baird and McGannon (2009) argued that studies of aggression in sport require a localized, contextual understanding, I argue that understanding ethics in sport requires a nuanced approach, which does not seek to 'measure' the ethics of a sporting subculture using a predetermined model of ethics.

Future directions

In this chapter, I have outlined a critical psychological approach for understanding ethical subjectivities within Ultimate's subculture. The Foucauldian approach I have advocated moves away from universalized conceptions toward a contextualized examination of subjectivity and ethical self-creation. This contextualization allows for consideration of both online and off-line aspects of Ultimate's subculture in the production of ethical subjectivities. This is significant because sport psychology has paid little attention to ethical subjectivities. Importantly, this subcultural approach has shown that ethics within Ultimate is not limited to on-field behaviors; instead, it is (re)produced throughout different facets of the subculture. As I have argued throughout this chapter, a reductionist approach would not allow for the consideration of such possibilities. However, as this chapter offers only a brief introduction to ethical subjectivities, it is worth considering some possibilities for further research.

First, with regards to Ultimate, two fledgling professional leagues, *Major League Ultimate* and *American Ultimate Disc League*, have recently emerged.

Both leagues have implemented significant rule changes (see American Ultimate Disc League, 2013; Major League Ultimate, 2013), introducing referees and replacing Spirit of the Game with alternative versions of fair play. While neither of these leagues has a certain future, it is an open question as to how these changes might affect Ultimate's subculture and, in particular, the role of the confession.

Second, understandings of ethical athletic subjectivities need greater attention. The approach I have outlined builds on a small number of existing Foucauldian studies within sport psychology (e.g., McGannon, 2012; McGannon & Busanich, 2010; McGannon & Mauws, 2000; McGannon & Spence, 2012), and collectively these offer a productive way forward. A further issue to consider is possibilities for developing alternative modes of representation of ethical subjectivities. In this regard, narrative (e.g., Smith & Sparkes, 2009), autoethnographic (e.g., Douglas, 2009), and poetic (e.g., Sparkes & Douglas, 2007) forms of representation could be explored. Finally, the examination of ethical subjectivities would also benefit from developing theoretical alternatives to Foucault, by drawing on the work of such theorists as Bauman (1993), Levinas (1998), Derrida (2005), or Critchley (1999).

In summary, the approach I developed was critical insofar as it offered a critique of universalistic psychological models of ethics in sport and explicitly incorporated an analysis of power relations. In this way, I analyzed ethics, truth, and subjectivity in terms of their contextual construction within Ultimate's subculture. Such an approach is productive as it reveals possibilities and understandings that cannot be predicted in advance, and, as such, it contributes to the ongoing development of methodologically and theoretically diverse approaches within sport psychology.

Notes

1 Some elite tournaments in North America offer teams 'observers,' who are able to resolve disputed calls between players. However, World Championships and World Club Championships, which are both organized by the World Flying Disc Association, are fully self-officiated.
2 It is also important to note that this represents a limited view of ethics insofar as it ignores other ethically problematic practices associated with sport and often ignored within mainstream sport psychology, such as racism, sexism, and abuse of positions of privilege (see Kontos, 2010; Peters & Williams, 2009).

References

American Ultimate Disc League. (2013). AUDL Rulebook. Retrieved from http://theaudl.com/media/downloads/AUDL_Rulebook_v2_0.pdf.

Baird, S. M., & McGannon, K. R. (2009). Mean(ing) to me: A symbolic interactionist approach to aggression in sport psychology. *Quest, 61*, 377–396.

Bara, Y. (2012, September 17). Back to reality: A case of the Mondays. *Skyd Magazine*. Retrieved from http://skydmagazine.com/2012/09/back-to-reality-a-case-of-the-mondays/.

Bauman, Z. (1993). *Postmodern ethics*. Oxford: Blackwell.

Besley, A. C., & Peters, M. A. (2007). *Subjectivity & truth: Foucault, education, and the culture of self.* New York: Peter Lang.

Bombjay, G. (2010). Ultimate Frisbee . . . not a sport. [Web log message]. Retrieved from http://undsptd.com/ultimate-frisbee-not-a-sport/.

Coulomb-Cabagno, G., & Rascle, O. (2006). Team sports players' observed aggression as a function of gender, competitive level, and sport type. *Journal of Applied Social Psychology, 36*, 1980–2000.

Critchley, S. (1999). *Ethics, politics, subjectivity: Essays on Derrida, Levinas and contemporary French thought.* London and New York: Verso.

Crocket, H. (2012). Playing with ethics? A Foucauldian investigation of ethical subjectivities in Ultimate Frisbee. Unpublished doctoral dissertation, University of Waikato, Hamilton, New Zealand. Retrieved from http://researchcommons.waikato.ac.nz.

Crocket, H. (2013). "This is *men's* Ultimate": (Re)creating multiple masculinities in elite open Ultimate Frisbee. *International Review for the Sociology of Sport, 48*, 318–333.

Crocket, H. (in press a). Foucault, flying discs and calling fouls: Ascetic practices of the self in Ultimate Frisbee. Manuscript submitted for publication.

Crocket, H. (in press b). "I had no desire to be having this battle with this faceless man on the soccer field anymore": Exploring the ethics of sporting retirement. *Sociology of Sport Journal.*

Denison, J. (2010). Planning, practice and performance: The discursive formation of coaches' knowledge. *Sport, Education and Society, 15*, 461–478.

Derrida, J. (2005). *The politics of friendship.* (G. Collins, Trans.). London and Brooklyn, NY: Verso.

Douglas, K. (2009). Storying my self: Negotiating a relational identity in professional sport. *Qualitative Research in Sport and Exercise, 1*, 176–190.

Fisher, L. A., Butryn, T. M., & Roper, E. A. (2003). Diversifying (and politicizing) sport psychology through cultural studies: A promising perspective. *The Sport Psychologist, 17*, 391–405.

Foucault, M. (1978). *The history of sexuality: An introduction.* (R. Hurley, Trans.) (Vol. 1). London: Penguin.

Foucault, M. (1984). *The history of sexuality: The use of pleasure.* (R. Hurley, Trans.) (Vol. 2). London: Penguin.

Foucault, M. (1988). *The history of sexuality: The care of the self.* (R. Hurley, Trans.) (Vol. 3). London: Penguin.

Foucault, M. (1993). About the beginning of the hermeneutics of the self: Two lectures at Dartmouth. *Political Theory, 21*, 198–227.

Foucault, M. (2000a). The ethics of concern of the self as a practice of freedom. In P. Rabinow (Ed.), P. Aranov & D. McGrawth (Trans.), *Ethics: Subjectivity and truth* (Vol. 1, pp. 281–301). London: Penguin.

Foucault, M. (2000b). Sex, power, and the politics of identity. In P. Rabinow (Ed.), R. Hurley (Trans.), *Ethics: Subjectivity and truth* (Vol. 1, pp. 163–173). London: Penguin.

Gentile, P. (2009). Ultimate Frisbee: The lamest sport ever. [Web log message]. Retrieved from http://www.collegemagazine.com/blogs/2009/03/03/ultimate-frisbee-the-lamest-sport-ever/.

Gilbourne, D., & Andersen, M. B. (Eds.). (2011). *Critical essays in applied sport psychology.* Champaign, IL: Human Kinetics.

Gilbourne, D., & Richardson, D. (2006). Tales from the field: Personal reflections on the provision of psychological support in professional soccer. *Psychology of Sport & Exercise, 7*, 325–337.

Greenough, J. (2013, January 7). Costs, costs, costs (a reality check). *Skyd Magazine*. Retrieved from http://skydmagazine.com/2013/01/costs-costs-costs-a-reality-check/.

Henriques, J., Hollway, W., Urwin, C., Venn, C., & Walkerdine, V. (1984). Introduction to section two: Constructing the subject. In J. Henriques, W. Hollway, C. Urwin, C. Venn, & V. Walkerdine (Eds.), *Changing the subject* (pp. 91–118). London: Methuen.

Hutcheon, L. (1994). *Irony's edge*. London: Routledge.

Kavussanu, M. (2008). Moral behaviour in sport: A critical review of the literature. *International Review of Sport and Exercise Psychology, 1*, 124–138.

Keeler, L. A. (2007). The differences in sport aggression, life aggression, and life assertion among adult male and female collision, contact, and non-contact sport athletes. *Journal of Sport Behavior, 30*, 57–76.

Kirker, G., Tenenbaum, G., & Mattson, J. (2000). An investigation of the dynamics of aggression: Direct observations in ice hockey and basketball. *Research Quarterly for Exercise and Sport, 71*, 373–386.

Kontos, A. P. (2010). Historicizing sport psychology. In T. V. Ryba, R. J. Schinke, & G. Tenenbaum (Eds.), *The cultural turn in sport psychology* (pp. 29–52). Morgantown, WV: Fitness Information Technology.

Korber, J. (2012). Why spectator Ultimate is here to stay. *Ultiworld*. Retrieved from http://ultiworld.com/2012/11/06/why-spectator-ultimate-is-here-to-stay/.

Krane, V., & Baird, S. M. (2005). Using ethnography in applied sport psychology. *Journal of Applied Sport Psychology, 17*, 87–107.

Leonardo, P. A. (2007). *Ultimate: The greatest sport ever invented by man*. Halcottsville, NY: Breakaway Books.

Leonardo, P. A., & Zagoria, A. (Eds.). (2005). *Ultimate: The first four decades*. Los Altos, CA: Ultimate History.

Levinas, E. (1998). *Otherwise than being*. (A. Lingis, Trans.). Pittsburgh, PA: Duquesne University Press.

Maffesoli, M. (1996). *The time of the tribes: The decline of individualism in mass society*. (D. Smith, Trans.). London: Sage.

Major League Ultimate. (2013). MLU rulebook. Retrieved from http://mlultimate.com/wp-content/uploads/2013/02/MLU_rulebook-v09.pdf.

Markula, P., & Pringle, R. (2006). *Foucault, sport and exercise: Power, knowledge and transforming the self*. London and New York: Routledge.

McGannon, K. R. (2012). Am "I" a work of art(?): Understanding exercise and the self through critical self-awareness and aesthetic self-stylization. *Athletic Insight, 4*(1), 79–95.

McGannon, K. R., & Busanich, R. (2010). Rethinking subjectivity in sport and exercise psychology: A feminist post-structuralist perspective on women's embodied physical activity. In T. V. Ryba, R. J. Schinke, & G. Tenenbaum (Eds.), *The cultural turn in sport psychology* (pp. 203–230). Morgantown, WV: Fitness Information Technology.

McGannon, K. R., & Mauws, M. K. (2000). Discursive psychology: An alternative approach for studying adherence to exercise and physical activity. *Quest, 52*, 148–165.

McGannon, K. R., & Spence, J. C. (2012). Exploring news media representations of women's exercise and subjectivity through critical discourse analysis. *Qualitative Research in Sport, Exercise and Health, 4*, 32–50.

Muggleton, D. (2000). *Inside subculture: The postmodern meaning of style*. Oxford: Berg.

Peters, H. J., & Williams, J. M. (2009). Rationale for developing a cultural sport psychology. In R. J. Schinke & S. Hanrahan (Eds.), *Cultural sport psychology* (pp. 13–22). Champaign, IL: Human Kinetics.

Pringle, R., & Crocket, H. (2013). Coaching with Foucault: An examination of applied sports ethics. In P. Potrac, W. Gilbert, & J. Denison (Eds.), *Routledge handbook of sports coaching* (pp. 16–26). London: Routledge.

Pringle, R., & Hickey, C. (2010). Negotiating masculinities via the moral problematization of sport. *Sociology of Sport Journal, 27*, 115–139.

Rinehart, R. E. (2000). Emerging arriving sport: Alternatives to formal sports. In J. Coakley & E. Dunning (Eds.), *Handbook of sport studies* (pp. 504–519). London: Sage.

Ryba, T. V., & Wright, H. K. (2005). From mental game to cultural praxis: A cultural studies model's implications for the future of sport psychology. *Quest, 57*(2), 192–212.

Ryba, T. V., Schinke, R. J., & Tenenbaum, G. (Eds.). (2010). *The cultural turn in sport psychology*. Morgantown, WV: Fitness Information Technology.

Shardlow, F. (2008). *Clip of the day*. Brighton, UK: Pushpass Productions. Retrieved from http://www.pushpass.co.uk/clip-of-the-day/index.php.

Shields, D. L. L., & Bredemeier, B. J. (1995). *Character development and physical activity*. Champaign, IL: Human Kinetics.

Shogan, D. (2007). *Sport ethics in context*. Toronto: Canadian Scholars Press.

Skyd Magazine. (2013). Tournament central: ECBU 2013. Retrieved from http://skydmagazine.com/2013/06/tournament-central-ecbu-2013/.

Smith, B., & Sparkes, A. C. (2009). Narrative analysis and sport and exercise psychology: Understanding lives in diverse ways. *Psychology of Sport & Exercise, 10*, 279–288.

Sparkes, A. C., & Douglas, K. (2007). Making the case for poetic representations: An example in action. *The Sport Psychologist, 21*, 170–190.

Theo, T. (2009). Philosphical concerns in critical psychology. In D. Fox, I. Prilleltensky, & S. Austin (Eds.), *Critical psychology: An introduction* (2nd ed., pp. 36–53). London, Thousand Oaks, New Delhi and Singapore: Sage.

Thornton, A. (2004). "Anyone can play this game": Ultimate Frisbee, identity and difference. In B. Wheaton (Ed.), *Understanding lifestyle sports: Consumption, identity, and difference* (pp. 175–196). London and New York: Routledge.

Thorpe, H. (2009). Understanding "alternative" sport experiences: A contextual approach for sport psychology [Special issue]. *International Journal of Sport and Exercise Psychology, 7*, 359–379.

Thorpe, H. (2010). Psychology of extreme sports. In T. V. Ryba, R. J. Schinke, & G. Tenenbaum (Eds.), *The cultural turn in sport psychology* (pp. 363–386). Morgantown, WV: Fitness Information Technology.

Wheaton, B. (Ed.). (2004). *Understanding lifestyle sports: Consumption, identity, and difference*. London and New York: Routledge.

Wheaton, B. (2007). After sport culture: Rethinking sport and post-subcultural theory. *Journal of Sport and Social Issues, 31*, 283–307.

Wilson, B. (2008). Believe the hype? The impact of the internet on sport-related subcultures. In M. Atkinson & K. M. Young (Eds.), *Tribal play: Subcultural journeys through sport* (pp. 135–152). Bingley, UK: JAI.

Wright, P. (2008, May 13). [BD] COTD: Fire v Chevron – Rodders' layout grab. *Britdisc Archive*. Retrieved from http://www.fysh.org/pipermail/britdisc/2008-May/006122.html.

Young, K. M., & Atkinson, M. (2008). Introduction: A subcultural history. In M. Atkinson & K. M. Young (Eds.), *Tribal play: Subcultural journeys through sport* (pp. 1–46). Bingley, UK: JAI.

14 Continuing the dialogue on criticality and subculture in sport and physical activity

Robert J. Schinke and Kerry R. McGannon

As one ponders the topics and perspectives written for this compilation concerning the interpretive and cultural turn in sport and exercise psychology, it becomes clear why a critical cultural sport psychology (CSP) should be embraced and further developed in light of the value CSP brings to understanding and encouraging sport and physical activity participation. Brett Smith writes:

> the consequences of doing "safe" or "risky" research may be profound. It might result in a sterile or fertile field. Having a lot of "safe" research but not much research that takes "risks" may mean that our work becomes predictable, formulaic, and insipid rather than innovative, creative and exciting. And if we all march to the same drumbeat, then developing and enriching our understandings of the psycho-social worlds of people involved in sport/exercise could be severely limited.
>
> (Smith, 2010, p. 95)

Indeed, we proposed in Chapter 1 that CSP is quickly becoming a subculture unto itself, given its goals of creating space for researchers and practitioners to consider the richness in various sport/physical activity environments through theoretical, methodological and practical lenses that are unorthodox or less known but also innovative and creative. What follows are the co-editors' final (in this book) reactions to this unique, albeit challenging and fluid, compilation. In the spirit of reflexivity, we briefly ponder what we have learned about ourselves and our own research approaches, how these locate within a broader academic domain, how critical "takes" formed the process of putting together the current volume, and how our own thinking was challenged and expanded. We then conclude by offering a few tentative takeaways, but not definitive points.

Introspection and reflexivity

The editors have engaged in dialogue with authors from 12 chapters as part of this compilation. These discussions were at times both energizing and challenging from the perspective of the authors and the co-editors. However, all parties survived the process and we believe that relationships remain intact. Perhaps the brightest part of these dialogues might be found within the outcome of this book and what we see as the potential to add to the growth of critical dialogue within CSP. Each chapter reveals a unique "take" on how a specific topic, such as hazing, concussion, sport disability, male athletes' eating disorders, professional golf, Army performance, the training of practitioners, Ultimate, sex variation, mixed martial arts, or ultramarathons, might be considered through a proposed critical lens. As we suggested in Chapter 1, writings about subculture are never straight-forward, nor value free, nor do they seek to be per se. At times, the editors felt that several contributed chapters could have been taken to a different, or additional, critical place, such as through the unpacking of a topic with a more skeptical tone, acknowledging power issues, or perhaps through deepened forms of author reflexivity. In response, the contributing authors correctly felt that they were being as critical as they needed to be in order to problematize a taken-for-granted aspect, or notion, within the chosen sport discipline or sport circumstance. Through dialogue, our co-editors and contributing authors came to a recognition – something we knew beforehand, but then were reacquainted with through reminding: that there are a vast number of critical lenses (and views of criticality) one might consider and choose from, with each as worthy as the next, within the CSP genre. As we conclude this compilation, we understand with additional clarity our own preferences and views, and that these ought not to be hegemonic, definitive, or dogmatic. In line with the wider goal of CSP being open to differ-ence and diversity, we believe that advocating for certain or "best" approaches and/or narratives over others serves to exclude scholars from a dialogue (as opposed to debate, negotiation, and reconciliation) and omits the intellectual connoisseurship we believe should be present within the academy (Schinke, Smith, & McGannon, 2013; Sparkes & Smith, 2013). It is by opening up space for unique topics from multiple vantage points (i.e., theories, methodologies, methods) that we attempt to reveal just how the present book provides further space for various forms of subculture and the various undercurrents that exist and are developing within CSP.

Othering is the counterpoint of what we wish to do in this current volume, as well as in our own work. By "othering" we mean any action or reaction by which an individual or group is mentally or overtly classified as "not one of us" or "part of the desired." Rather than remembering that every person is a complex bundle of unique emotions, ideas, motivations, reflexes, priorities, and many other nuanced characteristics, it can sometimes be easier to dismiss them as being in some way "less than"/lesser than we are, and, in so doing, positions of domination and subordination can be reinforced or reproduced (Johnson, Bottorff, Browne, Grewal, Hilton, & Clarke, 2004). Avoiding the process and/or end point of "othering" is something that we believe is another important dimension, if not essence, of CSP. Consequently, we thank the contributing authors for their unique takes on the critical and how that critical "take" related to each of their topics: it has taught us about the developing subculture of CSP, our own preferences, and what the unique critical lenses adopted by the contributing authors may open up in the wider goal of creating a critical CSP. Collectively, we hope that the reader is left with the idea that there is space for many and multiple theoretical, methodological, and practical approaches within the growing subculture of CSP – and we hope that this book is viewed, and used, as a catalyst in that regard.

Recently Robert and a few colleagues engaged in a commentary exchange with a few scholars outside the parameters of CSP. The process was quite fascinating, especially as Robert delved further into a response to the critique. At the same time, Robert's initial reaction was one of feeling insulted, dismissed, and somewhat othered. However, as the anger and indignation subsided, the initial commentary became useful in several of its clarifications, just as any critical review of one's own or another's work can be useful. However, the tone of the commentary was also problematic and subsequently problematized. The commentary was read in this manner because the authors suggested in their tone that understanding should be singular – a form of post-positivism. As we noted in Chapter 1 when discussing the underlying parameters of post-modernism and social constructionism within which cultural praxis and CSP is positioned, framing one's own views as truthful or the "one" best way to explore and understand a particular issue or phenomenon closes space for dialogue concerning multiple and/or different perspectives. In turn, this closes down much-needed growth in order to create further understanding in sport and exercise psychology – particularly in terms of cultural topics and issues (Smith, 2010). Equally, given the epistemological, theoretical, and methodological preferences that underpin our work, at times we too struggled to acknowledge that we have our own preferences and perspectives in terms of how each topic might be looked at and/or approached within the present volume. During these struggles, the largest challenge was to try to remember that we sought to be aligned with wider views as to what might constitute "being critical" – that critical approaches are difficult to define and, as such, there is not one way to define or approach CSP work through a critical lens, nor should there be (Kincheloe, McLaren, & Steinberg, 2011). At the same time, as outlined in the introduction, we alluded to the fact that an "anything goes" approach was not what we sought either. We grounded (and still do) the offerings within the current volume broadly in various elements of cultural praxis, which has at its heart the goal of embracing diversity and difference to create and/or open up inclusive and socially just sport environments (Ryba & Wright, 2005).

Where do we reside in relation to this compendium in light of the above points and as we arrive at its completion? As one might expect in a text positioned within a critical lens and a subculture such as CSP, we are not satisfied with our own understanding of how to proceed in each of our separate or collaborative versions of CSP. Thus, we do not regard this offering, nor our own journeys as CSP scholars, as "finished" or complete. There are far too many unknowns in this emerging scholarship trajectory, and regarding this volume or the points made within as final or "best" would be the antithesis of a critical CSP discourse. For example, there is not enough known about the complexities of silencing, the cultural construction of one or more identities (see McGannon & Spence, 2010) as experienced by clients, research participants, and even scholars (see Sparkes, 2013), or the unpacking of different terms and their meanings often held "sacred" in sport psychology (e.g., mental training, mental toughness, resilience). At the same time, we are invigorated by the endless possibilities that remain open to us and the increasing number of colleagues engaged in this subcultural critical dialogue, as evidenced by a forthcoming special issue in *Psychology of Sport and Exercise*, scheduled for publication in 2014.

What ultimately resonates with us is that CSP is a subculture with many intricate strands (i.e., multiple voices, multiple theories, diverse methodologies, and a wider series of approaches to practice that infuse with the client's cultural identities), which seek to "tease" out the complexities concerning sport researchers, practitioners and participants, and the contexts they inhabit. Kerry and I meet with like-minded scholars at the international conferences, and at times it feels as if we are part of a deviant, "underground movement" – a band of sisters and brothers seeking to push the domain forward and/or in new and different directions – by centralizing the complexities and undoings that are a significant, and sometimes overlooked, part of sport and exercise psychology. Though at times we struggle, as do our colleagues, with being among the pioneers in this developing and growing area of CSP scholarship against the backdrop of power structures within the academy (Sparkes, 2013), we are also grateful to the contributing authors for having taken this ride before us and with us, and to those who have paved the way for additional forms of thinking and ways of "doing" sport psychology. As was pointed out by many, if not all, the authors within the present volume in various ways, counter-narratives – in theory, research, and practice – need to be made available and shared by a CSP research community, so that researchers and practitioners can look at themselves, each other, sport and physical activity participants, and the domain as a whole in new and multiple ways (Smith, 2010).

Takeaways from the content

Returning to discussion points from Chapter 1, we now seek to reconsider/ re-examine a few key points. We begin by re-examining the meaning of the terms "dark side of sport," "physical activity," and "exclusion," upon reflection of various chapters. Next, we return to the theme of silencing and its counterpoint of making what was previously silenced, and perhaps unsaid, more visible and vocal. We then conclude with a few suggestions concerning how one might proceed in further critical CSP scholarship.

Let's shed light on the dark side of sport, physical activity, and exclusion. Several of the chapters in this book reveal topics that we referred to as "the dark side of sport." We agree that sport and physical activity offer many positive life lessons and experiences to athletes, coaches, parents, and the public at large. However, there is no denying that, when one considers such topics as concussion, eating disorders, emotional abuse, or hazing, and the ties to taken-for-granted discourses, institutional practices, and politics, athletes can be subjected to experiences that are

less than positive, placed in positions where they are subordinated or disempowered, and, in more than a few instances, scarred – both physically and mentally.
The reader is likely not all that surprised by the inclusion of these topics within a
compilation where the emphasis is placed on critical lenses and the sorts of topics
that may be included in CSP. Let's consider the topic of concussion. As the authors
of Chapter 9 have revealed, this topic is growing in popularity in sport psychology,
sport science, and even popular culture, in part because we are only just beginning
to understand the long-term consequences of having experienced one or a series of
concussions through sport, but also because sport organizations are coming under
fire and scrutiny within the media for not protecting or informing athletes ade-
quately (McGannon, Cunningham, & Schinke, 2013). Sports such as ice hockey,
football, and boxing are only now beginning to be recognized as dangerous playgrounds for today's and tomorrow's youth and young adults. Moreover, these
"dangerous playgrounds" have at times been perpetuated by taken-for-granted narratives and practices in sport that have silenced athletes, or by counter-narratives
that relate to athlete safety, health, and well-being (e.g., encouraging athletes to
play through the pain in order to appear tough, committed, "real" athletes). As CSP
is concerned with the role of power and politics and how these contribute to the
taken-for-granted in sport (Fisher, Butryn, & Roper, 2003) and physical activity
(McGannon & Spence, 2010), concussion is an issue ripe for further exploration
using CSP and the various elements of cultural praxis outlined within our introduction and within the various chapters herein (McGannon et al., 2013). Yesterday's
and today's athletes are now coming forward, sharing their experiences of being
pressed back into sport prematurely and the consequent symptoms associated with
post-concussion syndrome. Similarly, such topics as emotional abuse, as unpacked
in Chapter 2, are hard to speak about and are at times kept hidden or even perpetuated by social agents, current sport policies, or a lack of sport policies; they are by
their very nature touchy, delicate, and likely to cause discomfort in many a reader.
The largest challenges, we believe, associated with these topics are that youth and
parents might not fully understand the risks (re)created through careless engagement in sports in light of the power and institutional practices that may keep these
risks from either being fully understood or made public, perhaps until it is too late
for the athlete. Then there is hazing, considered in Chapter 3, an act that is complex
and can actually be encouraged through the use of specific language practices at
the local level (e.g., within sport teams) and wider discourses that seem to write out
the harm being done to another, on both physical and psychological levels, as an
acceptable and necessary part of being a committed and tough athlete. As such, two
of the benefits to be gained from this book are more care for all concerned and the
opportunity to continue to problematize the taken-for-granted (e.g., the medical
model, sport policies, gender issues, local and social practices of sport participants,
the dominant sport narratives concerning athlete identities) so that space can be
opened up to understand further the complexity of these cultural issues at the social
psychological level.

Equally concerning are the hidden risks associated with ultramarathon running
– which may be viewed as risks by someone outside of the running context or

even by those within the context, but which are something to be embraced as part of one's athletic identity (Busanich, McGannon, & Schinke, 2012). The focus in Chapter 6 was female ultramarathon runners and how the sport served to empower women in light of their exclusion from competitive endurance running. Sports such as ultramarathon open safe spaces for people – in this case women – to learn more about themselves and offer opportunities to revisit power relations (e.g., women's exclusion from sport). There are sports where disadvantaged people can both excel and seek to shed a constraint previously imposed on them, such as being classed, raced, or gendered. However, an additional way to consider ultramarathon, as well as other sports, is that it can open up the athlete to unknown damage under the guise of being beneficial. The fact that runners experience hallucinations as they run and push their bodies is problematic, but at the same time athletes know this and embrace it, even when it is regarded as moving beyond one's known physical limits and empowering for some. Though sport might offer opportunities for people to overcome their hardships or social disadvantage, these fairy-tale narratives mask the dark side of sport. Yet at the same time, regarding both positive and negative narratives as co-existing, as opposed to "either or," reveals the complexity of a critical CSP discourse and its importance to understanding how and why athletes risk physical failure, personal damage, or psychological distress (Busanich et al., 2012; McGannon et al., 2013; Papathomas & Lavalee, 2012).

Sports have their dark sides, particularly when sport participants are marginalized and/or othered, and whether researchers, practitioners, or policy-makers choose to explore these "sides" or not. And yet for some, the notion of what constitutes a "dark side" does not enter into their vocabulary, instead being viewed as an important and necessary part of being and becoming an athlete in certain sport cultures and contexts. Through critical approaches, such unspoken or taken-for-granted parts of sport and physical activity can be pushed to the fore in ways that encourage more holistic thinking when exploring experiences within the context of politics and power (Fisher et al., 2003). Researchers might then choose to shadow athletes and coaches and see how exploitation, harassment, self-harm, harm of others, or danger is experienced, when it is embraced, minimized, trivialized, or altogether overlooked, and then seek to understand what is it about the sport's environment, culture, or systemic structures that contributes to the (re) production of damaging behaviors and/or the othering, silencing, or marginalizing of cultural identities. Through critical explorations into sport contexts using tools suggested in cultural praxis, we could be bettering lives, and creating sports and inclusive spaces within them, where more athletes and physical activity participants are left intact (Ryba, Stambulova, Si, & Schinke, 2013). Thereafter, practitioners, coaches, parents, and athletes could better understand the risks associated with certain sports and within certain club/team environments. At the same time, the very notion of "risk" and how its meaning is socially and culturally constructed with implications (e.g., paternalism toward athletes, protection of certain political interests), and toward what end within sport and exercise contexts, is something to ponder further (McGannon et al., 2013). In a sense, it is through a critical lens that policy decisions can be made, or through which current institutional and political structures can be questioned and deconstructed. Such questioning and deconstruction has the potential to impact the health and well-being of developing and established participants, creating a sport world and environment that is inclusive and welcoming of diversity and difference. This form of thinking has been employed for some time by scholars within sport psychology, including Fisher et al. (2003), McGannon and Mauws (2000), Smith (2010), Ryba and Wright (2010), and Schinke and Hanrahan (2009) as a cultural studies of CSP, and by Stambulova and Ryba (2013) as the potential third wave in cultural sport scholarship. We need to continue to embrace this notion of a third wave, as many scholars have been doing for years now, and to continue to contribute toward, and develop, a critical discourse within CSP.

Let's examine contributors to silencing in sport. Within the compilation we saw time and again how performance contexts and certain practices of participants, researchers, or practitioners can either exclude or minimize people's identities and their experiences, and, with that, their very participation within, or disengagement from, sport and physical activity. Returning to Chapter 7, which focused on disability and impaired bodies, arguments might be made by some that encouraging people in wheelchairs to remain active and in waiting is beneficial: they could remain fit and enthusiastic in their lives while they are inhabiting bodies that are limited, constraining and so a cause of frustration. There is also the possibility of the fairy-tale ending, where people in wheelchairs are told that they will eventually be cured and able to stand again. On the other hand, in contrast to that narrative, what happens to a person confined to a wheelchair when she/he realizes that all of the hope instilled by others was false hope, without basis? The authors raised critical questions about people in the medical profession who support unrealistic thinking, and about narratives of false hope and how that impacts the everyday, embodied lives of individuals. When a medical practitioner attempts to bestow hope, especially when that hope is unfounded, is the person having his or her dignity taken from the body she/he lives in? From such work, one possible outcome is that medical professionals will become more and/or further reflective about the implications of the taken-for-granted narratives they use (see Anderson, Knowles, & Gilbourne, 2004), why they are using such narratives, and how these might impact the individuals with whom they work. Furthermore, in terms of power issues within this context, what are medical practitioners gaining from these forms of unrealistic narratives, and who may be subordinated and impacted as a result?

Within the aforementioned chapter, and also Chapters 4 and 8, the co-editors are beginning to understand how performance environments and sport policies sometimes silence people through the various taken-for-granted discourses and narratives that circulate concerning their identities and certain labels placed upon them. Performers and practitioners inhabit bodies and identities, and live in worlds that may make practitioners and policy-makers uncomfortable within the context of certain dominant sport narratives that circulate. Our co-editors pondered why outsiders or those positioned as "on the fringes" of an experience tend to feel so uncomfortable about the challenges experienced by others. Furthermore, rather than exploring discomfort or difference, it seems that professionals and policy-makers working within (and on) performance environments at times omit or trivialize what is foreign or different, such as an alternative standpoint or an unfamiliar identity/body, or try to treat everyone the same and erase or downplay the significance of diversity and difference (Butryn, 2010). Graduate students sometimes also overlook and sometimes silence the cultural standpoints of their colleagues, as recognized in Chapter 11. It seems easier to omit discomfort, diversity, and difference, and what it is within the circumstance that makes us uncomfortable with someone else's uniqueness or difference, than to examine them. The reader might, through understanding, learn when performance environments are being closed or exclusionary to some, as opposed to being open and inviting to only a select few. Furthermore, introspection and a better awareness of one's own preferences, and of how these include some and exclude others, permit the reader, be this person a policy-maker, a researcher, or a practitioner, to consider how she/he has contributed to closings and openings for themself and someone else, and then how to engage in social justice by remedying past mistakes (Schinke, McGannon, Parham, & Lane, 2012). Within the co-editors' dialogues with the contributing authors, we are now left to ponder whether the content conveyed might at times have skirted critical issues, partially because we too were uncomfortable with or unaware of particular topics that could also have been included. Hence we, like the reader, must consider how to support more openness and a freer exchange of ideas and perspectives, in keeping with the tenets of cultural praxis, where space is opened up to include multiple cultural identities and the plurality of difference referred to in Chapter 1 (see also McGannon & Johnson, 2009; Ryba & Wright, 2010; Schinke et al., 2012).

The challenge going forward is for researchers and practitioners to look for ways in which taken-for-granted or less examined aspects of sport and sport culture – however defined – may lead to silencing certain identities and/or encourage certain practices that create environments and sport contexts that are less inclusive or healthful for sport and physical activity participants, as noted in Chapters 7, 8, 11 and 12 (see also McGannon & Spence, 2010; Ryba & Wright, 2005, 2010). The ambition can then become to encourage more openings and even to write about previous closings, so as to benefit from what we have learned about inclusion and exclusion. Certainly, as Schinke et al. (2012) have recognized, more scholarship in the area of researcher and practitioner reflexivity has the potential to create safer and more inclusive practices, while also encouraging and exemplifying healthier performance environments. Furthermore, reflexivity permits each one of us to look more carefully at the institutional practices and power structures we are (re)creating and encountering as people existing within and sometimes rallying against sport policies and institutional practices (McGannon & Johnson, 2009). One way in which researchers and practitioners could undertake cultural praxis, as identified in the introduction to this chapter, is for them to engage in critical pedagogy, a sort of co-participatory spirit taken up in the exchange of ideas and the development of better solutions (see Kincheloe et al., 2011; Schinke et al., 2013).

Final remarks

The most basic ambition/goal of this compilation was to further discussion in the growing area of CSP by contributing to, and encouraging, more nuanced discussions about sport and performance topics through the use of a critical lens. In the past, some of our focus was on general cultural characteristics, such as nationality (Schinke, Yukelson, Bartolacci, Battochio, & Johnstone, 2011) and race and ethnicity (Schinke et al., 2006), and on the media as a sociocultural site that (re)creates certain identities for athletes, which can have implications for sport practices (McGannon, Curtin, Schinke, & Schweinbenz, 2012; McGannon et al., 2013). We hope that this book encourages others, as it did us, to look beyond earlier and current writings within the CSP topics that are critical – however defined. In turn, each topic might be considered within its own cultural underpinnings and multiple way of knowing and understanding. Building upon earlier work about cultural praxis through understandings of sport politics (e.g., Fisher et al., 2003), feminism (Gill, 2001; Krane, 2001), reflexivity and post-structuralism (e.g., McGannon & Johnson, 2009), race marginalization (e.g., Schinke et al., 2009), and broader discussions about the omission of culture (e.g., Duda & Allison, 1990) that paved the way for critical approaches and today's CSP, we hope that the present book invites colleagues to continue to look critically at the discipline of sport and exercise psychology. Perhaps these emerging dialogues might continue to clarify the various narratives that we each draw upon to frame ourselves, and our experiences, as we reside within, and sometimes challenge, sport institutional policies and practices (Sparkes, 2013). Moreover, we hope that the book invites colleagues to view CSP as a positive and emerging subculture within the larger discipline of sport and exercise psychology. We view the subculture of CSP as one that we are fluidly (re)creating to open up opportunities for more candid discussions about topics and emerging concerns related to culture, social justice, and diversity that will affect us all and the sport and physical activity participants with whom we work.

References

Anderson, A., Knowles, Z., & Gilbourne, D. (2004). Reflective practice for sport psychologists: Concepts, models, practical implications, and thoughts on dissemination. *The Sport Psychologist, 18*, 188–203.

Busanich, R., McGannon, K. R., & Schinke, R. J. (2012). Expanding understandings of the body, food and exercise relationship in distance runners: A narrative approach. *Psychology of Sport & Exercise, 13*, 582–590.

Butryn, T. M. (2010). Integrating whiteness in sport psychology. In T. V. Ryba, R. J. Schinke, & G. Tenenbaum (Eds.), *The cultural turn in sport psychology* (pp. 127–152). Morgantown, WV: Fitness Information Technology.

Duda, J. L., & Allison, M. T. (1990). Cross-cultural analysis in exercise and sport psychology: A void in the field. *Journal of Sport and Exercise Psychology, 12*, 114–131.

Fisher, L. A., Butryn, T. A., & Roper, E. A. (2003). Diversifying (and politicizing) sport psychology through cultural studies: A promising perspective. *The Sport Psychologist, 17*, 391–405.

Gill, D. L. (2001). Feminist sport psychology: A guide for our journey. *The Sport Psychologist, 15*, 363–372.

Johnson, J. L., Bottorff, J. L., Browne, A. J., Grewal, S., Hilton, B. A., & Clarke, H. (2004). Othering and being othered in the context of health care services. *Health Communication, 16*, 255–271.

Kincheloe, J. L., McLaren, P., & Steinberg, S. R. (2011). Critical pedagogy and qualitative research: Moving to the bricolage. In Norman K. Denzin & Yvonna S. Lincoln (Eds.), *Handbook of qualitative research* (4th ed., pp. 163–177). Thousand Oaks, CA: Sage.

Krane, V. (2001). One lesbian feminist epistemology: Integrating feminist standpoint, queer theory and cultural studies. *The Sport Psychologist, 15*, 401–411.

McGannon, K. R., & Johnson, C. R. (2009). Strategies for reflective cultural sport psychology research. In R. J. Schinke & S. J. Hanrahan (Eds.), *Cultural sport psychology* (pp. 57–75). Champaign, IL: Human Kinetics.

McGannon, K. R., & Mauws, M. K. (2000). Discursive psychology: An alternative approach for studying adherence to exercise and physical activity. *Quest, 52*, 148–165.

McGannon, K. R., & Spence, J. C. (2010). Speaking of the self and physical activity participation: What discursive psychology can tell us about an old problem. *Qualitative Research in Sport and Exercise, 2*, 17–38.

McGannon, K. R., Cunningham, S. M., & Schinke, R. J. (2013). Understanding concussion in socio-cultural context: A media analysis of a National Hockey League star's concussion. *Psychology of Sport and Exercise, 14*, 891–899.

McGannon, K. R., Curtin, K., Schinke, R. J., & Schweinbenz, A. N. (2012). (De-)Constructing Paula Radcliffe: Exploring media representations of elite athletes, pregnancy and motherhood through cultural sport psychology. *Psychology of Sport and Exercise, 13*, 820–829.

Papathomas, A., & Lavallee, D. (2012). Eating disorders in sport: A call for methodological diversity. *Revista de Psicología del Deporte, 21*, 387–392.

Ryba, T. V., & Wright, H. K. (2005). From mental game to cultural praxis: A cultural studies model's implications for the future of sport psychology. *Quest, 57*, 192–212.

Ryba, T. V., & Wright, H. K. (2010). Sport psychology and the cultural turn: Notes toward cultural praxis. In T. V. Ryba, R. J. Schinke, & G. Tenenbaum (Eds.), *The cultural turn in sport psychology* (pp. 3–27). Morgantown, WV: Fitness Information Technology.

Ryba, T. V., Stambulova, N., Si, G., & Schinke, R. J. (2013). ISSP position stand: Culturally competent research and practice in sport and exercise psychology. *International Journal of Sport and Exercise Psychology, 11*, 123–142.

Schinke, R. J., & Hanrahan, S. J. (Eds.). (2009). *Cultural sport psychology*. Champaign, IL: Human Kinetics.

Schinke, R. J., Smith, B., & McGannon, K. R. (2013). Future pathways for community researchers in sport and physical activity research: Criteria for consideration. *Qualitative Research in Sport, Exercise and Health, 5*, 460–468.

Schinke, R. J., McGannon, K. R., Parham, W. D., & Lane, A. (2012). Toward cultural praxis: Strategies for self-reflexive sport psychology practice. *Quest, 64*, 34–46.

Schinke, R. J., Yukelson, D., Bartolacci, G., Battochio, R. C., & Johnstone, K. (2011). The challenges encountered by immigrated elite athletes. *Sport Psychology in Action, 2*, 1–11.

Schinke, R. J., Peltier, D., Hanrahan, S. J., Eys, M. A., Recollet-Saikkonen, D., Yungblut, H., & Michel, G. (2009). The progressive integration of Canadian indigenous culture within a sport psychology bicultural research team. *international Journal of Sport and Exercise Psychology, 7*, 309–322.

Schinke, R. J., Michel, G., Gauthier, A., Pickard, P., Danielson, R., Peltier, D., . . . Peltier, M. (2006). The adaptation to elite sport: A Canadian Aboriginal perspective. *The Sport Psychologist, 20*, 435–448.

Smith, B. (2010). Narrative inquiry: Ongoing conversations and questions for sport and exercise psychology research. *International Review of Sport and Exercise Psychology, 3*, 87–107.

Sparkes, A. C. (2013). Qualitative research in sport, exercise and health in the era of neoliberalism, audit and new public management: Understanding the conditions for the (im)possibilities for a new paradigm dialogue. *Qualitative Research in Sport, Exercise and Health, 5*, 440–459.

Sparkes, A. C., & Smith, B. (2013). *Qualitative research methods in sport, exercise and health: From process to product*. London: Routledge.

Stambulova, N. B., & Ryba, T. V. (Eds.). (2013). *Athletes' careers across cultures*. London: Routledge.

Index

Note: Page numbers followed by 'f' refer to figures.

Printed by PGSTL